Turning on Learning

Five Approaches for Multicultural Teaching Plans
for Race, Class, Gender, and Disability

SECOND EDITION

CARL A. GRANT
University of Wisconsin, Madison

CHRISTINE E. SLEETER
California State University, Monterrey Bay

JOHN WILEY & SONS, INC.

NEW YORK • CHICHESTER • WEINHEIM • BRISBANE • SINGAPORE • TORONTO

Cover photo: Joseph Mozdzen/Photobank, Inc.

Photo credits: p. 62 (upper left, upper right), p. 63 (lower right) by Scott Cunningham/Merrill; p. 62 (lower left) by CEM Photo/Merrill; p. 62 (lower right), p. 63 (upper right) by Mary Hagler/Merrill; p. 63 (upper left) by Kevin Fitzsimons/Merrill; p. 63 (lower left) by Anne Vega/Merrill.

Library of Congress Cataloging-in-Publication Data
Grant, Carl A.
    Turning on learning : five approaches for multicultural teaching plans for race, class, gender, and disability/Carl A. Grant, Christine E. Sleeter. — 2nd ed.
        p.   cm.
    Includes bibliographical references and indexes.
    ISBN 0471-36445-2
        1. Multicultural education — United States — Curricula — Handbooks, manuals, etc. 2. Teaching — Aids and devices — Handbooks, manuals, etc.   I. Sleeter, Christine E., 1948 –   . II. Title.

    LC1099.3.G73   1997
    370.19′341 — dc21   97-1574
                                                                              CIP

Printed in the United States of America

10 9 8 7 6

*To the many teachers who have found
this book helpful and supportive*

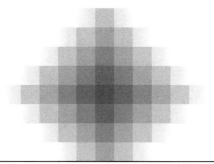

Preface

This book is the practical, lesson-based companion to *Making Choices for Multicultural Education: Five Approaches to Race, Class, and Gender* (Merrill/Prentice Hall, 1994; revision due © 1999). *Turning on Learning* grew out of the requests of teachers and preservice education students for specific illustrations of how to work with diversity and excite their students. Over the years, we have communicated with many teachers, administrators, teacher educators, and teacher education students around the country, who have repeatedly challenged us to show them how to apply our ideas in their classrooms. Theories have value only when they can be demonstrated and used in daily practice and when they offer concrete possibilities. This book provides these possibilities.

The text is grounded in theories and philosophies supporting multicultural education. Attention is given to classroom concerns related to race, class, gender, disability, language, and sexual orientation.

Turning on Learning contains many lesson plans that cover a variety of subject areas and grade levels 1–12, as well as action research activities that investigate the various dimensions of teaching. Many of the lesson plans are written by classroom teachers, and all of them have been examined by practicing teachers. But the book is more than a how-to manual. Rather, it is designed to help the teacher or teacher education student teach from a multicultural perspective. Each lesson plan offers a "Before" version—the lesson as it is usually taught—and an "After" version—how the lesson can be improved to "turn on" learning. A discussion explaining why the changes were made follows each lesson plan.

NEW TO THIS EDITION

In this second edition, we have made the greatest number of additions to the chapters addressing the last three approaches to multicultural education—single-group studies, multicultural education, and education that is multicultural and reconstructionist. This is because of the increased demand for teaching approaches that relate to social justice. Further, readers will note that some of the lesson plans in this second edition rework "before" lessons that are somewhat multicultural, strengthening them considerably.

It is hoped that readers will use not only the lesson plans in this book but also the process for modifying teaching in their own daily curriculum and instruction. We are confident that, in the process, more students will become excited about learning and enthusiastic about living in and bettering their world.

ACKNOWLEDGMENTS

We are indebted to a great many people who contributed valuable ideas to *Turning on Learning*. Our sincerest thanks go to the following educators for the lesson plans, ideas, and information they provided: Chris Aamodt, Claire Alldred, Deborah Bicksler, Mary F. Braun, Karen Campion, David Castaneda, Margaret Conway, Anne Fairbrother, Lola Ferguson, Maureen Gillette, Dorothy Goines, Virginia Kester, Jacquelyn King, Ozetta Kirby, P. Lloyd Kollman, Lisa Loutzenheiser, Gloria Nájera, Connie Olson, Debra Owens, Vicki Peterson, Jo Richards, Linda Roberts, Henry St. Maurice, Sue Senzig, Bob Suzuki, Kathro Taylor, Paoze Thao, Robin White, Kimberley Woo, and Lynette Selkurt Zimmer.

We are grateful to numerous practicing teachers and preservice education students who reviewed the lesson plans and gave us their reactions and valuable suggestions. We thank our undergraduate and graduate students at the University of Washington, the University of Wisconsin–Madison, and the University of Wisconsin–Parkside, as well as teachers with whom we shared drafts of the lesson plans in workshops across the country. We owe much to our colleagues who reviewed the manuscript and offered numerous suggestions for improvement: Barbara Kacer, Western Kentucky University; Angela Clark Louque, University of Redlands; Alba Rosenman, Ball State University; Will Roy, University of Wisconsin, Milwaukee; and Vilma Seebert, Kent State University.

Finally, we owe deep thanks to those who have typed, reviewed, given suggestions, and helped get this manuscript together. We thank Janet Dewane and Amy Hutler for preparing the initial manuscript on a word processor and for their patience through the many revisions and last-minute insertions. Judy Gaal's help with entering revisions into the word processor is also appreciated. We appreciate Chris Kruger's work in making revisions. We also appreciate the help and feedback of Lola Ferguson, Joy Lei, and Michael Tucker on drafts of earlier lesson plans.

Carl A. Grant
Christine E. Sleeter

Contents

CHAPTER 3

Human Relations   56

CHAPTER 4

Single-Group Studies   108

x   Contents

Lesson Plans

What Turns Your Students On?

Can you imagine what it would be like to be a student in your own classroom or in one with which you are familiar? If you are like most educators, you probably find it somewhat difficult to imagine yourself as the student. You may have trouble remembering who you were as a student and realizing that a full quarter century may have elapsed since you were the age of students now in school. Even if you are a college student, your elementary, middle, and high school years probably seem a long time ago.

Placing ourselves in the role of student often involves more than a leap across time to a role we no longer occupy. For many of us, it involves trying to identify with someone who differs from ourselves visibly and who is growing up in a world that is unfamiliar, strange, and maybe somewhat threatening to our own ideas of a "good" world in which to grow. There is about a 90 percent chance that you, the reader, are white—in 1986 the teaching profession was 89.6 percent white, and the percentage of teachers of color has been declining (National Education Association, 1987). Many of you live in middle-class conditions and have never experienced poverty. Very few of you were ever in special education. Most of our older readers probably grew up in two-parent families in which the mother's main role was to raise children and the father's was to support them financially. And most of our readers certainly did not grow up with MTV—television, perhaps, but not over thirty channels, including some that feature pornography and rock videos.

The gap between your own experiences and personal identity and those of your students may be small or it may be tremendous. But there is a gap, and it will continue to grow as the student population becomes more diverse. The Children's

Defense Fund reports the following information about children born in the United States:[1]

Everyday, 2,833 children drop out of school.

Everyday, six children commit suicide.

Everyday, 1,407 babies are born to teen mothers.

Everyday, 100,000 children are homeless.

Every 34 seconds, a baby is born to a mother who did not graduate from high school.

Every 25 seconds, a baby is born into poverty.

Every two hours, a child or youth is killed by firearms.

Our intent is not to cause alarm but to invite you to examine how you are meeting and working with students; we also invite you to become aware of what life in today's schools is like from students' perspectives. We have observed teachers who are willing to learn from their students, who view teaching and learning as a two-way interchange. As "students of their students," these teachers do an excellent job of building instruction around their students' interests and perspectives. Their classrooms are exciting places because they "turn on" learning.

On the other hand, we have also observed teachers who tend to overlook their students' identities and experiences, who teach as if their students were just like themselves. When the gap between teacher and student is not bridged, learning gets "turned off." Symptoms of turned-off learning include students' seeming inabilities to grasp concepts, to exert effort, and to display enthusiasm; repeated lateness or absence; boredom; and work that is sloppy or of poor quality. Further, gifted and talented students tend to underperform, doing just enough to get by. When students are turned off, teaching feels like either a chore or a battle.

Unfortunately, the latter type of teaching approach is more common than the former, and with the student dropout rate increasing, the situation is not likely to get better unless an effort is made to improve it. We term this ineffective teaching approach "business as usual," and its frequent use has been documented by recent studies of schools, where researchers have observed classrooms and interviewed teachers and students (Anyon, 1981; Cuban, 1984; Everhart, 1983; Goodlad, 1984; Grant & Sleeter, 1996; Lareau, 1989; Oakes, 1985; Payne, 1984; Solomon, 1992; Valli, 1986; Weis, 1990). Teaching strategies using the business-as-usual approach are fairly standardized and routine—teachers talk, and students sit and listen or read and complete worksheets. Students are tested mainly on what they have memorized and are usually marched through the material, with few, if any, adaptations for their individual learning styles, rates, skills, and interests. Although there is some variety and individualization at the elementary level, there is very little at the secondary level.

---

1. Prepared by the Children's Defense Fund (January 1996), 25 E Street NW, Washington, DC 20001, (202) 628-8787.

Further, course content is fairly uniform among schools and is not selected on the basis of student interest or experiential background. In fact, course content becomes increasingly removed from students' day-to-day experiences as they progress through the secondary grade levels, even though older students become more concerned about their personal identities and their relationships with their immediate environment. Course content also tends to emphasize the white wealthy male experience, or it presents information in a sterile, passive manner that neither invites nor encourages student participation. Although attempts during the past three decades to make curricula multicultural and nonsexist have removed many blatant omissions and stereotypes and have added culturally diverse pictures, examples, and some story content, most texts have not substantially enlarged the center of attention beyond European Americans and, to a lesser extent, African Americans.

In the business-as-usual approach, students tend to be grouped for instruction in ways that reproduce social stratification patterns in the larger society. For example, in the elementary grades, ability grouping in reading and math usually reinforces race and social-class differences, and groups are usually taught in ways that help them become increasingly different over the years. The use of tracking is widespread in our secondary schools. In tracking, certain students—primarily those of white and middle- or upper-class backgrounds—are taken from their elementary school ability groups and prepared for college; other students—primarily those of lower-class and minority backgrounds—are prepared for blue- or pink-collar labor; yet others are prepared for the "general" labor market. Special education often constitutes a track below the lower track for students whom the regular program is unable to accommodate, whereas gifted programs offer the most socially advantaged children the best instruction. Students who manage to be placed in the upper groups are often similar to their teachers and are more likely to find school stimulating. Other students—the numbers increase in the higher grades—often find school boring, irrelevant, and without meaning. However, it is not the idea of education that turns students off, as most recognize the value in learning and want to learn. What turns many students off is teaching that is routine and passive, course content that is unconnected to daily life, and a lack of intellectual challenge.

We interviewed students in a desegregated, working-class school environment and asked them about their perceptions of school (Grant & Sleeter, 1996). We found them critical of what the typical classroom offers but cognizant of what makes them want to learn. Regarding the business-as-usual teaching approach, students made comments like the following.

JODY: I got science first hour, and you know you're gonna be doing an experiment or taking notes or something. It's one of three things: you take notes, you read, or you do an experiment, and that's it. And you know what's coming up and it's not no fun, it's better if you get surprised.

SHIRLEY: We always do a certain thing through the week [in English]. Like the first day we do these little things, we read and then we have to answer questions about it. And the second day, he's got it planned day through day so if you miss Tuesday you know what you did Tuesday because you always do the same thing. Tuesday we have to work out of a workbook. And Wednesday we finish up the workbook, turn in the assignment, and start on our spelling test. Like, we write down words and get their meanings and stuff. And it goes on like that. It's boring in his class.

ANGELA: [Social studies was boring] because I just sat there. We just sat down and listened to him and that gets boring.

PHIL: A lot of the reason why the kids screw up in class is because they can see no practical use for what they are learning.

The students also appraised various teaching strategies for us, indicating which ones helped them to learn and which ones turned them on to learning (Table 1.1). (Although different groups of students may rate activities differently, teachers are often unaware of or overlook students' appraisals.)

As noted earlier, some teachers stimulate student learning effectively, and students know which teachers do so. The students we interviewed (Grant & Sleeter, 1996) commented about the classes in which they felt they had learned the most. For example, one student, Kristen, commented on teaching strategies and curriculum content:

KRISTEN: Multicultural [education] I like because it's different and [I like] publications because it's fun.

RESEARCHER: What makes publications fun?

KRISTEN: You get to go out and report and interview people, write stories to put in the [school newspaper].

RESEARCHER: Why do you like multicultural education?

TABLE 1.1   Students' Appraisals of Classroom Activities

Like, learn from this activity	Neutral or mixed appraisals	Don't like, don't learn from this activity
Small-group projects	Independent projects	Listening to lecture without taking notes
Whole-class discussions in which kids do most of the talking	Recitation (teacher asks questions and kids respond)	Watching films (especially science films)
Listening to speakers	Taking lecture notes	
Interviewing people	Doing dittoes	
Labs, experiments	Reading	
	Reading, then answering questions	

Source: Adapted from *After the School Bell Rings* (2nd ed.) (p. 139), by C. A. Grant and C. E. Sleeter, 1996, New York: Falmer Press.

KRISTEN: You get to study all the different people and stuff you never knew before—things that people say about people that are in books and stuff that you think is true, and we learn the truth about it. Like how the whites treated the Indians a long time ago. (p. 162)

Grace spoke with us about tests, and her comments may come as a surprise:

RESEARCHER: What do you think about those kinds of tests that you got today? You have to write definitions and then answer questions on the last part. They weren't really questions that you could answer by giving one or two words. It looked like they were questions you really had to think about.

GRACE: Yeah. We had to write long definitions for them and then you had to write what you thought on the last ones.

RESEARCHER: Would you rather have a test like that where you write down what you think or where you write down answers?

GRACE: What I think.

RESEARCHER: In other classes, are you asked to write down what you think like you were in this one?

GRACE: No, in most of the classes they give you notes and you have to study those notes and then what is in those notes you have to write on the test.

RESEARCHER: What is different about the class you were just in?

GRACE: I guess it's harder. (p. 167)

Hal expressed a definite interest in being able to formulate questions to direct his learning:

RESEARCHER: So you feel that interviewing is a good way to learn?

HAL: Yeah, because you're asking questions that you want to know and they're giving you answers that are interesting about what you're asking and stuff.

RESEARCHER: How about listening to speakers in class?

HAL: Yeah, because again you're asking questions that you want to know. One of my friends' dad came here and he was from Lebanon and we got to ask questions about it. It's easier to remember than learning from a book because they're telling us stuff that you really don't care about. This way you're asking what you want to know. (p. 168)

Lupe underscored the value of active participation in learning:

LUPE: In our government class we have to take a vote and the whole class is all together in it. We make up our own tests and take

	votes and stuff. That was only in one class. We only did it one time.
RESEARCHER:	What did you think about that?
LUPE:	I like it because that way you get more ideas. (pp. 168–169)

Finally, Alvin emphasized the importance of curriculum content being multicultural:

RESEARCHER:	Do you think it's important for other kids here to know about what the blacks do, who the heroes are, the contributions made?
ALVIN:	Yeah, because some people think that blacks are troublemakers. They don't know what they do or nothing. (p. 171)

Consider again the question with which we opened this chapter: What would it be like to be a student in your own classroom or in one with which you are familiar? What is school like for Brad, or Juanita, or Yvonne, or Carlos, or Ngoc? Does it turn them on to learning, or does it teach them routines and ignore the importance of using their own minds? If this first chapter has stirred some emotion, we encourage you to study this book carefully and to use it to help you examine and experiment with your teaching.

CONCERNS AND CHALLENGES

A concern you may have is that the home and neighborhood circumstances of some students make it hard for them to concentrate on school. Some students have personal problems that can frustrate the patience and creativity of dedicated teachers. For example, it is hard for a student to get turned on to math if he or she is hungry, worried about a problem at home, feels incapable of doing well in school, feels abandoned by a loved one, is worried about being pregnant or concerned about his or her safety in traveling to and from school, or is preoccupied with being popular. Although this book does not deal specifically with the problems that students bring to school, it is important to consider carefully how these factors can limit students' abilities, as well as the extent teachers use them as excuses for not trying to turn students on to learning.

Consider the following example. Several years ago one of the authors took up ice skating during a stressful time of life. The author would often arrive at the ice rink feeling moody, depressed, and preoccupied. After an hour of intense skating instruction and practice, the author would discover that personal problems had drifted to the back of the mind, while the activity and fun of the immediate learning situation took over. Skating instruction not only pushed aside personal worries for a while, but it also left the author with a refreshing feeling of having learned something new, having accomplished something. Thank goodness the skating instructor never labeled the author as too "emotionally disturbed" (not to mention too old!) to learn! In fact, the skill, enthusiasm, persistence, and interest of the skating instructor contributed to the author's well-being by providing a delightful alternative to the author's problems for an hour and by helping the author achieve something in spite of whatever else might have been going wrong that day.

So it is with good teaching. It may not solve a student's problems, and it may only partially divert a student from them, but it can provide an opportunity for the student to develop self-respect and to enjoy life and companionship for several hours a day. Entertainment should not be confused with teaching, however; many of us confused these during the 1960s, when schools were first desegregated. Teachers at that time were overly concerned with making students like them and with showing students that they liked them also. The affective side of teaching is important, but the cognitive side—helping students develop to the best of their academic ability—is equally important. Teaching and learning can be stimulating and enjoyable for virtually any student and teacher.

THE PLAN OF THE BOOK

The book does not use a "recipe" approach to turning on learning. Although it contains many practical and useful ideas for successful teaching, its primary intent is to help you develop your own analytical and creative teaching skills.

In the remaining five chapters of *Turning on Learning*, we provide a framework for examining five different teaching approaches that address human diversity— race, ethnicity, gender, social class, disability, and sexual orientation. In our work with teachers, we have observed that they have varying perspectives of human differences and of how to handle them in the classroom. Their perspectives can be grouped into five approaches, each having its own distinct goals, assumptions, and practices.

Chapter 2, "Teaching the Exceptional and Culturally Different," addresses how to help students who do not succeed in the existing classroom or societal mainstream. The approach discussed here builds bridges between the capabilities of the student and the demands of the school and wider society, so that the student can learn to function successfully in these contexts. Chapter 3, "Human Relations," is concerned with helping students to get along with one another better by appreciating each other and themselves. This approach concentrates on building positive feelings among people. In Chapter 4, "Single-Group Studies," groups that tend to be left out of the existing curricula are discussed. This approach teaches students about such groups as women, African Americans, Asian Americans, and people with disabilities. Chapter 5, "Multicultural Education," combines much of the first three approaches. It suggests changes to most existing school practices for all students so that the school and classroom may become more concerned with human diversity, choice, and equal opportunity. It is hoped that such changes will bring about greater cultural pluralism and equal opportunity in society at large as today's students become tomorrow's citizens. Finally, Chapter 6, "Education That Is Multicultural and Social Reconstructionist," addresses social inequalities among groups in society at large as well as in students' own experiences. The primary goals of this approach are to prepare students to work actively in groups and individually, to deal constructively with social problems, and to take charge of their own futures.

We encourage you to read all of the chapters. Unless a particular chapter title strikes you as especially interesting, you will probably find it most helpful to read the chapters in sequence, since to an extent the approaches build on each other. Once you have finished reading the book, you will probably find that one approach appeals more to you than the others, although you may also like aspects of other approaches. The approach that appeals to you the most should provide a point of departure for your own professional growth. Study that approach; work with its ideas; make it as much a part of your teaching as you can. If after you have worked with the approach you find it limited in ways you did not recognize initially, you may wish to reconsider the other approaches.

You need not practice only one approach. However, if you find yourself drawing bits and pieces from all the approaches without giving careful thought to any one approach in particular, ask yourself whether you are really engaging in business as usual. We have found that teachers who remain eclectic prefer either business as usual or simply have not spent enough time studying each approach. We also encourage you to read our companion book, *Making Choices for Multicultural Education: Five Approaches to Race, Class, and Gender* (1994), to investigate further the thinking behind each approach.

THE ORGANIZATIONAL PLAN

Each chapter begins with an explanation of the teaching approach. Following are Action Research Activities that investigate some aspect of teaching that helps to implement the approach (and possibly subsequent approaches). The activities can help you to gather information about students, the curriculum, the school, or the school's community that will enable you to examine your classroom behavior and to teach more effectively. Following the activities are several pairs of sample lesson plans that appear in a before-and-after format. The "Before" lesson plans represent samples of curriculum and instruction as they usually exist—business as usual. Because they are based on the observations of teachers, popular curriculum guides and textbooks, and lesson plans developed by teachers, they may be familiar to you. The "After" lesson plans illustrate ways that existing curriculum and instruction can be changed to implement the approach described in each chapter and to turn on learning. Finally, each "After" lesson plan is followed by a discussion of why the plan was changed.

The primary goal of this book is to help you examine existing patterns of curriculum and instruction and then learn how to change them to respond better to human diversity—to turn on more learning. By studying the lesson plans and discussions of changes carefully, you will learn how changes to business as usual can enable you to reach more students and to make a positive difference. You will also benefit from examining your own curriculum and instruction. Take a lesson or unit that you are planning to teach next week or next month and treat it as a "Before" plan. Then think of as many ways as possible that you can change the plan to implement the approach described in the chapter. Spend time developing a good, workable "After" plan for yourself, and then try it out in the classroom. Do this over a period of time with several lessons and units, until you get the feel of the practices described in each chapter and until you can see what changes are improving your own teaching. As you become comfortable with some new ideas, try out additional ones.

Do not limit yourself to studying the lesson plans in your own subject area or grade level. The lessons in this book are illustrations of ideas—they are not simply recipes to follow. For example, if you teach ninth-grade math, you may find some good ideas about adapting instruction to students' learning styles in an elementary social studies lesson. Think about how you can use those ideas to help teach ninth-grade math.

We also encourage you to work with your colleagues. Discuss with them the approaches that make the most sense to you and why. You may not reach consensus, but you will probably find yourself thinking about what you are trying to accomplish when you teach. Exchange ideas; observe each other teach, if possible, when trying something new. Throughout the book we demonstrate the importance and value of students learning to work cooperatively—the same can be said of teachers. Finally, do not feel that you have to master all the ideas in the text. Rather, use the book as a tool to help you grow.

References

Anyon, J. (1981). Social class and school knowledge. *Curriculum Inquiry, 11*, 3–42.

Cuban, L. (1984). *How teachers taught.* New York: Longman.

Everhart, R. (1983). *Reading, writing, and resistance.* Boston: Routledge and Kegan Paul.

Goodlad, J. I. (1984). *A place called school.* New York: McGraw-Hill.

Grant, C. A., & Sleeter, C. E. (1996). *After the school bell rings* (2nd ed.). New York: Falmer Press.

Lareau, A. (1989). *Home advantage.* London: Falmer Press.

National Education Association. (1987). *NEA study of the status of public school teachers.* Washington, DC: Author.

Oakes, J. (1985). *Keeping track.* New Haven: Yale University Press.

Payne, C. (1984). *Getting what we ask for.* Westport, CT: Greenwood Press.

Sleeter, C. E., & Grant, C. A. (1994). *Making choices for multicultural education: Five approaches to race, class, and gender* (2nd ed.). Upper Saddle River, NJ: Merrill/Prentice Hall.

Solomon, R. P. (1992). *Black resistance in high school.* Albany, NY: SUNY Press.

Valli, L. (1986). *Becoming clerical workers.* Boston: Routledge and Kegan Paul.

Weis, L. (1990). *Working class without work.* New York: Routledge and Kegan Paul.

Teaching the Exceptional
and Culturally Different

How can you maintain a high level of teaching performance in the following situations?

> You have a new student who recently moved to the United States from Laos. She speaks only a handful of English words, and her life experiences are quite different from yours as well as from the other students' in the class.

> Three of your students spend a portion of their school day in learning disabilities classes. One of the students attends a class for the emotionally disturbed, and the other two are visually impaired.

> Most of the students in your class are Mexican Americans (and you are not). Some of their manners of responding to you are unfamiliar to you.

> You are transferred to a new school and most of your students live at or below the poverty level, unlike the socioeconomic background with which you are most familiar.

> A group of students in your class seems tuned out, unmotivated, and academically behind.

Most teachers encounter situations like these during the course of their careers. The situations share a common characteristic: one or more of the students differ from the teacher's conception of what is "usual" or generally expected. In such situations, old routines and strategies do not work or do not function as well. For example, students may be unable to read the material that the teacher is accustomed to using, or they may find the material uninteresting and irrelevant to their own experiences and goals. Students may speak a language or dialect foreign to the teacher and sometimes use this language when the teacher feels that they should use Standard English. Students may "act out" when the teacher does not expect it, but they themselves may not consider it as acting out. Students may not participate in classroom activities that the teacher believes to be motivating; they may talk or whisper among themselves when the teacher expects silence, or they may sit passively when the teacher is trying to conduct a discussion. Perhaps they find the subject matter boring or fail to understand explanations the teacher thought made sense.

The teaching approach discussed here (**Teaching the Exceptional and Culturally Different**) addresses these kinds of situations. It involves changing one's instructional patterns and classroom procedures to fit the students and facilitate their academic success. (Chapter 2 of *Making Choices for Multicultural Education* [Sleeter & Grant, 1994] develops debates and theoretical ideas behind this approach in some detail.) We use the term **exceptional** to refer to students in special education, but the term can also refer to any student who is not succeeding academically. The term **culturally different** refers to students whose cultural background—race, ethnicity, language, or social class—differs from that of the teacher. The term also implies that there is sufficient cultural difference between the teacher and the students that effective teaching and learning breaks down—although, of course, this does not necessarily happen when the teacher and students differ racially or ethnically.

All five approaches in this text emphasize processes for identifying and building on students' strengths. All students have learning strengths—they come to our classrooms having already learned a good deal in their lives. But, as teachers, we may not recognize their strengths and therefore fail to capitalize on them as resources for learning. The approach in this chapter focuses on strengths and patterns students bring in terms of learning style, interests, language, and everyday life experience.

The long-term goals of this approach are to enable students to succeed in learning the traditional curriculum in traditional classrooms and to be successful in the existing society. Students' success in assimilating into the broader society is often determined by how well the teacher helps them to learn and accept the ways of the mainstream culture. Some readers may view these goals as too limited. At the same time, some of you may embrace many of the ideas and insights in this chapter. Some may find another approach more appealing, as certain approaches discussed in Chapters 3–6 use the ideas from this approach for adapting instruction to students, but advocate additional changes for different, long-range goals.

BRIDGES TO THE CURRICULUM

The approach to teaching exceptional and culturally different students involves building **bridges to the curriculum** that enable students to succeed and to adapt to the requirements of the traditional classroom. In some cases, these bridges are temporary; in other cases, building these bridges entails broadening a teacher's repertoire of what counts as "normal" ways of teaching and learning.

Learning Styles

Common sense and the education literature tell us that our students have different **learning styles.** Students who differ from ourselves, in particular, may prefer to learn in ways that differ from our own preferences. For example, some students learn a concept better when they read about it, others learn better when they actually observe the concept (e.g., oxidation of material), and still others need to use a combination of modalities, such as discussing, touching, and writing. We also know that some students need a great deal of structure (such as a time schedule, a task schedule, or writing guidelines), whereas other students prefer little structure, employing their creativity when doing an assignment.

Learning style is a complex idea and involves how people perceive, process, store, and retrieve information. In a learning situation, what cues does an individual attend to? How does the individual connect cues? What strategies does the individual use to make sense of new information or ideas? With what "old information" in the individual's head is the new information connected and stored? Everyone develops ways of approaching these information–processing tasks, but we do not all develop the same ways (Hollins, 1996).

One way to view learning is as information processing. Howard Gardner's (1993) idea of multiple intelligences is another way. According to Gardner, there are at least seven different kinds of intelligence, and everyone has a profile of strengths and weaknesses. These include linguistic intelligence and logical–mathematical intelligence (which schools focus on most heavily), musical intelligence, interpersonal intelligence, intrapersonal intelligence, spatial intelligence, and bodily–kinesthetic intelligence. Students who are not as strong in verbal skills as they are in other intelligence areas often do not do as well in the classroom as they might be if classrooms supported other intelligence areas as well as they support verbal skills. Teachers who vary their teaching strategies can capitalize on additional areas of intelligence and, in the process, have greater success teaching their students.

Learning styles overlap somewhat with cultural background and gender. Although not all members of a cultural or gender group learn in the same way, patterns exist concerning how members of different groups tend to approach tasks. These patterns develop because of factors such as child-rearing practices and the roles that children are expected to occupy as adults (Boykin & Allen, 1988; Fennema & Peterson, 1987; Hale, 1982; Philips, 1983; Shade, 1989). Rather than generalizing about your own students based on research on group differences, however, it is much more useful to investigate directly your own students' learning style preferences.

Action Research Activity 2.1 can help you to begin to examine your students' learning styles. Based on your discoveries, you probably will want to emphasize teaching strategies that involve students more actively. In other words, we all can afford to cut back on the routines of lecturing, reading the text, and answering the questions. Instead, we should teach students the benefits of working cooperatively with others. Once students learn to work together, they are much more likely to be academically successful, and you will enjoy the intrinsic rewards that come from your effort. Multimedia computer programs such as *HyperStudio* lend themselves very well to increased student involvement and appeal to multiple learning styles. Examples of adaptations to student learning style are found in several lessons later in the chapter: "Sentences, Subjects, and Predicates" (p. 23), "Word Usage" (p. 33), "Mong History" (p. 37), "Functions" (p. 43), "Polymers" (p. 47), and "Cardiovascular Health" (p. 51).

Curriculum Relevant to Students' Experiential Backgrounds

Successfully learning and understanding what is taught in school are paramount to obtaining a good job and participating fully in society. Students must learn well the basics—reading, mathematics, writing, and language—regardless of *how* they learn them. Good teachers know how to identify topics, examples, or introductions to lessons that are of interest to their students. They are also good at locating and using curriculum materials that make the students want to learn. This may sometimes mean using materials that are not part of the mainstream collection (for example, we observed a teacher gain the interest of Mexican American students by using both the European American and the Mexican versions of the fall of the Alamo). There are many ways to find out more about your students' experiential backgrounds and interests. Action Research Activity 2.2 is one tool you can use. Lesson plan examples of how you relate curriculum more directly to students' backgrounds appear later in the chapter: "Word Usage" (p. 33), "Functions" (p. 43), and "Cardiovascular Health" (p. 51).

Skill Levels

In any given class, some students will perform below or above grade level. How can you accommodate a range of skill levels? Should you teach to the mid-range of the class? Refer some students to special education? Seek the help of parents or an aide?

We have observed teachers who work successfully with a wide range of student skill levels, and one of their keys to success is using others—parents, older students, student teachers, and aides—to help meet students at their varying levels of competence. They also use varied grouping patterns rather than permanent ability groups (e.g., to teach specific skills such as spelling, temporary skill groups can be formed). Students are also grouped heterogeneously to encourage tutoring and high aspirations among low-achieving students.

We stress the importance of teachers meeting the skill level of students because we still observe students who, for example, read at the fourth-grade level but are asked to learn new material from seventh-grade textbooks. Further, these students may try to hide their learning problems from teachers. For instance, they may carry around the seventh-grade textbook because they are embarrassed to let their friends know they are reading a fourth-grade textbook. Teachers must be alert to these tendencies while at the same time help students to raise their skill levels. The lesson plans "Polymers" (p. 47) and "Cardiovascular Health" (p. 51) demonstrate adaptations for diverse skill levels.

Language

Most U.S. Americans, and most teachers, are proficient in only one language. Thus, with a student who speaks little English, the teacher must usually adjust. Teachers who are not accustomed to communicating with people who speak a different dialect may find themselves confused about how to work with students who use other dialects.

Of course, the child who speaks little English needs, first and foremost, to learn English in a nonthreatening, supportive environment. Generally, students respond positively to teachers who are interested in learning about their backgrounds. Teachers who have difficulty working with students who speak little English, or who are unprepared to teach non-English-speaking students, can learn to do so successfully. Peer tutors can be helpful not only for translation and communication but also as language role models who can convey to students a sense of friendship—that is, that the teacher cares enough to provide a "friend" the student can consult when language problems arise. Cooperative learning activities give students an opportunity to process material with each other in their own language as well as in English. Visual cues, such as demonstrations and pictures, give students nonlinguistic sources of information to bolster their newly acquired English vocabulary. ESL (English as a Second Language) and bilingual teachers are excellent professional resources whom the teacher should not hesitate to turn to when necessary. One of our colleagues periodically consulted with ESL and bilingual teachers to discuss ideas and events that would help her to understand better how to work with limited-English-speaking students. The lesson plan "Cardiovascular Health" (p. 51) shows how to work with students who are in the process of learning English.

Because limited-English-speaking students are likely to be the major persons responsible for English communication in their families, teachers of these students should prepare notices for home in both languages. In addition, teachers should ask the home-school coordinator or a bilingual staff member to help encourage parents to meet with them to discuss classroom goals and activities. The authors once spoke at a PTA meeting with an audience of over one hundred parents. About one-third were European American, one-third African American, and one-third Mexican American, many of whom did not speak English and did not attend school meetings regularly. We spoke in English but with an ongoing translation in Spanish. Both the English-speaking and the Spanish-speaking parents told us they found the experience gratifying. The next PTA meeting drew an equally diverse parent group; the large turnout of Spanish-speaking parents was attributed mainly to the bilingual format of the previous meeting.

English-speaking students who do not speak Standard English need to learn how to speak it. It is likely that they can understand Standard English when spoken to them, even though the teacher may have difficulty understanding their dialects. Action Research Activity 2.3 will help you identify linguistic patterns your students have mastered to assist you in teaching them a second dialect—Standard English. Teaching the new dialect is much like teaching a foreign language—the differences between the two "languages" must be made clear, and continued practice is essential (see the lesson plan "Word Usage" on p. 33). However, teachers must be careful not to punish or criticize students for having mastered their home dialect; rather, they should view it as a language base on which mastery of an additional dialect can be built. Some teachers choose to explain to students that there is "everyday talk" (or "street talk") and "school talk" (or "formal talk"). Delpit (1995) reports that one teacher of Athabaskan Indians referred to the student talk as "Heritage English." This teacher helps the students to appreciate their language by savoring the words and discussing the nuances of their language. However, it must be made clear that "everyday talk" is to be used with friends or outside of school and "school talk" must be used in school. Most students accept this distinction without too much reservation.

Cultural Capital and Expectations

When we invest monetary capital, we expect to receive a return on it. Similarly, some types of knowledge bring a greater return in our society than do other types of knowledge. For example, algebra may not seem practical in everyday life, but a knowledge of algebra is useful if one wants to attend college. Teachers should strive to guide exceptional and culturally different learners toward acquiring the knowledge that will help them most later in life. When your students leave high school they will compete with other students for college entrance, jobs, and scholarships, and teachers need to prepare them for how to compete. Students' low expectations of their abilities or teachers' overconcentration on teaching them about their own cultures to the exclusion of the mainstream culture can be detrimental to these students. Ideas for teaching traditionally hard subjects more effectively are presented in the lesson plans such as "Functions" (p. 43) and "Polymers" (p. 47).

Success Stories

The ultimate goal of this approach is to incorporate all students into the U.S. mainstream. Students who do not do well in school need extra help and encouragement. Role models can help; for example, low-income students can learn about successful people who had grown up in poverty, female students can learn about successful women in various fields, and students of color can learn about successful people from their own communities. Role models like these can encourage students to become part of the mainstream and can discourage them from giving up (see "Mong History," p. 37, and "Polymers," p. 47).

If It's Boring or Demeaning, Avoid It!

Although teachers can recognize students who seem bored, disinterested, or put down, often these symptoms are attributed to students being "behind." Teachers may give them worksheets and drill them each day, and when they seem bored or resentful, teachers protest: "They need it!" But do they really?

When we try to learn something new and difficult—such as how to drive a car or memorize lines for the community play—often what we need to do is relax for a while and then approach learning from a different angle. Students often need to learn in the same way, with the help of a patient teacher who strives to avoid creating boredom. Students need to experience success, not busy work, whose main purpose is to get both teacher and student through another school day. In fact, boring or demeaning schoolwork discourages students from wanting to learn and from meeting their full potential. In contrast, variety, games, enthusiasm, and active involvement encourage learning and are necessary to avoid boredom. Further, rewarding students for their accomplishments is beneficial to both teacher and student. If you have difficulty finding new ideas, try to imagine yourself as a student and then ask what would interest you—this often leads to good, creative thinking. Or, ask yourself how you would teach your students if they were gifted—and then teach that way. The issue of boredom is addressed further in the lesson plans "Sentences, Subjects, and Predicates" (p. 23), "Word Usage" (p. 33), and "Cardiovascular Health" (p. 51).

Relationships with Students

For many students, a caring relationship with the teacher is a prerequisite to learning. If the teacher does not seem to like the students personally, some students will not try in school. In many classrooms, teachers establish caring relationships with all their students; but in many others, teachers expect students to care about academics without necessarily having a warm relationship with the teacher. Students then tune out, and the teacher becomes frustrated because they are not working. Jaime Escalante (1990), who achieved acclaim for his success in teaching college–level math in an East Los Angeles barrio high school, attributes part of his success to his loving his students and teaching them accordingly. His students knew he cared and believed in them, so they worked for him.

We know quite a few teachers who would like to establish warm relationships with students but are bothered by students' classroom behavior. They become frustrated when students talk out of turn, jostle each other as they walk down the hall, blurt out answers, and so forth. Cultural differences in communication and interaction style can short–circuit good classroom relationships as teachers interpret student behavior as disruptive, aggressive, passive, cold, and so forth. And when teachers are frustrated or irritated with students, students know it and react accordingly. Action Research Activity 2.4 has helped many teachers become sensitive to cultural patterns their students use in the classroom, as well as cultural patterns the teacher uses and considers "normal." Becoming aware of how cultural differences in interaction style play out in the classroom will not by itself make you care about your students, but it can help you get past feelings of frustration that hinder many caring relationships from developing.

Connections with the Home and Community

Although space does not permit us to fully develop the idea of making connections with students' homes and the community, its importance needs to be emphasized. Teachers should familiarize themselves with the communities in which they teach by spending time there, getting to know parents, and finding out what parents want for their children. It is also useful to compare parents' wishes in regards to schooling with your own or your parents'. In general, parents in all socioeconomic and cultural groups want their children to receive the best education possible. Also inquire about the system parents use for making sure homework gets done; if they do not have a system, help them develop one. Tell parents about what goes on in your classroom, and make sure your conversations with them are two-way interchanges and that you speak in a way they can understand.

ACTION RESEARCH ACTIVITY 2.1

Learning Styles

This activity is an introduction to investigating learning styles. The following items describe things to investigate, but you need to decide how to investigate them. Collect the requested information on several students, using the record sheet shown in Figure 2.1. You may notice patterns based on gender and ethnic background, but do not stereotype certain groups as learning a certain way. Use the patterns you discover in your students' learning style preferences as guides for selecting teaching strategies.

Working Alone Versus Working with Others.   Many students work best cooperatively with a partner or small group, whereas others work best individually. The student's preference should be respected, although those who have not learned to work cooperatively may enjoy and benefit from the experience.

Preferred Learning Modalities.   The term **preferred learning modalities** refers to the sensory channels or processes that students prefer to use for acquiring new information or ideas. They can be investigated in the following ways:

Give students choices and record which ones they choose most often.

Record the success with which students have learned under each condition.

For each student, record data you collect about the following items related to the student's preferred style of learning.

Student's name _____

		Method of Data Collection	Findings
1. Style of working:	Alone With others		
2. Learning Modality:	Watching Reading Listening Discussing Touching Moving Writing		
3. Content:	People Things		
4. Need for structure:	High Low		
5. Details versus generalities			

FIGURE 2.1   Learning Styles Record Sheet

Ask students which they prefer to use for gaining or expressing new ideas or information.

Content About People Versus Content About Things.   Students' interest in content can be investigated in the following ways:

Offer students choices (e.g., a story topic or math story problems) and observe which one they select most often.

Ask students which topic they usually prefer (but do not force them to choose—for some, it makes no difference).

Structured Versus Nonstructured Tasks.   Some students prefer tasks that are structured, whereas others prefer to create their own structure. The best way to investigate this preference is to give the student choices between highly structured work and open-ended work and determine which is chosen most often. Sometimes the teacher may simply ask students, particularly older students, but other students may not completely understand the teacher's question. Students who seem lost or do poorly on open-ended assignments probably need structured work; those who seem bored with structured assignments probably need open-ended work.

Details Versus the Overall Picture.   Some students do meticulous work well, are attentive to details, and can work through small steps to arrive at the larger idea; other students need to view the larger, more general picture first and may become bored or lost with details or small steps. For instance, when writing stories, some students use grammar and mechanics correctly, but their stories may not have much point; whereas other students may produce good overall story ideas but their first drafts are weak in grammar and mechanics. Students' preferences for details or generalities are best investigated through observation. Although all students eventually need to work on both details and generalities, some will have trouble learning these concepts if the teacher emphasizes one or the other prematurely.

ACTION RESEARCH ACTIVITY 2.2

Students' Experiential Background

Spend time in the neighborhood where your students live, observing and listening. Look and listen for things you can use as examples or as lessons to help teach concepts in your curriculum. It may be difficult to refrain from making judgments, but the more open you are, the more you will find that can be used to help the students. Pay attention to such things as geometric shapes in building designs, the kinds of plant life and rocks that are present, the types of stores that are present, the styles of music played, the kinds of games children play, and so forth. Record your observations in Table 2.1.

TABLE 2.1

Observations	Related Academic Concepts	Ideas for Using Observations
1.		
2.		
3.		
4.		
5.		
6.		
7.		
8.		
9.		
10.		

ACTION RESEARCH ACTIVITY 2.3

Dialect Difference

If your students speak a dialect of English with which you are unfamiliar, this activity can help you gain some understanding of its linguistic patterns. (A dialect is not the same thing as an accent or partial mastery of English by a speaker of another language.) Listen closely to how people say things. Below you will find a list of things to listen for. See how many patterns you can detect. You may notice patterns that are not listed; if so, keep track of them also.

Phonemes (sounds)

■ Are some consonant sounds pronounced differently than you are used to? Does it matter if the sound is at the beginning, middle, or end of the word?

■ Are some vowel sounds pronounced differently than you are used to?

■ Are consonant sounds that you pronounce dropped when they appear in certain places in words (such as at the end)?

Grammar

■ Compared with the way you speak, are there differences in the way the past tense is indicated?

■ Are there differences in the way the possessive is indicated?

■ Pay attention to how "do" and "be" are used; look for patterns that differ from what you are used to.

■ Are there differences in word order?

■ Pay attention to patterns indicating the negative.

■ Are there differences in use of pronouns?

■ Are there differences in use of adverbs or adjectives?

Vocabulary

■ Listen for words you are unfamiliar with; find out what they mean.

■ Listen for words you are familiar with but seem to have a different meaning than you are used to.

■ Listen for phrases you are unfamiliar with or you do not use.

■ Pay attention to words and phrases you use regularly that are not used regularly by the students you are working with.

■ Pay attention to figurative or creative use of language.

Nonspoken Language

■ Are facial expressions used differently than you are used to?

- Are gestures used differently than you are used to?
- Are voice inflections used differently than you are used to?
- Is rhythm or speed of talking different than what you are used to?
- Does the person prefer to be at the same distance from you that you are used to? Closer? Farther?
- Does the person talk as loudly/softly as you are used to?

Social Context

- Does the person switch dialects around different people or in different settings? If you notice a pattern and feel comfortable doing so, find out if he or she is aware of doing this.

ACTION RESEARCH ACTIVITY 2.4

Interpersonal Communication Style

This activity is appropriate when observing two or more members of the same sociocultural group interacting with each other. Watch people on more than one occasion to discern communication patterns that are commonly used.

Watch people talking naturally, and if you can do so unobtrusively, write descriptions of their behavior as they talk. Look for things such as the following:

What distance do they maintain between each other?

What kinds of gestures are used?

In what contexts do people touch each other? How do they touch, and where? (Some cultural groups touch a lot, others very little.)

What do they do to indicate they are listening?

How does a person "get the floor" when he or she wants to speak? (e.g., does the person simply start talking? wait for an opening? use a hand gesture?).

What level of loudness or softness of speech do people maintain?

If possible, watch an adult giving directions to, or reprimanding, a child who is a member of the adult's same sociocultural group.

What does the adult say?

What nonverbal behavior does the adult use?

How does the child respond?

Compare the patterns you observed with patterns you expect or take for granted from your own cultural background. How do you react when students exhibit interaction patterns you observed? All of us can learn to code-switch between two different cultural patterns. In what ways might your students need to learn to code-switch when in school, and how can you help them learn to do this? In what ways might you need to learn to code-switch?

LESSON PLAN

Sentences, Subjects, and Predicates

Subject Area: Language Arts

Grade Level: 2–4

Time: Two class periods

Objectives

1. Students will distinguish a complete sentence from a phrase and demonstrate such on a worksheet of phrases and sentences.

2. Students will identify subjects and predicates of sentences.

Suggested Procedures

1. Explain to the class that today they will learn what a complete sentence is and that it has two parts: a subject and a predicate.

2. Write the following sentence on the board: "The girl is sitting on the bench." Ask students who or what is doing the action (the girl); explain that the subject is who or what the sentence is about. Ask the students what the girl is doing (sitting on the bench); explain that the predicate tells what the subject does.

3. Go through several similar sentences on the board, asking students to identify the subjects and the predicates. When students gain an understanding of these concepts, give them a worksheet and have them underline the subject and circle the predicate of each sentence.

4. Display several pictures around the classroom. Tell the class they will practice how to distinguish between a complete sentence (which has both a subject and a predicate) and a phrase (which does not have both of these). For the first picture, ask the class to suggest a caption; write it on tagboard beneath the picture. Have students identify whether the caption is a complete sentence or a phrase. Then have the class suggest another caption that is a phrase if the first caption was a sentence, or a sentence if the first caption was a phrase.

5. Go through the pictures, calling on individuals to suggest captions and identify whether the caption is a phrase or a complete sentence. Each picture should acquire two captions: one sentence and one phrase.

6. Hand out a worksheet with some complete sentences and some phrases. Ask students to identify whether each item is a complete sentence or a phrase. Have students underline the subjects and circle the predicates of the complete sentences.

Evaluation

Assess individual mastery of concepts by evaluating each student's worksheet and responses when called on to perform orally.

AFTER

Sentences, Subjects, and Predicates*

Subject Area: Language Arts

Grade Level: 2–4

Time: Two class periods

Objectives

1. Students will distinguish a complete sentence from a phrase and demonstrate such on a worksheet of phrases and sentences.

2. Students will identify subjects and predicates of sentences.

Suggested Procedures

1. Explain to the class that today they will learn what a complete sentence is and that it has two parts: a subject and a predicate.

2. Randomly choose ten students to be "subjects" and another ten to be "predicates."

3. Hand out one large flashcard to each child. Students who are "subjects" receive flashcards that say "SUBJECT" on one side and display a specific subject on the other side. The ten subjects are:

   a. the chair

   b. my sister

   c. a yellow car

   d. all giraffes

   e. this book

   f. the football game

---

*Source: Karen Campion, Milwaukee School District, Milwaukee, WI.

    g.   smoke

    h.   a clown

    i.   the sky

    j.   storms

Students who are "predicates" receive flashcards that say "PREDICATE" on one side and display a specific predicate on the other side. The ten predicates are:

    a.   has a broken leg

    b.   looks just like me

    c.   ran out of gas

    d.   have long necks

    e.   was hard to read

    f.   ended in a tie

    g.   rose from the chimney

    h.   has a big red nose

    i.   is blue today

    j.   scare me

4. Explain to students that they are only half of a sentence and need to search for their other half to be complete. If they are a subject, they need to search for their missing predicate. If they are a predicate, they need to search for their missing subject.

5. Students search around the class for their missing half and sit down next to each other when they have found them. When the entire class is seated, students are ready to present their sentences to the rest of the class.

6. Choose one pair of students to come to the front of the class. The two students stand next to each other and hold up their flashcards to make a complete sentence. The class reads the sentence out loud (e.g., "The chair has a broken leg").

7. Explain to students that the subject is who or what the sentence is about. Ask the "subject" in the pair of students to raise his or her hand. Explain to the class that the predicate tells what the subject is about or what it does. Ask the "predicate" in the pair of students to raise his or her hand.

8. Have either the subject or the predicate student move to the corner of the room, and ask the class to read what is on the flashcard (e.g., "has a broken leg"). Explain that without the subject, the predicate is lost—or is not a complete sentence. Subject and predicate need each other for the whole sentence to make sense.

9. Have another pair of students come to the front of the class, and repeat steps 6–8, but instead of continually explaining, change the questions. For example,

ask what a subject is. Do this until all the pairs of students have come before the class.

10. Review or close the lesson by practicing with sentences on the board. Each student circles the subject and underlines the predicate of his or her own sentence on the board. The teacher evaluates and assists when necessary.

11. Pair students randomly. List topics on the board, such as animals, people, jobs, games, and weather. Have pairs of students choose topics, and provide them with scissors and old magazines. Ask the students to cut out magazine pictures related to the topic they chose. One student from each group is asked to write a caption that is a phrase, not a sentence. The other student is asked to write a caption that is a complete sentence. Students need to cooperate with each other and share ideas. The teacher should give assistance if needed, especially to students writing phrases. The students are asked to glue their pictures on colorful construction paper and to attach the captions underneath them.

12. Each pair of students then shows their pictures to the group and reads the two captions they wrote. The other children are asked to decide which caption is a complete sentence. After they have chosen the correct one, the class decides what is the subject and what is the predicate. Pictures and captions remain hanging on bulletin boards for visual reinforcement.

13. Hand out a worksheet with some complete sentences and some phrases. Read the directions to students and have them determine whether the items are complete sentences or phrases; then have them point out the subjects and predicates.

Evaluation

1. Assess group learning by presentations and by class response to questions during the activity.

2. Assess individual mastery by evaluating each student's worksheet.

WHY THE CHANGES?

Sentences, Subjects, and Predicates

Learning Style

The "Before" lesson plan requires students to learn mainly by observing a demonstration, then performing it alone. The modalities used are mainly reading and writing, although the pictures provide some nonliterary visual stimulus. The recitation format in procedure 5 introduces some competition, since each individual's performance is publicly evaluated and the peer group determines who knows the answers and who does not. While these strategies work for some students, they do not work well for many others.

The "After" lesson plan makes several adaptations for the learning style of the students in the teacher's class, which the "Before" plan does not do. The activities involve everyone with as little lecturing as possible. The lesson uses a people-oriented approach rather than a task-oriented one. The learning is from whole to part, in that the lesson teaches a complete sentence by having each part find its partner. It also emphasizes cooperating and sharing information by having students work together and present to the class, and it incorporates more visual learning with the poster and magazine activity.

Boredom

The "After" lesson would probably interest most students because it involves them actively and it offers alternatives to board work and worksheets. Both lessons teach the same concepts in roughly the same amount of time; however, academic integrity and time constraints are not sacrificed in making a more interesting lesson.

LESSON PLAN

BEFORE

The Importance of Math to Everyday Life

Subject Area: Mathematics

Grade Level: 4–8

Time: About 20 minutes

Objective

Students will appreciate the importance of mathematics to daily life.

Suggested Procedures

1. Ask students to list at least five uses of math in everyday life (e.g., making coin change, converting cooking measurements, figuring mileage, appraising, computing, measuring, traveling).

2. Ask each student to provide three examples of where and how math use occurs. For example, if a student lives in the Mountain Time Zone and if he or she wishes to watch a program on MTV scheduled for 9:00 P.M. Eastern Standard Time, what mathematical concept would be used to determine the time that the program would air in the Mountain Time Zone?

Evaluation

1. Assess students' understanding of math use through discussion.

2. Assess students' appreciation of the importance and usefulness of math through the seriousness with which they apply themselves.

AFTER

The Importance of Math to Everyday Life

Subject Area: Mathematics

Grade Level: 4–8

Time: One or two class periods

Objectives

1. Students will appreciate the importance of mathematics to daily life.

2. Students will learn that the ability to use higher levels of math often helps one acquire a prestigious and high-paying job.

Suggested Procedures

1. Ask students to list at least five uses of mathematics in everyday life (e.g., making coin change, converting cooking measurements, predicting, determining value, computing, measuring, traveling).

2. Ask students to provide examples (evidence) of where and how these uses occur. Ask students to provide examples of who is mostly responsible for using math in this manner. On the board, develop the chart shown in Table 2.2.

3. Ask students to analyze the chart to determine the following:
   a. Have they seen both men and women performing the job? If so, which gender performs it the most?
   b. Have they seen people of color perform the job? If so, who?
   c. Which jobs pay the most? Which race(s) and gender mostly occupy the jobs?

TABLE 2.2 Chart for Using Math Daily

Uses of Math	How	Kind of Math	Person Using	Schooling	Salary
1. Navigation	Airplane	Geometry	Pilot	College and flight school	Beginning annual: $55,000
2.					
3.					

4. Discuss with students that one reason white, European American males dominate some of the higher-paying jobs is that they tend to continue with math use through high school and college. Help students to realize that both sexes and any race can hold any of these jobs but that acquiring a good math background is a prerequisite, and now is a good time to start doing that.

5. Ask students to choose the jobs on the list that they would most like to have and to investigate further the math they would need to know to do the job.

6. Group students across race, gender, and class lines (where possible) to discuss the use of math in daily life and how it affects their ability to attain the profession they chose.

Evaluation

1. Assess students' understanding of math through discussion.

2. Assess students' appreciation of the importance and usefulness of math through the seriousness with which they apply themselves.

3. Through discussion, assess students' understanding of how a knowledge of math influences the achievements of groups of people.

WHY THE CHANGES?

The Importance of Math in Everyday Life

Relevance

The students being taught seem uninterested in mathematics. The "Before" lesson plan tries to inspire students to take math more seriously in the present, which is good. The "After" lesson plan also tries to connect math with students' futures. Often students do not realize the extent to which subject matter can relate to future job opportunities, nor do they often have much knowledge of a range of job options or salaries. By providing students with such information, the "After" lesson plan tries to make math seem useful for students' futures as well as present lives.

Role Models

The "After" lesson plan has students identify the race and gender of role models in math-related careers and critically think about the role models with relationship to math study. Females and students of color tend to take less math in school than white, European American males, which has consequences for jobs people attain. The "After" plan helps students see a link between the presence or absence of role models available to them and what people do to achieve certain roles. The idea is to encourage them not to be limited by an absence of role models in areas of interest to them.

Cultural Capital

Students often view upper-level math skills as useless because they believe such skills are not useful in everyday life. However, math skills are useful in many careers and for success in college. A lesson such as this one teaches how knowledge that has no immediate practical use can still be useful later in life.

LESSON PLAN

BEFORE

Scientific Problem Solving

Subject Area: Science

Grade Level: 5–8

Time: One week

Objectives

1. Students will use scientific processes to solve problems.

2. Students will design, set up, and perform a science experiment correctly.

3. Students will write up a science experiment using the correct format.

Suggested Procedures

1. Discuss with students the meaning of the scientific method or process by demonstrating several experiments. For example, make a battery or show the principles of a jet engine. While demonstrating the experiment, display a write-up of the steps and procedures on an overhead projector for students to follow.

2. Set up an experiment. For example, use a pulley to show how to lift heavy objects. Provide an outline of the procedure for conducting the experiment on a worksheet and have students complete the write-up.

3. Provide students with illustrations of science experiments and have them write up the procedures and results of the experiments.

4. Provide students with a science question that can be investigated by experimentation. Show them a variety of laboratory materials and explain how the experiment would be set up to investigate that question.

5. Provide students with science questions to be investigated using available laboratory materials. Ask each student to select one question, set up and conduct an appropriate experiment, and write up the procedures and results.

Evaluation

Observe each student's experiment and check the correctness of his or her write-up.

AFTER

Scientific Problem Solving

Subject Area: Science

Grade Level: 5–8

Time: Ongoing

Objectives

1. Students will appreciate science concepts as useful.

2. Students will understand that thinking like a scientist means solving problems in an orderly manner.

3. Students will show how scientific processes apply to their everyday lives.

4. Students will design, set up, and perform a science project, device, or experiment correctly.

5. Students will present a science project or experiment in a scientific manner.

Suggested Procedures

1. Discuss with students the importance of a knowledge of science to everyday life. Have students brainstorm applications of science to their own lives; make a list on the board.

2. Take a field trip to a local site at which students can observe the application of science principles (e.g., a farm, lake, hospital, health club, city power plant, water filtration plant). Through discussion of what students observe, make sure they see the connection among some natural resources, scientific knowledge, and their everyday lives.

3. Bring to class a car battery, chain and pedals from a bicycle, a nutcracker, a flush pump from a toilet, a motor from a refrigerator, and so on. Use these items to illustrate science principles that will be or have been taught in class. Ask students to explain, using these examples, how science affects their everyday lives. Make sure they understand the principles of science used in each device.

4. Review the science principles you have taught in class, such as the use of a fulcrum and lever or direct versus alternating electrical currents. Organize students

into groups and have each group locate in their home environment and bring to class an example of how at least one of these principles is used in everyday life. Ask each group of students to present the examples to the class and to explain the science principles that the devices use. Make certain that the student groups include both boys and girls, and discuss the gender neutrality of the materials they bring to class. For example, a car battery or an iron are gender neutral regardless of their connection to particular sex roles in the past.

5. Have students work in small groups to construct a project, device, or experiment that uses science principles to meet an everyday need. The small groups can each work collectively on a project, or the individuals within each group can work on their own projects using the other group members as consultants. For the students conducting the experiments, plan to spend time helping them formulate hypotheses, identify variables, and the like. Use the problem they have selected to investigate as a context for teaching them how to think like a scientist.

6. Have each student or group present their project in the class. During the presentation, students should explain to the class the science principles involved and how they relate to everyday life. Students should use this presentation time to talk and act in a formal manner—like a scientist.

Evaluation

1. Assess students' appreciation of the usefulness of science through discussions of the field trip as well as students' ability to locate and discuss examples of science from their own everyday lives.

2. Assess students' skill at designing and carrying out science applications through their projects.

3. Assess students' skill at formally presenting science projects through their oral presentations.

WHY THE CHANGES?

Scientific Problem Solving

Learning Style

The students being taught seem uninterested in science and don't see the point for studying it. In the "Before" lesson plan, students observe the teacher and then work individually on worksheets and experiments. The "After" lesson plan encourages cooperative learning, active participation, oral presentation, and hands-on activities. Many students find these active, collaborative teaching strategies much more engaging.

Relevance

The "Before" lesson plan teaches important concepts for students to learn. However, the "After" lesson plan relates scientific inquiry not only to experiments done in school but also to everyday life. The "After" plan shows students how science functions in their own environment and emphasizes that it is used to make life more understandable and convenient. The "After" plan discourages students from viewing science as a mystery or as the sole domain of a specialized group of people.

Cultural Capital

Students need to learn the more traditional kinds of classroom experiments and procedures for writing up experiments. The "After" plan does not stress this as heavily as the "Before" plan. The "Before" plan is best taught to students following the "After" plan—that is, after students have internalized the idea that science is useful to them, interesting, and accessible. When teaching the more traditional experiments and skills, the teacher should continually relate them to everyday life to reinforce their usefulness. The teacher should also continue to use teaching procedures that match students' learning styles, such as cooperative learning.

LESSON PLAN

BEFORE

Word Usage

Subject Area: Language Arts

Grade Level: 6–12

Time: Ongoing

Students: Those who do not habitually use Standard English in their daily speaking and writing

Objectives

1. Students will use correct Standard English.

2. Students will refrain from using incorrect English or slang.

Suggested Procedures

1. Explain to students that the slang they use when speaking is not correct, and that the class will learn and practice correct English.

2. Throughout the school year, spend time on one part of speech at a time; show correct usage, have students practice locating and correcting errors, and ask them to use correct sentences both orally and in writing. For example, if you are working on correct verb usage, use an overhead projector to show sentences in which there are errors. Ask the class, sentence by sentence, to identify the errors and to offer corrections. Create worksheets of incomplete sentences in which students are to fill in blank lines with the appropriate verbs; offer three or four verb choices for each item. Once students have completed the worksheets, review them orally in class. Then ask students to write an essay entitled "My Favorite Saturday," in which they are to pay particular attention to verb usage. Students who make excessive errors in their essays should correct them with the teacher's help and rewrite their essays. The teacher may also assign additional exercises from a grammar book.

3. Correct students regularly when they lapse back into their earlier speech patterns. Continue to emphasize the importance of always using correct Standard English.

Evaluation

1. Assess mastery of word usage through quizzes and essays.

2. Assess word usage carryover into daily life through oral usage.

| **AFTER** | ## Word Usage |

Subject Area: Language Arts

Grade Level: 6–12

Time: Ongoing

Students: Those who do not habitually use Standard English in their daily speaking and writing

Objectives

1. Students will learn what it means to code-switch and when it is useful to do so.

2. Students will use correct Standard English in circumstances in which it would be to their benefit.

Suggested Procedures

1. Ask students to suggest situations in which they might want to persuade the following audiences: peers, adults in their neighborhood, and authority figures in the wider society. Ask them to describe differences in the style of speech used

by these different audiences and to discuss how people react if one uses the wrong style of speech with the wrong audience. Point out how the concepts of dialect and language difference apply to the situations that students suggest; stress that one dialect or language is not inherently better than another but that one's purpose and audience should help determine which dialect or language one uses. Explain that code-switching means switching from one dialect or language to another, depending on one's purpose and audience.

2. Have students suggest an issue or concern they wish to address to the three audiences. Ask them to role-play orally how they would persuade each audience. (If word processors are used to teach language arts, consider the possibility of using global search-and-replace functions to code-switch. Also, with some spell-checking software, custom dictionaries can be built for each code.) Then have each student write a persuasive paragraph addressed to each audience, using the dialect or language style most likely to achieve the most positive reaction by each audience.

3. Divide students into small reading groups and have them critique each other's papers. Pay particular attention to the papers that use Standard English; provide correct usage for phrases that the group is unable to provide. Based on feedback from the group and yourself, students should rewrite the papers. If you are using word processors, present different drafts using different codes. Plan rewrites for each draft. Since rewriting with word processors is less demanding, you can ask for more versions and drafts.

4. Collect the papers. Evaluate them, paying particular attention to Standard English usage in paragraphs directed toward authority figures. If there are errors that most students are making, have whole-class lessons on these and repeat this sequence. Work individually or in small groups with specific errors that individual students may be making. When teaching specific Standard English patterns, first show students how Standard English differs grammatically, phonetically, and/or syntactically from their dialect. Then have them practice translating back and forth between dialects. Use games for any drill that may be needed on specific skills.

5. Ask each student to identify a particular authority figure whom he or she wishes to persuade to a particular point of view, either orally or in writing. Examples include persuading a prospective employer to hire oneself, persuading the principal to handle a school problem in a certain way, and persuading the city council to deal with a particular problem. Ask students to construct a persuasive argument, in Standard English, that they will deliver either orally or in writing. Provide help as needed.

Evaluation

1. Assess students' understanding of code-switching through the first written assignment.

2. Assess students' ability to use Standard English through each oral and written assignment.

3. Assess students' enjoyment through the effort they put into the assignments.

WHY THE CHANGES?

Word Usage

Learning Style

The "After" lesson plan adds the features of oral language use, role-play activities, and working cooperatively with peers to the individual writing used in the "Before" lesson plan. These features are important for two reasons. First, social situations require more oral than written language; second, most speakers of non-Standard English dialects prefer oral learning and working with others.

The "After" plan also encourages students to work together, to critique and give feedback to each other on language use, rather than having them receive all information and feedback from the teacher. Again, this makes use of a preference for learning with others. It also attempts to teach non-Standard English speakers to help each other code-switch appropriately, rather than relying on someone else for direction. Word processors can facilitate both practice and collaborative learning, as noted in the "After" lesson plan.

Relevance

The "Before" lesson plan does not make use of students' prior knowledge of language use other than their knowledge of Standard English. However, the "After" lesson plan uses students' awareness that people speak differently in different contexts and uses their collective prior experience with Standard English. Since most or all students will have had considerable exposure to Standard English (e.g., through the media), they probably know more about the subject than they use. In addition, the teacher uses the language that students already know to teach elements of a dialect they have not yet mastered.

The "Before" plan implicitly teaches students that the language spoken in their home and community is wrong, bad, and inferior. Often this forces students to do things the teacher's way or their home's way, and many students reject the teacher's way if forced to make a choice. The "After" plan teaches that both ways are acceptable in the right context; emphasis is placed on judging context, learning a new dialect (Standard English), and learning to code-switch.

Skill Levels

The "Before" plan assumes that students do not know a skill until it is taught to them. The "After" plan requires the teacher to pay attention to students' oral and written language, spending time teaching only those skills that students have not already mastered on their own.

Boredom

The "Before" plan runs the risk of boring students because it overuses work-sheets, establishes a weekly routine for teaching discrete skills, and has little connection to students' own language use. However, the "After" plan involves students actively in role-playing real situations and invites them to help define what kinds of situations would be real—the active involvement and the connection to daily life help prevent boredom. The teacher may, however, need to drill individuals on particular skills in the "After" plan. This can become boring, although teachers are encouraged to make games out of any such drill work.

LESSON PLAN*

BEFORE

Mong History

Subject Area Social Studies

Grade Level: 8–12

Time: Five class periods

Students: Culturally and linguistically diverse, with some Mong students in the class

Objectives

1. Students will explain who the Mong are, when and where they came from (geography), and why they came to the United States (history).

2. Students will describe early Mong history.

3. Students will describe recent Mong history.

4. Students will identify the major trends that shaped the Mong society.

5. Students will pinpoint the geography or the area of concentration where the Mong lived and are now living.

6. Students will take accurate notes during lectures and films.

Suggested Procedures

1. Have a world geography map available for each appropriate class period to draw students' attention to the subject matter. Start eliciting students' prior

*Source: Paoze Thao, California State University. Monterey Bay.

knowledge (elaboration) about who the Mong are. Have students contribute information they already know about the Mong and their relations with the United States. Write their contributions on the board and highlight new vocabulary as it occurs.

2. Explain to students that they will hear a short lecture on the earlier Mong history (previewing and advance organization). They will listen, take notes, compare their notes with their classmates, and then write short summaries (summarizing) of the lecture. The lecture they will hear is normally organized into three parts: introduction, content, and conclusion. Use the following steps:

   a. Read a paragraph to students and have them take notes.

   b. Check their comprehension of the paragraph and ask them for the meanings of the new words (inferencing) presented and relate them to what they already know.

   c. Read the second paragraph and ask students to repeat the second step.

   d. Read the third paragraph and ask students to repeat the second step.

   e. Read the entire short lecture. Ask students to take notes. Tell the students about the importance of linguistic markers. Write some of them on the board as they hear them in the lecture. For example, "Today, I'm going to talk about . . . " indicates the topic. When they hear the word "important," it means that the following statement is the main idea (selective attention).

3. Explain to students that they will hear a short lecture on the recent Mong history. Students should use a Timelines List (T-List) to take their notes (note-taking). Ask students to follow procedure 2.

   Then, explain the T-List procedure to students. In this T-List, students will write the main ideas (selective attention) on the left-hand side and the corresponding details on the right-hand side of the T-List.

4. Explain to students that they will continue to hear a short lecture on the major trends that shaped the Mong society. Tell students to jot down phrases and make abbreviations when taking notes (note-taking). Tell them to practice taking notes by eliminating words unnecessary for comprehension. Show the videos *Journey from Padong* and *The U.S. Secret Army in Laos*. Have students continue to take notes by using the T-List format.

5. Have students identify and pinpoint the area of concentration for the Mong that students already know. Then, lecture on the demography of the Mong. Students continue to take notes.

Evaluation

1. Divide students into small groups of three to six (maximum) to compare their notes, discuss the lectures, pool information, and fill in any missing information on the T-Lists.

2. Ask students to answer the self-evaluation questions. These questions relate to the parts of the lecture that are easy and difficult to understand (visualizing or making mental pictures).

3. Ask students to write brief summaries based on their notes. Then, ask them to work in pairs to revise and edit their summaries.

4. Assess students' additional sources of information about the relations between the Mong and the United States during the Vietnam conflict.

AFTER   ## Mong History

Subject Area: Social Studies

Grade Level 8–12

Time: Six class periods

Students: Culturally and linguistically diverse, with some Mong students in the class

Objectives

1. Students will explain who the Mong are, when and where they came from (geography), and why they came to the United States (history).

2. Students will describe early Mong history.

3. Students will describe recent Mong history through oral history accounts.

4. Students will pinpoint the geography or the area of concentration where the Mong lived and are now living.

5. Mong and non-Mong students will cooperate with each other to complete a task.

6. Students will gather information about Mong people from Mong sources.

7. Mong students will participate actively in the classroom discussions.

8. Students will take accurate notes during lectures and films.

Suggested Procedures

1. Have a world geography map available for each appropriate class period to draw students' attention to the subject matter. Start eliciting students' prior knowledge (elaboration) about who the Mong are. Have students contribute information they already know about the Mong and their relations with the United States. Encourage the Mong students to share a specific episode of their own history with the entire class (elaborating prior knowledge). Write their contributions on the board and highlight new vocabulary as it occurs.

2. Explain to students that they will hear a short lecture on the earlier Mong history (previewing and advance organization). They will listen, take notes, compare their notes with their classmates, and then write short summaries (summarizing) of the lecture. The lecture they will hear is normally organized into three parts: introduction, content, and conclusion. Use the following steps:

   a. Read a paragraph to students and have them take notes.

   b. Check their comprehension of the paragraph and ask them for the meanings of the new words (inferencing) presented and relate them to what they already know.

   c. Read the second paragraph and ask students to repeat the second step.

   d. Read the third paragraph and ask students to repeat the second step.

   e. Read the entire short lecture. Ask students to take notes. Tell the students about the importance of linguistic markers. Write some of them on the board as they hear them in the lecture. For example, "Today, I'm going to talk about . . . " indicates the topic. When they hear the word "important," it means that the following statement is the main idea (selective attention).

3. Explain to students that they will hear a short lecture on recent Mong history. Students should use a Timelines List (T-List) to take their notes (note-taking). Ask students to follow procedure 2.

Then, explain the T-List procedure to students. In this T-List, students will write the main ideas (selective attention) on the left-hand side and the corresponding details on the right-hand side of the T-List.

4. Show the videos *Journey from Padong* and *Education at the Crossroads: Needs for Professional Development* (Thao, 1996). Tell students to take notes.

5. Divide students into small groups of three to four (cooperating). Half the class will be responsible to do tape-recorded ethnographic interviews with Mong parents and Mong community leaders to record their oral histories as encountered by them. In their small groups, have the students design the questions (questioning for clarification) that will be used. (You will need to have arranged ahead of time for individuals to be interviewed.)

6. The other half of the class is to do research on the Internet to search for information on the "Mong/Hmong Home Page." Students can also search for Lao history on the Internet. Useful Web sites include the following:

   http://www.stolaf.edu/people/cdr/hmong

   http://minyos.xx.rmit.edu.au/~s914382/hmong/lao.htm

7. Then, students are to report back to the whole class.

8. Encourage students to attend the Mong New Year celebration taking place every year around November and December in major cities, where ten of thousands of Mong gather together (e.g., Twin Cities [Minnesota]; Fresno, Sacramento, Merced [California]; Milwaukee, Sheboygan, Eau Claire, Wausau, Green Bay, Appleton, La Crosse, Oshkosh [Wisconsin]). This is to get students to see the dynamics of the Mong actually living in the United States.

Evaluation

1. Assess students' general understanding of the specific episode of Mong history that was assigned for each group to perform the specific tasks. Assess the quality of students' oral presentation, the ethnographic interviews collected, and the amount of information students obtained from research through the Internet.

2. Assess students' understanding of earlier Mong history, recent history, and their ability to connect parents' contributions toward the Vietnam conflict with ideas in the video *The U.S. Secret Army in Laos* through oral discussion or a quiz.

3. Ask students to identify the geographic areas where the Mong lived and are now living.

4. Assess Mong students' active class participation through anecdotal observations.

WHY THE
CHANGES?

Mong History

Learning Styles

The Mong have long been influenced by the French educational system. During French colonialism (1892–1947), the French introduced the European model, which was implemented in Laos for nearly fifty years. The system was highly centralized and very selective. Curricula were based on the French educational pattern, and instruction was conducted in the French language. Since education was focused mainly for the elite to carry out services for the French functionaries, only a few Mong benefited from this system. Because of this influence, Mong parents were instructed by the teacher-centered "rote memorization method"—there was very little interaction between teachers and students. Many Mong parents attained one to two years of formal education in Laos, and the French educational system still influences the way some Mong parents want their children to be educated. Many Mong students thus lack the kinds of learning strategies, higher-order thinking skills, research skills, and critical reasoning skills that are absolutely necessary for high academic success in schools and higher education.

Traditionally, English as a Second Language (ESL) and content-area instruction have been functioning independently. That is, ESL has not been integrated with content-area instruction. Though many Mong students were born in the United States, they are still being classified as limited-English-proficient (LEP) students. To implement a successful program for Mong students, there is an urgent need for ESL or bilingual teachers to collaborate with content-area instructors to carry out the instruction. The intent is to accelerate the process of learning and teaching to make a smooth transition from the Basic Interpersonal Communication Skills (BICS) to the Cognitive Academic Language Proficiency (CALP), as defined by Cummins (1991), as soon as possible.

Both the "Before" and "After" lesson plans are designed to prepare all students, including the culturally and linguistically diverse student population, to achieve high academic excellence in the content areas. The "After" lesson plan integrates ESL with the content areas within the context of the Cognitive Academic Language Learning Approach (CALLA). The heart and soul of this approach is to teach students three types of learning strategies: metacognitive (advance organization, selective attention, organizational planning, self-monitoring, and self-assessment), cognitive (resourcing, elaborating prior knowledge, taking notes, grouping, making inferences, summarizing, imagery, and linguistic transfer), and social/affective (questioning for clarification, cooperating, and self-talk).

In addition, the "After" lesson plan provides an opportunity for mainstream students and other culturally and linguistically diverse students to gain a better understanding of their peers' historical background and the reasons why their classmates are in the United States today. This lesson also provides an opportunity for Mong students to experience their history through their ethnographic interviews, with a direct connection to their parents and community leaders. This will motivate the Mong students (some of whom may not know their own history), to have self-esteem, self-worth, and pride as part of American society.

Resources

National Clearinghouse for Bilingual Education (NCBE). 1118 22nd Street NW, Washington, DC 20037. Tel. (800) 321-6223.

Web site: http://www.ncbe.gwu.edu.

E-mail address: askncbe@ncbe.gwu.edu.

Print

Chamot, Anna Uhl, & O'Malley, J. Michael. (1986). *A Cognitive Academic Language Learning Approach: An ESL content-based curriculum.* Washington, DC: National Clearinghouse for Bilingual Education.

Chamot, Anna Uhl, & O'Malley, J. Michael. (1994). *The CALLA handbook: Implementing the Cognitive Academic Language Learning Approach.* Reading, MA: Addison-Wesley.

Cummins, James. (1991). Conversational and academic language proficiency in bilingual contexts. In J. H. Hulstijn & J. F. Matter (Eds.), *Reading in two languages* (pp. 75–89). AILA Review 8. Amsterdam: Free University Press.

Kagan, Spencer. (1992). *Cooperative learning.* San Juan Capistrano, CA: Resources for Teachers, Inc.

Kraus International Publications. (1993). *English as a second language curriculum resource handbook: A practical guide for K–12 ESL programs.* Millwood, NY: Author.

Quincy, Keith. (1995). *Hmong, history of a people.* Cheney, WA: Eastern Washington University Press.

Thao, Paoze. (1994). *Mong resettlement in the Chicago area (1978–1987): Educational implications.* Ph.D. dissertation, Loyola University of Chicago.

Audiovisual

Journey from Padong. (Available from University Film and Video, University of Minnesota, 1313 Fifth St. NE, Suite 109, Minneapolis, MN 55414, (612) 627-4270. Rental fee $15.)

Thao, Paoze. (1996). *Education at the crossroads: Needs for professional development.* Sacramento, CA: Lug Moob Video.

Wallace, Mike. (1983). *The U.S. secret army in Laos.* New York: CBS 60 minutes.

LESSON PLAN

BEFORE

Functions

Subject Area: Algebra

Grade Level: 9–12

Time: One class period

Objectives

1. Students will explain what the term **function** means in algebra.

2. Students will identify domain and range, given sets of quantities that vary together.

3. Students will construct statements using functional notation.

Suggested Procedures

1. On the board, write the following:

    income, amount of tax

    height, weight

    time elapsed, distance traveled

Using an overhead projector, show sets of numbers for each pair on the board. Explain that, although all three examples are different, they have something in common; that is, they are sets of two numbers that vary together. Explain that a mathematician needs to focus on both sets simultaneously. For example, an accelerating car travels distance over time; one cannot understand this if one pays attention only to distance or only to time.

2. Define the three items in a function: domain, range, and rule.

3. Show how mathematical sentences can be constructed. For example, I = income, T = tax; the tax on an income of $15,000 is $3,025; T ($15,000) = $3,025. Have students help construct additional sentences, using the sets of numbers on the projector. Stress that any letters can be used as long as students agree on what they stand for.

4. Explain that mathematicians have agreed on three letters to express functional relationships: x, y, and f. Write f(x) = y on the board and read it aloud. Show how the equation applies to relationships expressed in the previous step.

5. Assign homework.

Evaluation

Assess students' mastery of objectives through homework problems that require them to identify domain and range and to construct statements using functional notation.

AFTER

Functions

Subject Area: Algebra

Grade Level: 9–12

Time: One class period

Objectives

1. Students will compare and contrast street language with mathematical language.

2. Students will explain what the term **function** means in algebra.

3. Students will identify domain and range, given sets of quantities that vary together.

4. Students will contrast statements using functional notation.

Suggested Procedures

1. A day or two before the lesson, ask students for the names of four (or more) popular musicians. Ask them to describe in a phrase or two each musician's career (e.g., length of career, frequency of new recordings, number of times songs have hit the top-40 charts, and so on). Write the phrases on the board and save them. Then ask for volunteers to research the careers of these musicians. For each musician, students are to complete the chart shown in Figure 2.2, providing the number of songs recorded and the number of songs that made the top-40 charts. The teacher should point out that the numbers in each column of the chart are to be cumulative.

2. The day of the lesson, have volunteers put the chart for each musician's career on the board. Explain that their careers can be described in street language and in mathematical language. Review the street language phrases provided earlier; discuss the extent to which they convey precision.

3. Explain that mathematical language uses a different vocabulary and set of symbols: functional notation. On the charts on the board, point to the domain and the range; discuss the fact that these vary together. Also point out that the exact relationship varies over time and varies among musicians. Point out street language words that students used to express this.

4. For each musician, have students select letters to represent the domain and range and write sentences such as $P(17) = 2$, where P = the number of songs produced. Explain how parentheses are being used.

5. Explain that functional relationships generally have three parts (domain, range, and rule) and that they are expressed with the letters x, y, and f. Write $f(x) = y$ on the board and explain the relationship to the preceding step. Read this statement mathematically.

6. Explain how to solve for f and express f graphically. Students should learn to graph the musicians' careers and to write formulas describing them.

7. To make sure that students understand, ask for other sets of two quantities that vary together, such as age and height. Ask students to write formulas expressing these relationships.

FIGURE 2.2

Name of musician	Total number of songs produced	Total number of songs in Top 40

Evaluation

1. Assess students' comprehension of the term **function** through oral work.

2. Assess students' skills through homework problems that ask them to identify domain and range and to construct statements using functional notation.

WHY THE CHANGES?

Functions

Learning Style

The students being taught here are inner-city students, mainly from poverty-level homes. They are not yet sure why they should be learning algebra and how it relates to anything. They also find many traditional teaching strategies, in which they are passive, to be boring. The "Before" lesson plan asks the teacher to explain and demonstrate as students watch. In contrast, the "After" plan invites active student participation as they gather data and suggest descriptions. Active participation helps most students to learn.

Relevance

The "Before" plan does not suggest to students why they would want to know this information. The teacher attempts to make the lesson applicable to real life by using examples of income tax, height and weight, and acceleration, but students may or may not find the examples relevant or interesting. In the "After" lesson plan, however, the teacher capitalizes on student interest through music. Further, by inviting students to gather information on musicians, the teacher has (1) used the lesson to show students a use for data they care about and (2) allowed students to contribute expertise in an area they probably know more about than the teacher.

In the "After" plan, the teacher asks students to generate other sets of quantities that vary together to make sure students understand the concept. The "Before" plan requires them merely to apply a rule to examples provided by the teacher.

Expectations

The "Before" plan allows more time for students to complete homework in class, which has the advantage of making the teacher available for help. It does this, however, at the expense of interesting instruction that involves students actively. Perhaps the teacher does not expect much homework to get done at home and therefore streamlines whole-class instruction to allow class time for homework. The "After" plan allows more opportunity for the teacher to note and correct mistakes during the lesson, when everyone can benefit from additional explanation. The teacher of the "After" plan expects that students will complete homework at home and therefore uses class time for active instruction of everyone. If the teacher follows through on homework, assigns reasonably interesting work, and explains it thoroughly, it is quite likely to get done.

Language

In the "After" plan, the teacher also makes use of street language, offering mathematical language as a different, more precise but less colorful, alternative. Again, the lesson takes a familiar part of the students' world—their language—and relates it to algebra.

LESSON PLAN

BEFORE

Polymers

Subject Area: Chemistry

Grade Level: 11–12

Time: Two class periods

Students: Those of varying academic skill levels, many below average; those who seem uninterested in chemistry

Objectives

1. Students will explain the meaning of the term **polymer.**

2. Given a monomer, students will diagram the polymer chain that forms.

3. Students will learn to identify common materials that are polymers.

Suggested Procedures

1. Review orally the concept of double bonding. Explain that polymers are organic molecules that form when double carbon bonds are converted to single bonds and a long-chain molecule with single carbon-carbon bonds is created.

2. Have students read pages in a textbook on additional polymers.

3. Review the main concepts on the board, asking questions frequently to make sure students understand. Start with the conversion of ethylene to polyethylene;

diagram this. Then discuss and diagram polyvinyl chloride, polypropylene, polystyrene, Plexiglas, and Teflon.

4. Show examples of these materials; discuss their uses.

Evaluation

1. Assess students' understanding of polymers and chemical bonding changes through class participation in review.

2. Assess students' understanding of a polymer chain and their memory of common materials that are polymers through a quiz.

AFTER

Polymers

Subject Area: Chemistry

Grade Level: 11–12

Time: Three class periods

Students: Those of varying academic skill levels, many below average; those who seem uninterested in chemistry

Objectives

1. Students will explain the meaning of the term **polymer.**

2. Given a monomer, students will diagram the polymer chain that forms.

3. Students will learn to identify common materials that are polymers.

4. Students will enjoy chemistry and consider it as a career option.

Suggested Procedures

1. On a table, have the following items: film, floor tile made of PVC, beakers, Lucite, Teflon bearings, and a Teflon frying pan. Ask students what all these materials have in common; students should figure out that all are forms of plastic and all are either manufactured or naturally produced.

2. Some software programs for educational computers simulate the bonding process and permit students to control the steps (e.g., *Molecular Editor* for the Mac). If you cannot gain access to a sophisticated visual resource, use a metal board with magnetic letters, numbers, and sticks to make the formula for the monomer ethylene shown in Figure 2.3. Point out the double carbon bond and

FIGURE 2.3

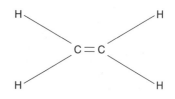

review the concept of double bonding. Explain that this is a monomer, in which **mono-** means "one." Put another monomer ethylene on the board and ask students how these might be joined. Lead students to see how polymers are constructed when double bonds break and monomers link in a chain. Point out that the prefix **poly-** means "many." (Whether using computer displays or magnetic pieces, all parts, including chemical bonds, must be used in linking monomers to form polymers; point out that pieces do not drop out and new pieces do not appear.)

3. Diagram the monomers vinyl chlorine, propylene, methyl methacrylate, and tetrafluoroethylene on the board. Have students work in pairs to figure out diagrams for polymer chains of each. (Students may use computer displays or magnetic pieces if this helps.)

4. Provide a study sheet on additional polymers; instruct students to read the pages and to complete the study sheet with a partner or alone.

5. With the whole class, review the polymer chains that students constructed in pairs, using students' input.

6. Have students suggest questions they would like to ask a chemist who works with these materials; make a list of students' questions. Encourage questions related to what the chemist does, how the chemist works with the materials, differences a chemist can see between monomers and polymers, what it is like to be a chemist, and so forth. On a subsequent day—after the chapter on polymers is completed—invite a female chemist as a guest speaker and allow students to ask questions.

Evaluation

1. Assess students' understanding of a polymer and of the chemical bonding changes when monomers form by observing student pairs work on problems, through whole-class review, and through items on a quiz.

2. Assess students' understanding of monomers and polymers and of materials that are polymers through study guide answers.

3. Assess students' interest through their questions and reactions to the guest speaker.

Resources

Software

Molecular Editor. Kinko's Courseware, 4141 State Street, Santa Barbara, CA 93110. Tel. (800) 292-6640.

**WHY THE
CHANGES?**

Polymers

Learning Styles

The "After" lesson plan uses a greater variety of teaching procedures than the "Before" plan. In addition to lectures and textbook readings, it includes a visual diagram and cooperative problem solving. Cooperative problem solving helps students who learn better working with others.

Relevance

Both lesson plans try to relate polymers to daily life by showing items made with polymers. However, the "Before" plan waits until the end of the lesson to do this, whereas the "After" plan begins by introducing familiar, everyday items.

Skill Levels

This type of class is not one in which the teacher can assign a grade-level text and expect students to learn from it. The teacher in the "After" plan has made three adjustments for diverse skill levels. The first adjustment involves a computer display or magnetic board, rather than writing formulas on the board. The magnetic board and computer display allow the teacher and students to move elements and bonds around to create polymers, which makes it easier for students to see the relationship between them. In the "Before" plan, in which the teacher writes formulas on the board, this relationship is not made as clear.

The second adjustment is the use of peer teaching. The "After" plan asks students to work on polymer chains in pairs and to complete study sheets with partners. The teacher should make sure pairs actually work together; he or she should re-pair students as needed.

The third adjustment involves choosing which monomers and polymers to study. Formulas for monomers and polymers in the "Before" plan vary, and some are quite complex. They are selected on the basis of the textbook and are more common materials. But for students who find the main idea confusing in itself, this variety of formulas only adds to their confusion. Although the "After" plan also selects monomers and polymers from the textbook, those selected have formulas similar enough so that the main idea can be seen more clearly.

Expectations

The "After" plan spends more time than the "Before" plan on emphasizing students' mastery of the material. If the students become interested enough in chemistry and successful enough in learning it, the extra effort is worthwhile.

Success Stories

The "After" plan tries to make the field of chemistry more relevant to students by inviting a guest speaker with whom some of them can identify. The speaker should be someone who can provide a positive role model for students who do not see chemistry as relevant to their lives. Students themselves write the questions for the speaker to address, which bridges the identification and communication gap between the students and the speaker.

LESSON PLAN

BEFORE

Cardiovascular Health

Subject Area: Health

Grade Level 10–12

Time: Five class periods

Students: Several Spanish-English bilingual students, as well as a few students from a learning disabilities (LD) class

Objectives

1. Students will identify the main parts of the cardiovascular system and their functions.

2. Students will describe several heart diseases or conditions and their causes.

3. Students will learn a healthy dietary and exercise program.

Suggested Procedures

1. Explain that the class will spend the next few days studying the cardiovascular system, related diseases, and disease prevention.

2. Assign pages in the textbook on the structure and function of the cardiovascular system and risk factors.

3. Review the major concepts in a reading assignment, asking questions frequently to check comprehension. Show the film *Heart—How It Works* (1955). Encourage

students to take notes on the discussion of the textbook assignment and the film.

4. Assign pages in the textbook on heart attack and heart disease.

5. Review the major concepts in the reading assignment; give a mini lecture, elaborating on what physicians do when someone has a heart attack.

6. Invite the school nurse as a guest speaker to talk about how exercise and diet can promote cardiovascular health.

Evaluation

Evaluate each student's mastery of the objectives through a quiz.

Resources

Heart—How it works. (1955). Delmar, CA: McGraw-Hill/CRM.

AFTER   Cardiovascular Health

Subject Area: Health

Grade Level: 10–12

Time: Five class periods

Students: Several Spanish-English bilingual students, as well as a few students from a learning disabilities (LD) class

Objectives

1. Students will identify the main parts of the cardiovascular system and their functions.

2. Students will describe several heart diseases or conditions and their causes.

3. Students will learn a health dietary and exercise program.

Suggested Procedures

1. Invite students to share the experiences of family members or friends who have heart disease. Explain that the class will study the cardiovascular system, diseases, and disease prevention.

2. Divide the class into three groups based on students' reading levels. Have three sets of reading materials ready. One set, written at the lowest reading level, describes heart diseases. A second set, written at an intermediary level,

describes the circulatory system. A third set, written at a more difficult level, describes the parts of the heart. Distribute the appropriate reading materials to each group. Have students read and then quiz each other until all group members have mastered the material.

3. Regroup students into four groups, such that each new group contains two or three members from the first group. Assign each group one of the following problems or tasks to complete collaboratively:

   a. Explain what types of exercise contribute to the health of the cardiovascular system. Suggest an exercise program for persons aged 15–25 that will promote cardiovascular health; give reasons for your suggestions.

   b. Explain what cholesterol does to the cardiovascular system. Develop European American and Mexican menus that are low in cholesterol.

   c. Develop a Spanish-English dictionary to help Spanish-speaking people with limited English communicate with an English-speaking doctor about common heart problems.

   d. Determine and describe the functions an artificial heart must perform. Describe the conditions under which one might be helped by an artificial heart.

   Have available any resource materials the groups might need, such as nutrition guides or newspaper articles on the artificial heart.

4. Have each group orally present its completed project to the class. Encourage students to use relevant diagrams, charts, or activities to involve the class. Make duplicated copies of students' exercise programs, menus, and dictionaries for the entire class.

5. Provide a study guide on the material students should know, as well as additional copies of the first reading assignment for students who wish to read what other groups read. Encourage students to study together and to quiz each other on the study guide.

Evaluation

1. Evaluate students' comprehension of main ideas through group projects.

2. Evaluate students' mastery of the objectives through a quiz.

WHY THE CHANGES?

Cardiovascular Health

Learning Style

Many students tend to learn better through cooperative learning than through individualistic learning. Cooperative learning also fosters peer tutoring, which helps low-achieving students. The "Before" plan does not use cooperative learning. The "After" plan uses quite a bit of it, although only in procedures 3 and 4 do all students participate; they have a choice in the other procedures. In the "Before" plan, the main role students occupy is as passive recipient. In the "After" plan, students are active participants in learning, which tends to promote better achievement.

The "Before" plan uses various teaching–learning strategies: reading, discussing, watching a film, listening to a speaker. In the "After" plan, the film and speaker are removed only for lack of time; both leave students passive, and a choice was made to increase time on active involvement. Films and speakers can be useful reinforcers or sources of new information, however, and should be left in if time permits.

Relevance

Little attempt is made in the "Before" plan to relate the curriculum to these particular students. The "After" plan includes several attempts: the introductory discussion, the use of the Spanish language in one project, the use of Mexican foods in a group project, and the invitation for students themselves to figure out a dietary and exercise program.

Skill Levels

The "Before" plan makes no provision for students' diverse skill levels, whereas the "After" plan does in two ways. First, reading assignments are made according to students' reading levels, although students later have to teach each other about what they read so no one misses content areas. Second, students are encouraged to study together with a study guide to direct work.

Language

The Spanish-English dictionary assignment helps bilingual students acquire English words. It can also sensitize English-speaking students to language barriers.

Boredom

The "After" plan is more interesting than the "Before" plan without sacrificing integrity. It also encourages more thinking—students learn better when the lesson itself is enjoyable.

References

Boykin, A. W., & Allen, B. (1988). Rhythmic-movement facilitated learning in working class Afro-American children. *Journal of Genetic Psychology*, *149*, 335–347.

Cummins, James. (1991). Conversational and academic language proficiency in bilingual contexts. In J. H. Hulstijn & J. F. Matter (Eds.), *Reading in two languages* (pp. 75–89). AILA Review 8. Amsterdam: Free University Press.

Delpit, L. (1995). *Other people's children*. New York: New Press.

Dunn, R. S. (1992). *Teaching elementary students through their individual learning styles: Practical approaches for grades 3–6*. Boston: Allyn & Bacon.

Escalante, J. (1990). The Jaime Escalante math program. *Journal of Negro Education*, *59*(3), 407–423.

Fennema, E., & Peterson, P. L. (1987). Effective teaching for girls or boys: The same or different? In D. C. Berliner & B. V. Rosenshine (Eds.), *Talks to teachers* (pp. 111–125). New York: Random House.

Gardner, H. (1993). *Multiple intelligences: The theory in practice*. New York: Basic Books.

Hale, J. E. (1982). *Black children: Their roots, culture, and learning style*. Provo, UT: Brigham Young University Press.

Hollins, E. R. (1996). *Culture in school learning: Revealing the deep meaning*. Mahwah, NJ: Lawrence Erlbaum.

Philips, S. U. (1983). *The invisible culture*. New York: Longman.

Shade, B. J. R. (1989). *Culture, style and the educative process*. Springfield, IL: Charles Thomas.

Sleeter, C. E., & Grant, C. A. (1994). *Making choices for multicultural education: Five approaches to race, class, and gender* (2nd ed.). Upper Saddle River, NJ: Merrill/Prentice Hall.

Human Relations

Do any of the following incidents resemble situations you have encountered?

A student who uses a wheelchair is mainstreamed into a fourth-grade class. She is excited and nervous on her first day. The student is introduced to the class and then wheels to her place in the front row. None of the other children speak to her, but they stare and giggle when they think she is not looking. On the playground, several students gang up to tease her.

A newly desegregated high school is the scene of a cold war. Although the European American and African American students inhabit the same classrooms and facilities, they rarely mix or talk to one another; when they do mix their interactions are superficial. For the most part, they ignore one another most of the time, but occasionally fights and verbal insults occur.

Some of the Latino students refuse to acknowledge their ability to speak Spanish—they seem embarrassed by their parents and by their Spanish surnames, which suggest they know Spanish (and many of them do). They are eager to look and act like their white European American classmates. Other Latino students take pride in their culture and language and are put off by their Latino brothers and sisters who act like their white classmates; they are also put off by some of their white classmates who distance themselves from them.

During recess, two girls ask a group of boys if they can play soccer with them. Some of the boys snicker, saying, "Girls can't play well enough to play with boys." A few boys point toward their less athletic male teammates, saying, "Those sissies are better soccer players than any girl."

If you have encountered similar situations, you may find yourself gravitating toward the **Human Relations approach** to teaching. Although this approach is not the only means by which to deal with the problems that exist among different groups of people, it is the only one that has as its primary concern the establishment of nondiscriminating interaction among different types of people.

PRIMARY CONCERNS OF THE HUMAN RELATIONS APPROACH TO TEACHING

The Human Relations approach is directed toward developing respect among individuals of various races, genders, classes, exceptionalities, and sexual orientation. It encourages students to see the beauty within people instead of looking only at the external surface. It also seeks to improve feelings and communication in the classroom and in the school as a whole. Specifically, it focuses on the following considerations:

- Respect for oneself and for others
- Positive student–student relationships
- Elimination of the stereotypes students often have about each other (which are often manifest in name-calling)
- Improved self-concept, especially related to individual and cultural differences
- Positive cross-group communication

The term *human relations* generally encompasses any aspect of interpersonal relations. The Human Relations approach to multicultural education is directed primarily toward interpersonal and intergroup relations centering on race or ethnicity, gender, social class, sexual orientation, and abilities differences. In this approach, teachers work with students in a number of areas.

Cooperative Learning

Recently, a fair amount of research suggests that **cooperative learning** improves student–student relationships across race, gender, and ability/disability lines as well as student achievement (Johnson, Johnson, & Maruyama, 1983; Slavin & Madden, 1979; Slavin, 1995). However, to be effective, cooperative learning must satisfy several conditions for cross-group contact, as suggested by Gordon Allport (1954) more than forty years ago. It must involve students in cooperative activities across lines of difference, involve students in roles of equal status, provide opportunities for students to learn about one another as individuals, and be strongly supported by the teacher. In addition, cooperative learning must be used consistently and frequently in the classroom.

Although there are different models for structuring cooperative learning, they all require students to interact in small groups to accomplish a common goal. They also require teachers to structure tasks so that each student is able to make a worthwhile contribution. Some of the lesson plans that appear later in this chapter illustrate the models for structuring cooperative learning. The **group investigation model** is presented in the lesson plans "Westward Ho!" (p. 88) and "Salamanders" (p. 84). This model requires students to contribute different talents, skills, interests, and roles to the creation of a group project or solution of a group problem. The **team games model** is used in the lesson "Factoring Polynomials and Making Friends at the Same Time" (p. 105). In this model, students practice academic skills while working together as a team. The **jigsaw model** is illustrated in "Solving Two Equations with Two Unknowns" (p. 101). In this model, students are grouped twice. First, each group masters different materials and each student becomes an "expert" in his or her group's area. Students are then regrouped so that each new group has at least one "expert" from the first set of groups. The new groups solve a problem or complete an assignment that requires pooling their expertise and sharing what they learned in the first group. (See also "Cardiovascular Health," chapter 2, p. 51.)

Cooperative learning involves much more than grouping students and asking them to work cooperatively. Rather, the group tasks need to be planned carefully so that each student has a needed role in the group, a contribution to make of which he or she is capable, and the incentive to work together with the group.

Attitudes, Prejudice, and Stereotyping

Teachers must be aware of what their students say and of their behavior to recognize stereotyping, which many students do without realizing it. Negative attitudes, prejudices, and stereotyping develop through a complex range of factors; in our companion volume, *Making Choices for Multicultural Education* (Sleeter & Grant, 1994), we review research and theory on these concepts. Students need to be made aware that stereotyping goes against the principles they learned in science—that judgments should be formed only after a comprehensive evaluation of the data.

Eliminating stereotypes usually involves helping students to see how they are using stereotyping and to understand that stereotyping involves making an oversimplified opinion or uncritical judgment, both of which are not characteristic of students with inquiring minds. As preschoolers, they begin to notice differences among people and begin to form attitudes and interpretations of those differences. Stereotypes represent peoples' attempts to understand what they see and experience and are formed on the basis of hearsay, narrow experiences, bad experiences, and interpretations of experiences that are a part of everyday discourse. Action Research Activity 3.1 is a useful tool to sensitize young people to their own tendencies to stereotype. Action Research Activity 3.4 is a questionnaire that looks at sex stereotyping.

Curricular interventions can help reduce prejudice and stereotyping. James Banks (1995) reviewed research on curricular interventions addressing racial and gender stereotyping. He concluded that research findings on the impact of curriculum on students' attitudes and stereotyping are inconsistent but optimistic. Some studies have found that interventions make no difference, while others found that they make a positive change. Banks recommends that teachers use well-designed curricular interventions and materials and pay attention to the impact of their interventions on their own students so that they can make adjustments as needed. Young children seem particularly influenced by curricular interventions—elementary teachers have a particularly important opportunity to develop open and democratic attitudes in children.

Lesson plans that help to correct the problem of stereotyping involve giving correct information to replace stereotypes and having students participate in activities that make them realize the inaccuracies of stereotypes. For example, a lesson seeking to counter-argue the stereotype that males are not nurturing could feature as guest speakers fathers who care for their children; also, male students could be allowed to practice holding a baby. A lesson on the inaccuracy of stereotypes about females being unathletic could involve a discussion of the excellent performance by women in the Olympic Games of 1996, where women showed exceptional athletic skills. In addition, some factual data are usually needed to replace stereotypes, as are activities that persuade students that factual data is preferable to stereotypes. The lesson plans "Toys" (p. 71), "Bones and Muscles" (p. 81), and "Stereotypes" (p. 97) are designed in this way.

Personal Feelings

As we all know, children can be cruel to one another and can hurt classmates' feelings without even realizing it. We hope that as students mature, they learn that such cruel behavior is wrong. A school district one of us is familiar with has implemented a "peace builders" program to teach students constructive ways of relating with people; this program is having a positive impact on how students treat each other. The teacher is an important influence on students' learning to eliminate cruel behavior and to replace it with peaceful and positive behavior. Lessons that focus on this usually involve conflict resolution, role-playing, and discussion of how feelings are hurt by name-calling and cruel actions. Action Research Activity 3.3 helps you investigate your students' experiences with name-calling, teachers' interventions, and students' ideas about how to handle it.

Students in grades 6–12 sometimes need lessons to help them understand how members of oppressed groups feel. For example, the lesson might segregate students on the basis of such characteristics as right-handedness versus left-handedness to help them understand the feelings and attitudes associated with being oppressed. By encouraging students to experience personally how it feels to be neglected or ridiculed, teachers can instigate more positive behavior among classmates and groups.

Individual Uniqueness and Worth

Each student is different and unique in his or her own way. If teachers fail to recognize students' uniqueness, the students will often make it clear to the teacher in some way. The Human Relations approach highlights the uniqueness and worth of each and every individual. Race, gender, and social class are important considerations, but the approach concentrates on **individual uniqueness** and **worth.** Many teachers point out that it is also important to stress what we have in common rather than focusing entirely on differences. Teachers who demonstrate value for the worth of their diverse students usually connect this with the common value that all students share. Students bring different gifts to the classroom, but all of them bring a desire to feel worthy, successful, and accepted.

Included in this chapter are several lessons that help students develop pride in themselves and an appreciation of peers. The lessons attempt to sensitize students to the similarities and differences among people, helping them to see that people are more alike than different and that differences are valuable. These kinds of lessons can take countless forms, but they often involve similar activities (e.g., students identifying something unique and valuable about themselves; determining what would make another student happy and attempting to fulfill that wish; creating collages and classroom displays expressing personal interests; arranging fairs that highlight students' accomplishments). The lessons "Paper Flowers" (p. 69) and "Billboards" (p. 94) also involve teaching about the contributions of ethnic and gender groups, especially those represented by students in the school. The main concern is to teach that everyone has something worthwhile to contribute.

Cross-Group Communication

Communication, whether it occurs among groups or between two individuals living in the same household, should not be underestimated. Major organizations (e.g., the United Nations) have been formed solely to promote **cross-group communication,** and some school staff members (e.g., bilingual teachers and home–school coordinators) spend most of their work day in this area. The people directly involved in establishing and promoting cross-group communication know that it is hard work.

Although it may be difficult to establish and maintain cross-group communication in the classroom, educators have some powerful advantages over those in other fields. The teacher is in charge, and students ordinarily look up to the teacher—these advantages help to create a classroom characteristic of open, civil, and honest interactions. The authors have observed teachers who are excellent at establishing cross-group communication in classes made up of several different kinds of groups. These teachers use a variety of techniques and strategies to achieve their success, including cooperative learning. They also teach communication skills (e.g., listening, sharing, inviting), and have students practice these skills in structured lessons. Another strategy is to teach students about cultural differences in communication style, allowing students of different cultural backgrounds to interpret correctly what others mean and to respond in a culturally appropriate manner. The lesson "Judging Differences" (p. 92) works toward this goal. Lesson plans that seek to promote cross-group communication usually involve factual information about communication skills and styles, demonstrations of communication skills, role-playing, and contact with people whose communication styles differ from the students'. Although these activities work well, cross-group communication must be a regular part of the daily curriculum to be successful.

In some of the lesson plans that follow, the "After" sections have different titles from those used in the "Before" sections. The change in title reflects a substantive change in the focus of the lesson to meet the needs of all students to "turn on" to learning.

ACTION RESEARCH ACTIVITY 3.1

Stereotyping

This activity is a survey that investigates the extent to which your students or co-workers stereotype people on the basis of race, gender, and disability. Figure 3.1 contains pictures of people and their names, along with a list of personality characteristics and work roles. Photocopy the figure, making as many copies as you need.

Scoring. The best response is no response. People who say they cannot complete the survey are usually refusing to stereotype, as are those who put *all* the characteristics under *every* name. For those who do stereotype in their responses, you can analyze their responses through the following patterns:

- Which persons received the success words and phrases (1, 4, 7, 10, 20, 22, 26, 27)?
- Which persons received the failure or anonymity words and phrases (8, 9, 11, 12, 13, 30, 31, 32)?
- Were sex-stereotypic personality traits and work roles chosen (e.g., women: cleans house [18] and bakes cookies [16])?
- Are there particular race stereotypes (e.g., African Americans: good in music [14] and plays basketball [34]; Asian Americans: owns a restaurant [26] and quiet [5])?

ACTION RESEARCH ACTIVITY 3.2

Sociometric Survey

To find out how well your students know and like each other, use the survey shown in Figure 3.2 (p. 65). Fill in students' names in the left-hand column and duplicate and distribute. Assure students that their responses will be kept confidential.

You can analyze the results of the survey in two ways. First, for each student, tally the total number of marks in each column. For example, which students are liked or known the most? The least? Are there identifiable characteristics of least-liked or least-known students? Second, look for segregation and grouping patterns, such as sex segregation, racial segregation, and so forth. Use this information for group-building activities. You may also want to investigate potential stereotypes that accompany social segregation or dislike of peers.

Maria Concha Hernandez

Martin Begay

Kenneth Steinmetz

Cheryl Smith

Directions: Select the words or phrases from the following list that describe each person. Write the word or phrase (or number) under the person's name.

1. strong
2. mean
3. shy
4. aggressive
5. quiet
6. loud
7. smart
8. stupid
9. unable to speak well
10. rich
11. poor
12. sad
13. needs help
14. good in music
15. good in math
16. bakes cookies

FIGURE 3.1   Stereotyping

Jane Fitzpartick

Pat Jackson

William Jones

Susan Noguchi

17. good at yard work
18. cleans house
19. teacher
20. principal
21. janitor
22. doctor
23. nurse
24. cares for children
25. car mechanic

26. owns a restaurant
27. president
28. secretary
29. police officer
30. thief
31. unemployed
32. stays home
33. goes skiing
34. plays basketball

ACTION RESEARCH ACTIVITY 3.3

Name-Calling

These are interview questions about experiences with prejudice. They work best with older students.

1. Tell me about a time in which some students were making fun of another student.

   What did the teacher(s) or supervisor(s) do about it?

   How did students react to what the teacher(s) or supervisor(s) did or did not do?

   Might the situation have been handled better, do you think? If so, how?

   Did the teacher(s) or supervisor(s) do anything to teach kids not to make fun of others like the one getting picked on? If so, what?

2. Can you think of times when girls/boys (opposite sex of the interviewee) have picked on other kids on the basis of sex or have stereotyped your sex unfairly?

   Tell me about it; what did they do or say?

   What, if anything, did the teacher(s) or supervisor(s) do about it?

   How effective were their responses?

   Would you have liked to have seen them do something different?

3. Have you been aware of other kids being prejudiced against other racial or ethnic groups?

   How did you know they were?

   What did the teacher(s) or supervisor(s) do about it?

   How effective were their responses?

   Would you have liked to have seen them do something different?

4. Can you think of times when kids with disabilities have been picked on or called names?

   What happened?

   What did the teacher(s) or supervisor(s) do about it?

5. In addition to what we have just talked about, are there other ways that kids make fun of each other? Other names you have heard them call other kids?

6. Tell me about the most effective thing you have seen an adult do to help kids who are different get along better and appreciate each other more.

Student's Name	Very well— a friend	Well, but not a friend	Not too well, would like to know better	Not too well, would *not* like to know better	Not at all
1.					
2.					
3.					
4.					
5.					
6.					
7.					
8.					
9.					
10.					
11.					
12.					
13.					
14.					
15.					
16.					
17.					
18.					
19.					
20.					
21.					
22.					

FIGURE 3.2   How Well Do You Know Your Classmates?

How do you know it worked?

Why do you think it worked? (In other words, what made it work?)

ACTION RESEARCH ACTIVITY 3.4

Sex Stereotyping

Have sex stereotypes disappeared at long last? Find out! You can do this activity as either an interview or a questionnaire. If you do it as an interview, use questions such as the following:

1. Are there any occupations you consider:

   especially appropriate for a woman? Why?

   especially appropriate for a man? Why?

   inappropriate for a woman? Why?

   inappropriate for a man? Why?

2. Around the house, which tasks do you think are more appropriate for:

   the females to do? Why?

   the males to do? Why?

3. In your household, which jobs do:

   the females do?

   the males do?

4. If there are very young children in the household, who should have the main responsibility for them?

   Why?

   Should that person also hold a job?

Questionnaire

Name: _____

Directions: Choose the best word from the two given to complete each sentence. If neither choice is best, write any word you think is best.

   1. Dr. Martin reads X rays. _____ helps people.
      (He, She)

   2. We need milk, butter, and eggs. My _____ will go to the store.
      (dad, mom)

   3. _____ is mowing the lawn.
      (Ann, Tim)

4. Dr. Meyer filled a cavity in one of Maria's teeth. _____ is a dentist.
   (She, He)

5. Steve's house is dirty. His _____ must clean it.
   (dad, mom)

6. _____ Johnson is our principal.
   (Mrs., Mr., Ms., Miss)

7. Jim's _____ is a firefighter.
   (aunt, uncle)

8. A police officer came to the door. _____ was wearing a blue uniform.
   (She, He)

9. An astronaut came to our school. _____ talked about rockets.
   (She, He)

10. _____ is a good baseball player.
    (Tina, Steve)

11. _____ enjoys playing on the computer at home.
    (Judy, Willie)

12. Carlos broke his watch. His _____ fixed it.
    (mom, dad)

13. The mechanic fixed our car. _____ knew what was wrong.
    (She, He)

14. Nurse Jackson took Rosa's temperature. _____ put Rosa to bed.
    (She, He)

15. _____ likes to bake cookies.
    (Joey, Julie)

16. _____ Kelley is our librarian.
    (Mrs., Mr., Ms.)

17. _____ is an artist.
    (Todd, Gwen)

18. _____ must take out the garbage.
    (Joan, Jim)

19. It is _____ 's turn to do the dishes.
    (Mike, Sue)

20. _____ is going camping this weekend.
    (Joy, Greg)

Nombre: _____

1. _____ Martinez lee los rayos x. _____ ayuda a la gente.
   (La doctora, El doctor)   *(Ella, El)*

2. Necesitamos leche, mantequilla, y huevos. Mi _____ ira a la tienda.
   (madre, padre)

3. _____ esta cortando la (el) cesped.
   (Ana, Carlos)

4. _____ Meyer lleno una carie en el diente de Maria. _____ es
   (El doctor, La doctora)   *(El, Ella)*

   un(a) dentist(a).

5. El cuarto de Steve esta sucio. Su _____ tiene que limpialo.
                                        (madre, padre)

6. _____ Rodriguez es nuestro(a) diretor(a).
   (El Sr., La Srta., La Sra.)

7. _____ de Luisa es un(a) bombero.
   (El tio, La tia)

8. Un(a) agente de policia llego a la puerta. _____ llevaba un uniforme
                                                (Ella, El)

   azul.

9. Un(a) astronaut(a) llegó a nuestra escuela. _____ hablo sobre
                                                 (Ella, El)

   cohetes.

10. _____ es un(a) buen(a) jugador(a) de beisbol.
    (Rosa, Miquel)

11. Las matemáticas son la matéria preferida de _____ en la escuela.
                                                  (Carmen, Mario)

12. Carlos rompio su reloj. Su _____ se lo arreglo.
                                (madre, padre)

13. _____ arreglo nuestro coche. _____ supo lo que estaba mal.
    (El mecanico/La mecanica)   *(El, Ella)*

14. _____ Jackson se le tomo la temperatura a Rosa. _____
    (La enfermera/El enfermero)   *(El, Ella)*

    alemandó a Rosa a acostorse.

15. A _____ le gusta hornear galletas.
     (Jose, Diana)

16. _____ Cruz es nuestro(a) bibliotecario(a).
    (El Sr., La Srta., La Sra.)

17. _____ es un(a) artist(a).
     (El, Ella)

18. Letoca a _____ de lavar los platos.
        (Susanna, Miguel)

19. _____ debé sacar la basura.
    (Ramon, Conchita)

20. _____ va a acampar este fin de semana.
    (Carlos, Maria)

LESSON PLAN

BEFORE

Paper Flowers

Subject Area: Art
Grade Level: 1–3
Time: One day

Objectives

1. Students will cut curves on paper accurately.
2. Students will create a colorful design.

Suggested Procedures

1. Pass out large pieces of construction paper, one to each student. Show them how to fold it in half to make a cover for their art work.
2. Demonstrate how to draw a flower shape using curves on colored paper. Show several different flower shapes; stress that they can be very different from one another. Show how to cut out a flower.
3. Make available colored paper, scissors, and paste. Tell students to draw several different flowers on different colors of paper, cut them out, and paste them to their covers.
4. When students are done, share covers.

Evaluation

Assess students' quality of design of covers, quality of cutting, and neatness.

AFTER

Paper Flowers[*]

Subject Area: Art
Grade Level: 1–3
Time: One day

Objectives

1. Students will cut curves on paper accurately.
2. Students will create a colorful design.
3. Students will appreciate their own uniqueness.

[*]*Source:* Dorothy Goines, Racine Unified Public Schools, Racine, WI.

Suggested Procedures

1. Write the word *unique* on the board and pronounce it. Ask for a definition. Develop a common definition after having students share their thoughts.

2. Discuss that people are all alike in some ways and unique in others; have students suggest ways we are alike and ways we are different.

3. Explain that we all have unique fingerprints. Have several ink pads available and ask each student to make a fingerprint on white paper. Compare fingerprints.

4. Explain that students' uniqueness will be used to create art folders decorated with unique flowers. Pass out large pieces of construction paper, one to each student. Have them fold it in half to make a cover for their art work.

5. Pass out colored paper. Have each student decorate a piece with his or her fingerprints.

6. Demonstrate how to draw a flower shape using curves. Show several different flower shapes; stress that flowers are also unique in many ways. Show how to cut out a flower.

7. Tell students to decorate different colors of paper with fingerprints and to draw and cut out flowers from their decorated paper. Encourage them to share flowers and paste them on their covers.

8. Finally, have students share covers. Point out the beauty and interest contributed by their unique fingerprints, unique fingerprint designs, and unique flowers.

Evaluation

1. Assess students' quality of design of covers and quality of cutting.

2. Assess students' reactions to uniqueness in their covers and flowers.

WHY THE CHANGES?

Paper Flowers

Individual Uniqueness and Worth

In the "After" plan, the art lesson becomes one about the value and beauty of uniqueness. Note that the discussion of uniqueness is presented in a positive and nonthreatening context: children usually find fingerprints fascinating, they usually enjoy art, and bright-colored paper flowers are visually pleasing. In this context, learning about individual differences is also a pleasant experience. A teacher with a class of students in which there is name-calling and stereotyping could start working on these problems with a nonthreatening individual difference, such as fingerprints, and in a relaxed and positive lesson, such as art. From there, one can move to more sensitive differences.

LESSON PLAN

BEFORE

Toys

Subject Area: Mathematics

Grade Level: 1–3

Time: Two hours

Objectives

1. Students will subtract two-digit numbers.

2. Students will count change correctly.

Suggested Procedures

1. Give each student a store catalogue or advertisement featuring toys. Instruct them to cut out five pictures of toys they would like to own and to paste each picture on a sheet of tagboard. Instruct them to copy the listed price next to each toy and to round it to the nearest dollar.

2. Set up a mock toy store. Have three students act as cashiers (the role can be rotated). Give each student $25.00 in play money. Allow students to buy as many "toys" as they would like. Use this activity to practice subtraction and counting change.

Evaluation
Given story problems involving subtracting money and identifying change, assess students' ability to solve them correctly.

AFTER

Toys[*]

Subject Areas: Social Studies, Mathematics

Grade Level: 1–3

Time: Four hours

---

[*]*Sources:* Connie Olson, Kansasville, WI, and Sue Senzig, Racine Unified Public Schools, Racine, WI.

Objectives

1. Students will recognize and describe sex stereotypes.

2. Students will understand how stereotypes are limiting and often inaccurate.

3. Students will identify sex stereotyping in toy commercials.

4. Students will subtract two-digit numbers.

5. Students will count change correctly.

6. Students will appreciate the interests and wishes of others.

Suggested Procedures

1. Seat students around tables. On each table, have several store catalogues or advertisements featuring toys. In selecting catalogues or advertisements, you should be sensitive to the price ranges that the students' families can afford, although this should not mean censoring exposure to toys outside their price range. Instruct each student to cut out five pictures of toys they would like to own.

2. Have girls select toys they think boys would like and boys select toys they think girls would like. Have them paste the pictures on one or two large sheets of tagboard. Compare the toys selected for girls with the toys selected for boys. Have children identify characteristics of "girl" toys and "boy" toys; list them on the board. Ask if girls and boys are really like the words on the board; draw out examples that show both sexes to be more complex. Point out that these words are stereotypes or show bias: they suggest that both sexes have limited interests and capabilities, that members of each sex are all alike, and that the sexes are very different from one another. Ask students to identify toys on the opposite sex's poster they would like.

3. Ask students about the people who help us decide which toys are right for us. One source students will probably name is television commercials. Tell students that television commercials can teach them to limit their interests by showing a certain toy being used by only one sex.

4. Instruct students to watch three toy commercials very carefully over the weekend. Give each student a copy of the "Toy Commercial Evaluation" sheet shown in Figure 3.3. When students have completed the form, help them to identify the following:

   ▪ Toys shown with both sexes

   ▪ Toys shown with one sex

   ▪ Toys shown with one sex that could be enjoyed by both sexes

5. Have children cut tagboard to separate the toys. Instruct them to price the toys in whole-dollar amounts, using the catalogues as a guide. Set up a mock toy store. Have three students act as cashiers (this role can be rotated). Give each student $25.00 in play money.

Commercial 1

Name of the toy _____

Who was in the commercial? (circle one)
    boys   girls   both boys and girls

How was the toy being used? _____

To whom do you think the company is trying to sell the toy? (circle one)
    boys   girls   both boys and girls

Commercial 2

Name of the toy _____

Who was in the commercial? (circle one)
    boys   girls   both boys and girls

How was the toy being used? _____

To whom do you think the company is trying to sell the toy? (circle one)
    boys   girls   both boys and girls

Commercial 3

Name of the toy _____

Who was in the commercial? (circle one)
    boys   girls   both boys and girls

How was the toy being used? _____

To whom do you think the company is trying to sell the toy? (circle one)
    boys   girls   both boys and girls

FIGURE 3.3   Toy Commercial Evaluation Sheet

6. Put two paper slips with each student's name in a hat. Have students draw two names. Instruct them to "buy" a toy for each name drawn; it should be something that that student would like, and students should not confine choices to sex stereotypes. Use this activity to practice subtraction and counting change.

After buying and giving and receiving gifts, students may spend their remaining play money in the toy store as they wish.

Evaluation

1. Assess students' skill in identifying sex stereotypes through their toy commercial evaluations.

2. Assess students' attention to the interests of others and their willingness not to stereotype by observing what they buy in the mock toy store.

3. Assess students' skill in subtracting money and identifying change through some story problems.

Toys

Stereotypes and Stereotyping

The toys in the "Before" plan lend themselves excellently to lessons on sex stereotyping. Therefore, an examination of stereotypes was added to the math lesson. The discussion of "girl" toys and "boy" toys helps students become aware of what a stereotype is and of stereotypes they probably encounter every day. The teacher should not force students to accept toys with which they are uncomfortable but should encourage students not to limit themselves or their peers because of stereotypes. Students are taught to analyze toy television commercials because many of their ideas probably come partly from the media.

Feelings

In the "After" lesson plan, the teacher pays attention to what families can afford when selecting the toy catalogues and designing the store. An effort should be made not to put students from low-income families in a position of having to choose things their families cannot afford. Also, the "After" plan encourages students to pay attention to the interests and feelings of others by "buying" toys for each other. The teacher needs to monitor this activity to make sure students are actually trying to please those for whom they are buying toys.

Cooperating and Sharing

The "Before" plan reinforces individual consumption; each student has his or her own catalogue to cut and works at his or her own desk. However, in the "After" plan, students work at tables and share catalogues. This in itself is not cooperative learning, but it does encourage the sharing of materials and ideas.

LESSON PLAN

Global Cooperation

Subject Area: Social Studies

Grade Level: 3–4

Time: Two days

Objectives

1. Students will learn that different countries specialize in products for world trade.

2. Students will value cooperation and interdependence.

Suggested Procedures

1. On a table, display items that come from different parts of the world, such as a banana, a rubber ball, a radio, and a wool sweater. Ask students if they know where the items are made.

2. Explain that different countries produce different products, and that countries trade products so that people can enjoy more than just what is produced in their own country. To illustrate this, select about six different countries that are located in different parts of the world and produce different products. Point them out on a map and show pictures of their main trade products.

3. Distribute blank world maps. Have students locate each of the six countries and paste their own pictures or magazine cut-outs of the countries' main products on the maps.

4. Instruct students to locate items at home that come from other countries and to bring a list of these items to class the following day.

5. On the following day, share lists, writing items on a master list on the board. Ask students to consider the following questions:

    What would happen if we stopped trading with a certain country?

    Why is it important for countries to cooperate?

    Do individuals in the family or local community need to cooperate and trade for similar reasons? Can you give examples?

Evaluation

Assess students' understanding of specialization, cooperation, and independence through class discussion.

AFTER   Global Cooperation[*]

Subject Area: Social Studies

Grade Level: 3–4

Time: Two days

---

[*]*Sources:* Chris Aamodt and Margaret Conway, Madison, WI.

Objectives

1. Students will appreciate the difficulties caused by maldistribution of products.

2. Students will learn that they must give up something to gain something else.

3. Students will value human life despite social and cultural differences.

4. Students will develop cooperation skills.

Suggested Procedures

1. Divide the class into four groups. Have each group pick a country's name, draw a flag for their country, and draw a picture or write a paragraph about its climate, land, and life-style.

2. Distribute trade cards for four products—blankets, bread, fruit, and medicine—as shown in Table 3.1.

TABLE 3.1

	Group 1	Group 2	Group 3	Group 4	Total
Blankets	6	0	2	2	10
Bread	1	1	1	7	10
Fruit	2	7	0	1	10
Medicine	1	2	7	0	10

3. The groups now must decide which products are important to them and then trade in the trade center in the middle of the classroom. Only one person from each group can be in the trade center, but all trades must be approved by the entire country.

4. Take away one country's bread (due to bad weather causing the wheat crop to fail), creating a famine in that country. The other countries must decide whether to help the starved country. If they refuse to cooperate, a flood will come to all except the starved country, which has the land with the highest elevation. The groups either cooperate or suffer from floods.

5. Discuss the following questions with the class:

   How did you feel inside your group?

   How did you feel toward the other groups?

   What were differences and similarities between the groups?

   What did the groups want from each other?

   What were the differences between products?

   How did you feel when the teacher took the bread?

How did the rest of you feel toward this group?

How did you solve the problem?

Have you ever wanted something you did not get? What?

How does that differ from wanting food or needing clothes?

Have you had to sacrifice or trade to get what you want?

Do your parents ever tell you to finish your food because there are starving children in other countries? Why do they say that?

How could we help people who do not have enough?

6. Have children sit in a circle. Put some candy in a bowl and pass it around the circle. No one can eat the candy until the bowl has made it all the way around the circle, but give this lenient rule: "You can take as many as you want." The bowl will probably not make it very far before it runs empty. At this point, give this problem to the students: "What are you going to do? Is it fair that a few have all the treats while others go away without any? Does cooperating mean you do not always get your way?" This should reinforce the idea of thinking of others.

Evaluation

Assess students' willingness to cooperate and share through discussion and through their behavior when the candy is passed around.

WHY THE CHANGES?

Global Cooperation

Cooperation

The "Before" lesson plan teaches about cooperation but it does not teach students to cooperate themselves—students work individually rather than with each other. In contrast, the "After" lesson plan has students work together in groups that constitute a "country," and it requires the "countries" to work together to deal with product distribution and famine. The students themselves participate in cooperating.

Another problem with the "Before" plan is that it reinforces the idea that global specialization is beneficial to all, even though the economies of Third World countries are in many cases devastated by shifting production from diversified products for local consumption to specialized products for trade. Often the main beneficiaries of global specialization are wealthy countries that can afford to buy imported luxury items. The "After" plan does not criticize global specialization directly but it also does not reinforce it. Rather, the lesson directs students' attention to the distribution of goods and asks them to consider how people can work together to distribute goods more fairly.

LESSON PLAN

The Life Cycle

Subject Area: Science

Grade Level: 3–4

Time: One class period

Objectives

1. Students will define the term *life cycle* as the major stages of growth that all living things experience.

2. Students will describe the stages of the life cycle of humans and insects.

Suggested Procedures

1. Discuss each stage of the human life cycle (i.e., childhood, adolescence, and adulthood) in relationship to students in kindergarten through college.

2. Ask students if they know what a butterfly is before it becomes a butterfly. Describe a butterfly's four-stage life cycle: egg, larva, pupa, adult. Point out that some insects (e.g., silverfish, grasshopper, and waterbug) have a three-stage life cycle: egg, nymph, adult.

3. Have students read pages in a textbook on the life cycle.

4. Ask students if they can identify the life-cycle stages of their family members (e.g., younger sister, teenage brother, parents).

5. Discuss the major changes in growth that are experienced during each stage of the human life cycle (e.g., voice change, balding).

Evaluation

On a test, ask students to define the life cycle and to describe the growth stages of insects and humans.

The Life Cycle

Subject Area: Science

Grade Level: 3–4

Time: Three or four class periods

Objectives

1. Students will define the term *life cycle* as the major stages of growth that all living things experience.

2. Students will describe the stages of the life cycle of humans and insects.

3. Students will state the developmental similarities, differences, and responsibilities associated with each life-cycle stage of humans.

4. Students will apply the appropriate meaning of respect to animals and humans of the different stages of the life cycle.

Suggested Procedures

1. Discuss each stage of the human life cycle (i.e., childhood, adolescence, adulthood) in relationship to students in kindergarten through college.

2. Ask students if they know what a butterfly is before it becomes a butterfly. Describe a butterfly's four-stage life cycle: egg, larva, pupa, adult. Point out that some insects (e.g., silverfish, grasshopper, and waterbug) have a three-stage life cycle: egg, nymph, adult.

3. Have students read pages in a textbook on the life cycle.

4. Ask students what would happen to an insect if it tried to do something in one life stage that is normally done in another. Some examples follow:

   A butterfly trying to fly while in the larva stage

   A nymph grasshopper trying to lay eggs

   A mosquito trying to bite your arm while in the larva stage

   Students will learn that insects cannot perform activities in one life stage for which they are not equipped. The insects' attempts will be futile, in that they would hinder growth into the next stage.

5. Group students across gender, socioeconomic class, ability/disability, and race and have them discuss similarities in the experiences of all people—regardless of gender, class, disability, or race—at each human life stage. Also ask the groups to discuss the responsibilities associated with each life stage and if there are appropriate behaviors or attitudes that are normally expected across human life-cycle stages. For example, are there proper ways that humans in the childhood stage should treat humans in the adult stage? Do humans at the adult stage have certain responsibilities to humans at the childhood stage? Help students to understand that respect and responsibility are important attitudes for humans to have for each other regardless of stage of development.

6. Have students discuss whether the amount of respect one gives to another person should differ according to that person's age, gender, race, or socioeconomic

status. For example, should their respect be the same for a white European American male adolescent and an African American male adolescent? A working-class elderly Latina and an upper-class white European American elderly woman?

7. Lead a discussion that includes both sexes on the differences that occur in each stage between males and females, such as boys developing a deeper voice and having to shave and girls growing taller than boys during adolescence.

Evaluation

1. In a quiz, ask students to describe the life cycle of humans and insects.

2. During class discussion, assess students' ability to associate correctly the different meanings of respect with the stages of the life cycle.

WHY THE CHANGES?

The Life Cycle

Respect

The "Before" lesson plan asks students to describe the meaning of the life cycle for insects and humans. The "After" lesson plan also helps students to see a relationship between the stages and the meanings of respect. The "After" plan provides an opportunity for the teacher to discuss the two meanings of respect in relationship to life cycle, race, and gender. For example, will the definition of *respect* that students' use be different for white European American teenage males than for African American teenage males?

Stereotyping

The "After" plan helps students to pay attention to stereotyping by encouraging them to examine the two meanings of respect in relation to race and gender.

Individual Uniqueness and Worth

The "After" plan has students examine appropriate behaviors and responsibilities at each stage of the life cycle to help them appreciate the inappropriateness of trying to "grow up" too fast or showing disrespect to members of other age groups. In other words, a third grader need not act like an eighth grader to be respectable, and adults should not act like adolescents. Further, adults and children have responsibilities to each other.

Cross-Group Communication

The "After" plan encourages boys and girls to discuss sex differences with each other to develop comfort and honesty in communicating with the opposite sex.

LESSON PLAN

Bones and Muscles

Subject Area: Health

Grade Level: 3–5

Time: Two class periods

Objectives

1. Students will describe the functions of bones and muscles.

2. Students will name and describe three kinds of joints and three kinds of muscles.

3. Students will identify the approximate number of bones and muscles in the body.

Suggested Procedures

1. Have students write their names. Then ask them to describe the characteristics that their hands need to do this. Make sure the discussion includes the following:

    Firmness, support (flesh cannot be like jelly)

    Flexibility (joints between firm parts)

    Voluntary movement of firm parts (something to move parts when you want to)

    Have students do jumping jacks; ask if the same properties are necessary to do the jumping jacks as are needed for writing their names.

2. Explain that bones and muscles are two body systems that perform these functions. Have students read pages in a textbook on this subject.

3. Review the text material orally in class. Stress the following points: functions of the skull, ribs, and pelvis to protect soft parts; different kinds of joints; different kinds of muscles; voluntary versus involuntary muscles. Make it clear that everyone has over two hundred bones and over six hundred muscles.

4. Have students complete a crossword puzzle on bones and muscles.

Evaluation

Through oral review and the crossword puzzle, assess students' comprehension of the material.

AFTER

Bones and Muscles

Subject Area: Health

Grade Level: 3–5

Time: Two to four class periods

Objectives

1. Students will describe the functions of bones and muscles.

2. Students will name and describe three kinds of joints and three kinds of muscles.

3. Students will describe alternative devices that perform similar functions to bones and muscles when these are impaired or absent.

4. Students will appreciate the similarities between people with orthopedic disabilities and people without such disabilities.

5. Students will feel comfortable discussing and handling devices used by people with orthopedic disabilities.

Suggested Procedures

1. Have students write their names. Then ask them to describe the characteristics that their hands need to do this. Make sure the discussion includes the following:

    Firmness, support (flesh cannot be like jelly)

    Flexibility (joints between firm parts)

    Voluntary movement of firm parts (something to move parts when you want to)

    Have students do jumping jacks; ask if the same properties are necessary to do the jumping jacks as are needed for writing their names.

2. Explain that bones and muscles are two body systems that perform these functions. Have students read pages in a textbook on this subject.

3. Ask students if they know of anyone who lacks working bones and/or muscles in their arms, hands, legs, or feet. Discuss why these disabilities occur (e.g., because of birth defects, amputations, skeletal or muscular diseases, injury). Ask

if the people whom students have mentioned have the same needs and desires to accomplish activities as anyone else; lead students to the conclusion that they do.

4. Show devices available for performing the same tasks as bones or muscles, such as prosthetic devices, braces, casts, and wheelchairs. Show how these devices work, enabling their users to perform much the same activities as other people. Show how they substitute for the bones and muscles that students read about in the text.

5. Have students keep a notebook on sport injuries and repairs. Assign a group of students (both boys and girls) to monitor the sports pages of newspapers and magazines to keep abreast of athletes who injure themselves. Have them discover how bone and muscle injuries are repaired (e.g., medical treatment, the length of rehabilitation time required, and the rehabilitation process).

6. Ask students to read children's books that teach about orthopedic disabilities while stressing the normalcy of people with disabilities. For example:

Barbara Adams, *Like It Is: Facts and Feelings About Handicaps from Kids Who Know* (New York: Walker, 1979), chap. 3 (on orthopedic disabilities).

Carol J. Bennett, *Giant Steps for Steven* (Mayfield Heights, OH: After School Exchange, 1980).

Bernard Wolf, *Don't Feel Sorry for Paul* (Philadelphia: Lippincott, 1974).

Audrey Osofsy, *My Buddy* (New York: Henry Holt & Co., 1992).

Mary Ellen Powers, *Our Teacher's in a Wheelchair* (Niles, IL: A. Whitman, 1986).

Evaluation

1. Through class discussion of devices, assess students' comprehension of the material.

2. Through class discussion of people with physical disabilities whom students know and of the readings on orthopedic disabilities, assess students' appreciation of similarities among people.

WHY THE CHANGES?

Bones and Muscles

Stereotyping

The "Before" lesson plan implicitly teaches that all "normal" people have a specific set of bones and muscles. Although it does not explicitly state that people who are missing some working parts are not "normal," students often think this is the case. The "After" lesson plan dispels stereotypes while suggesting material that directly relates to those stereotypes. The "After" plan necessarily takes longer than the "Before" plan to provide information about the devices that people with disabilities use and to allow students to examine them.

Should the "After" lesson plan be taught when the class includes a student with a physical disability? Ideally, the lesson should be taught before such a student is mainstreamed, to prevent teasing and name-calling. If a student with a physical disability is already a part of the class, the teacher should make sure that he or she will feel comfortable with the lesson. This varies widely among individuals. In schools that mainstream students with physical disabilities, often cordial and accepting relationships develop between the students with disabilities and those without. Further, it may be tempting to assume that a lesson such as this is not needed. However, students without disabilities still may know little about the devices people use, and a lesson such as this may well answer questions they do not feel comfortable asking.

Grouping

The "After" plan calls for a group of male and female students to monitor the sports pages for muscle and bone injuries. This procedure will make certain that both boys and girls are acquiring sports health information.

LESSON PLAN

BEFORE

Salamanders*

Subject Area: Science

Grade Level: 4–5

Time: One to two class periods

Objectives

1. Students will understand that salamanders may be classroom pets.

2. Students will identify salamanders as amphibians and describe their main characteristics.

Suggested Procedures

1. Ask students to define the word *amphibian* and to give examples of amphibians. Students may say that they are cold-blooded animals with a backbone that

---

*Source: Vicki Peterson, Madison, WI.

live both on land and in water. These examples may include frogs, beavers, and seals.

2. Ask students to explain what they know about salamanders and to explain the experiences they have had with salamanders.

3. Organize students into four groups; give each group a recording sheet, along with books and magazine articles about salamanders. Explain that they are to read and gather new information about salamanders. Encourage students to find words that are different from what other groups might record. Have students record this information using words and phrases that begin with the letters that spell *salamander* (an acrostic).

4. Have each group write out a brief explanation of the word(s) they record.

5. After 20–30 minutes have students share their research results. Have each group share each letter of the word *salamander.* They should respond alternately and give a brief explanation of the word(s) they chose.

6. The teacher could show the class live salamanders if they are available.

Evaluation

1. Assess students' understanding that a salamander is an amphibian and have them describe the characteristics of an amphibian through a short quiz.

2. Assess students' understanding about the way salamanders live through a short essay.

3. Assess students' appreciation of salamanders and other amphibians through classroom discussion and/or a short essay.

AFTER   ## Salamanders

Subject Area: Science

Grade Level: 4–5

Time: Three to four class periods

Objectives

1. Students will identify salamanders as amphibians and describe their main characteristics.

2. Students will identify locations throughout the world where salamanders exist.

3. Students will understand that salamanders look different depending on where they live, including locations within the United States.

4. Students will appreciate that people worldwide are interested in salamanders.

5. Students will understand that salamanders may be classroom pets.

6. Students will understand that when a person acquires honest and accurate knowledge about a living thing it may change the way he or she originally thought about the living thing.

Suggested Procedures

1. Ask students to define the word *amphibian* and to give examples of amphibians. Students may say that they are cold-blooded animals with a backbone that live both on land and in water. These examples may include frogs, beavers, and seals.

2. Call upon students to tell what they know about salamanders and to share experiences they have had with salamanders. Each student should be given a chance to comment.

3. Ask students to write their names on green Post–it notes. They are to indicate their attitudes toward salamanders by placing their squares on vertical graphs under columns labeled Positive, Negative, and No Opinion. Set this aside until the lesson is finished. Ask students to share how they developed their attitudes.

4. Organize students into four groups. To maximize achievement, the group members are selected by the teacher, mixing students by gender, race, social class, and academic skills. Each group is given a recording sheet along with a packet of World Wide Web and other articles about salamanders. Their assignment is to gather new information about salamanders. This information should be recorded using words and phrases that begin with the letters that spell the word *salamander* (an acrostic). They also need to be able to give a brief explanation of the word(s) they record. They are also given the challenge to find words that are different from what other groups might record. As another way to maximize achievement, cooperative group skills are discussed. The expectation is that the information that gets recorded on the sheet has been agreed upon by the whole group.

5. Students work together in their cooperative groups for about 20 minutes. After 20 minutes the research ends and each group shares its information.

6. The teacher should have the class observe and hold live salamanders.

7. Have students research information on salamanders that live in their area or salamanders that live in the location of a friend or family member.

8. Have each student make a life-size illustration of the salamander they are studying. They should include with the illustration a short written description on the natural surrounding and how the salamander has adapted to this surrounding.

9. Have students establish national or international pen pals through the Internet and share experiences and information about salamanders.

10. Have interested students participate in local/state/national salamander surveys that work toward documenting salamander populations. Have teams of students under adult supervision go to local ponds, learn collection techniques, and make collections of salamanders. Using survey data from the World Wide Web on the population of salamanders in this country and other countries, students can compare and contrast data on salamanders living in their area with data on salamanders living in other states and countries. Students can also investigate how the data they collect can contribute to the body of worldwide data on salamanders.

11. After students have completed their research and/or had time to observe a live salamander, ask them if their attitude has changed toward salamanders. Have students put their names on blue Post–it notes and put them on another vertical graph indicating their present attitude toward salamanders. Compare and contrast the two graphs. Ask students to share reasons why they changed or did not change their attitudes. Explain that when a person gathers knowledge about a subject (object or person) it often corrects the stereotypes and myths he or she holds and leads to a change in his or her attitude and behavior.

Evaluation

1. Assess students' knowledge of amphibians through a short quiz.

2. Assess students' knowledge and characteristics of salamanders through a short essay.

3. Assess students' attitude toward and appreciation of salamanders through class discussion.

WHY THE CHANGES?

Salamanders

Cooperative Learning

Both plans use cooperative grouping as a strategy for learning; however, the "After" plan asks teachers to make the groups diverse according to race, gender, class, and academic skill levels.

Eliminating Stereotypes and Stereotyping

The "Before" plan does not address stereotyping, and indeed science lessons usually do not, although often they lend themselves to this. The "After" plan encourages students to examine their attitudes toward a living thing and to see that sometimes knowledge learned about a living being may lead to a change in attitude toward it. Science generally encourages students to formulate opinions on the basis of information, and in this lesson, opinions and attitudes are actually recorded before and after students acquire information. What they learn from doing this can be applied to knowledge about people, as well.

Personal Feeling

The "After" plan has students examine and hold a live salamander after they have collected information on this animal. The expectation is that any apprehension students have toward salamanders will be eliminated and all students will develop a more positive feeling toward them, including the desire to have them as pets. The analogy is that personal contact along with information may lead a person to want to make friends with those who differ from oneself. Of course, having a friendship with a person is not the same as keeping a pet, in that human friendships are based on mutuality and equality; this distinction needs to be clear.

Cross-Group Communication

The "After" plan includes having students access the World Wide Web to collect information and to communicate (by way of computer and establishing pen pals) with individuals living in other states and other parts of the world who are interested in salamanders. Also, the "After" plan involves students in contributing information to a global knowledge bank that collects data on salamanders.

LESSON PLAN

BEFORE

Westward Ho!

Subject Area: Social Studies

Grade Level: 4–6

Time: Two weeks

Objectives

1. Students will identify on a map the trails used by wagon trains traveling west and the geographic features of the land encountered.

2. Students will describe why pioneers went west, how their trips were organized, and how they handled obstacles and problems during their travels.

3. Students will appreciate the importance of the early pioneers.

Suggested Procedures

1. Using a large map, review the locations of the main settlements during the early 1800s. Point out the Oregon country and explain why the pioneers were drawn to the west. Have students study the map and suggest hazards or problems that pioneers in covered wagons might face while heading west.

2. Read a textbook about the westward movement of pioneers. As the class comes to each topic in the text, discuss the following questions:

Why would people leave their homes to head west?

What did they need to take with them?

How did they organize themselves for travel? Who played what roles?

What main routes did they take? Why? How did they know these routes?

What geographic hazards did they face? How did they deal with them?

What kinds of threats did the American Indians pose? How did the pioneers respond?

What health hazards did they face? How did they respond?

3. Show a film that portrays a visual account of the pioneers' trip west.

4. Have students construct a wall mural of wagon trains heading west. As a class, decide what should go on the mural; each student should draw and color at least one contribution.

Evaluation

1. Assess students' ability to identify trails, describe geographic features, describe reasons for westward movement, and describe the process of westward movement through a test.

2. Assess students' appreciation of the importance of the early pioneers through their contributions to the mural.

AFTER

Westward Ho!*

Subject Area: Social Studies

Grade Level: 4–6

Time: Two weeks

Objectives

1. Students will identify on a map the trails used by wagon trains traveling west and the geographic features of the land encountered.

2. Students will develop attitudes and skills for cooperation.

3. Students will solve problems similar to those encountered by the pioneers going west.

---

*Source: Kathro Taylor, Berlin Public Schools, Berlin, WI.

4. Students will examine the stereotypes and negative attitudes associated with sex roles and American Indians.

5. Students will develop skill in writing paragraphs.

Suggested Procedures

1. Using a large map, review the locations of the main settlements of white European Americans, American Indians, and Mexican Americans during the early 1800s between the West Coast and the Mississippi River. Point out the Oregon country and explain why the pioneers were drawn to the west.

2. Divide the class into groups of five or six students, such that each group contains students mixed on the basis of academic skill level, race, sex, and social class. Explain that each group is to act as a wagon train and that the following roles need to be filled each day:

> Wagon master (leader)
>
> Mule skinner or bullwacker (assistant leader)
>
> Journalist (keeps log of daily activities)
>
> Trail guide (plots routes on a map)

Discuss the fact that leaders and guides were usually men but that women can perform these roles as well. Have students rotate roles each day so that everyone gets a chance to have a major role. Explain that the log will be used to evaluate each group; thus, the journalist of the day has the main responsibility of seeing that day's log is completed, but all group members can pitch in. If word processors are available, the log should be kept as much as possible on them. The log need not be straight narrative; letters, pictures, and diaries may also be entered.

3. Have each group organize for the trip west. Each team is given money to spend; members must decide on the destination of the trip, the supplies needed, and how the roles are allocated.

4. The trip west begins. Show a video, show pictures, or have students read a description of a rainy day, with wagons mired in mud. An axle is broken trying to free the wagon, and one team member injures a leg. Each team must decide what to do.

5. The next day's problem (on video, in pictures, or in story form) shows a raging river that the team must ford. The river frightens animals and could wash away supplies. Each team must decide what to do.

6. The next day, Plains Indians approach. Discuss with the class how the American Indians' perspectives of the westward movement may differ from the pioneers'. Suggest ways the parties might respond to one another. Include the possibility of hostilities occurring and the likely consequences. Consider also the likely consequences of responding cooperatively. Have each team develop a respectful and constructive plan for interacting with the American Indians that would encourage cooperation and minimize hostilities.

7. The next day's problem is the desert, with water supplies low and temperatures high. The team must decide what to do.

8. The last problem is a steep mountain grade that must be scaled; the trail is partly blocked by rock slides, and light snow is falling. The team must decide what to do.

9. The teams all arrive at their destinations and must plan for settlement. They must decide how to organize each settlement in a way that fosters cooperation, good relationships with the American Indians, and minimal sex role assignments.

10. Have students read textbook accounts of the westward movement and then relate them to their own "westward experience."

Evaluation

Evaluate each group's log in terms of cooperation, reasonableness of solutions, comprehension of geography, writing skills, and creativity.

WHY THE CHANGES?

Westward Ho!

Cooperative Learning

The "After" lesson plan uses the group investigation model; that is, students are presented with much the same information as in the textbook but, rather than being told how the pioneers coped, they must figure out what to do themselves collectively. Each group produces one product—the log—that is used to determine their grade. This provides motivation for all students to contribute to the production of a good log. Doing the log on a word processor facilitates cooperative writing. In the process, students develop better relationships with their peers and better problem-solving skills. Designating roles that must be filled helps keep the group on task, and it structures who will do what. Changing from individual textbook reading to cooperative learning not only builds classroom relationships and problem-solving ability but also encourages motivation.

Stereotyping

The "Before" lesson plan unintentionally reinforces several stereotypes: that the American Indians created problems for the settlers but not vice versa; that white European Americans were the only group of importance; that men were the leaders; and that students who cannot read well are unable to learn well. In contrast, the "After" plan deals with these stereotypes and does so without spending too much time. The "After" plan invites both sexes to share all roles. It also encourages the settlers to relate respectfully to the American Indians and to realize that hostility leads to hostile responses. The "After" plan points out that white European Americans were not the only racial group in the west.

LESSON PLAN

BEFORE

Taking Dictation

Subject Area: Language Arts

Grade Level: 4–6

Time: One class period

Objectives

1. Students will take dictation with accuracy.

2. Students will spell correctly when writing narratives.

Suggested Procedures

1. Explain what dictation is, and ask students to brainstorm situations in which one might use dictation skills.

2. Dictate a short piece of prose (about one paragraph) with which students are somewhat familiar. This should optimize student success rate while teaching them the importance of learning to take dictation. Have students immediately go back and check their spelling, punctuation, and accuracy.

3. Following the exercise, dictate to students a paragraph of information that is new to them but that contains words from their spelling or vocabulary list. Again, have students check their work. Discuss any difficulties students may be having.

Evaluation

Assess students' skill in dictation by reviewing their written work.

AFTER

Judging Differences

Subject Area: Language Arts

Grade Level: 4–6

Time: One day

Objectives

1. Students will learn that they cannot always judge people or things by their own ideas of what is right.

2. Students will recognize the confusion and unfairness that may come from legitimate but unrecognized differing interpretations of a situation.

3. Students will understand how it feels to be judged wrong by someone whose cultural frame of reference may differ from their own.

Suggested Procedures

1. Divide the class in half. Have one half pretend they are visitors from England, and the rest are themselves—students living in the United States.

2. Excuse the U.S. American students from the class and teach the "British" students the British spellings of the following words:

color	colour
center	centre
favor	favour
labor	labour

3. Later in the day, tell the students they will be taking dictation. Explain what dictation is and ask students to brainstorm situations in which one might use dictation skills. Inform students that five points will be deducted for any misspelled word. Dictate to all students the following sentences:

   The president of the labour union invited members to the city centre for the meeting. She said the meeting would be held in the room with the red coloured drapes. The city was doing the union a favour by allowing the meeting to be held there, since their meeting hall had burned down.

4. Have the U.S. American students exchange papers with the "British" students for correction. Have the students correct the papers as you read the passage. The "British" students should mark the words *favour, colour, centre,* and *labour* incorrect if they are not spelled the British way.

5. Return the papers and await the U.S. American students' reactions. Have students discuss how they feel about the corrections when they know their way is right.

6. The class should then discuss situations in which people who differ culturally are rebuked unjustly by others who do not recognize another frame of reference. Examples could include taking standardized tests, performing unfamiliar rituals, knowing what to do in a particular religious institution, pronouncing words in a nonstandard way because of dialect differences, or dressing in a particular way.

Evaluation

Assess students' understanding of cultural differences through class discussion and ongoing observation of their reactions to one another.

WHY THE CHANGES?

Judging Differences

Respect and Cross-Group Communication

Although there is nothing inherently wrong with the "Before" plan, the teacher decided to use dictation as a way of teaching students to recognize multiple cultural frames of reference and not to assume that one's own way is the right way. The "After" lesson is based on a real-life experience of the son of one of the authors, when he was a U.S. American student in England. A teacher treated British spelling as the only correct spelling and penalized the U.S. student for learning his spelling in the culture in which he was raised.

The "After" plan can be used most profitably when there are real cultural differences among students that they are judging negatively. After this lesson, which in itself is nonthreatening, students may be more receptive to discussing and learning about cultural differences among themselves or others they encounter.

LESSON PLAN

BEFORE

Billboards

Subject Areas: Language Arts, Art

Grade Level: 4–9

Time: Two to three days

Objective

Students will appreciate and use visual devices as symbols for communication.

Suggested Procedures

1. Have available pictures of signs and billboards, or take the class on a walking tour of an area where students can view several of these.

2. Lead a discussion of how messages are conveyed through visual images, words, logos, colors, sizes, and shapes. Have students describe their responses to various signs and billboards and explain what features triggered their responses.

Help students appreciate how visual devices can substitute for and often be more effective than verbal, discursive communication.

3. Each student should think of a message that he or she wishes to communicate and then design a sign or billboard to communicate that message. In art, students can produce their signs or billboards.

Evaluation

Assess the signs that students design for use as visual devices.

AFTER   ## Billboards[*]

Subject Areas: Language Arts, Art

Grade Level: 4–9

Time: Two to three days

Objectives

1. Students will appreciate and use visual devices as symbols for communication.

2. Students will appreciate the similarities and differences among themselves.

Suggested Procedures

1. The day before the lesson, ask students to wear their favorite T-shirt the next day.

2. Have students examine each other's T-shirts. Lead a discussion on how messages are conveyed on T-shirts through visual images, words, logos, colors, and the cut of the shirt.

3. Organize students into groups of about five, such that each member is wearing a different T-shirt. Have students discuss what their T-shirts are saying and why each person likes and wears his or her own T-shirt.

4. Have students wearing similar T-shirts stand together. Ask them to what extent their T-shirts symbolize things they have in common with each other and things that make them different from their peers.

5. Discuss with the class that we all have similarities and differences and that we express them in how we dress. Point out that T-shirts are particularly popular and effective for doing this because of their low cost and versatility. Help stu-

---

*Source: Ozetta Price Kirby, Racine Unified Public Schools, Racine, WI.

dents appreciate how visual devices can substitute for and often be more effective than verbal, discursive communication.

6. Ask the class to help design on the board a T-shirt that symbolizes the similarities among class members; if possible, the design should also reflect an appreciation of differences. The design should not impose some students' preferences on everyone else but should express ideas from the entire class.

7. As an art project, make these T-shirts for the entire class.

8. To extend the idea of this lesson, students may visit public places (such as a shopping mall) to list the messages on T-shirts and caps that people are wearing. Discuss with the class the messages conveyed through the symbols, logos, and words.

Evaluation

1. Assess students' understanding of visual devices for communication through the discussion of T-shirts.

2. Assess students' appreciation of the similarities and differences among people through the discussion of T-shirts and the quality of the T-shirt design produced by the class.

   Note: To the extent that this lesson requires materials (T-shirts) from home, make sure no one is asked to bring something that he or she cannot afford. The teacher may wish to make extra T-shirts available for this purpose.

WHY THE CHANGES?

Billboards

Individual Uniqueness and Worth

This language arts and art lesson was turned into a lesson about human similarities and differences, using a medium that students commonly use to express their self-identities: T-shirts. Most students have thought about visual devices and symbols when selecting T-shirts to wear, although they might not have thought about it in those terms. The "After" lesson plan uses this experiential knowledge that students already have and asks them to apply it to an analysis of their peers' T-shirts.

Cooperation

The "After" plan asks students to identify with each other as a class, to the extent that they can design collectively a logo symbolizing who they are. The creating and wearing of their own class T-shirts can be an excellent group-building device as well as a motivating activity.

LESSON PLAN

BEFORE

Introductions

Subject Area: Social Studies/Humanities

Grade Level: 7-12

Date: The first day of the school year, or the first day of the second semester in schools in which students change classes each semester.

Objective

Students will become acquainted with the teacher and with other students.

Suggested Procedures

1. The teacher introduces her/himself, telling students a little bit about her or his own personal background, and what the course will be like.

2. Students take turns introducing themselves to the rest of the class, telling their name, hobbies or interests, and something of interest they did during vacation.

3. The teacher passes out textbooks and gives students a brief overview of the text and its organizational structure. The teacher then introduces the first assignment or concept for the semester.

Evaluation

None, since this is simply an introductory activity.

AFTER

Stereotypes[*]

Subject Area: Social Studies/Humanities

Grade Level: 7–12

Date: The first day of the school year, or the first day of the second semester in schools in which students change classes each semester.

Objectives

1. Students will define the word *stereotype*.

2. Students will examine historical events that often served as the basis for stereotypes.

---

[*]*Source:* Kimberley Woo, Teachers College, Columbia University, New York, NY.

3. Students will become aware of their own stereotypes.

4. Students will think critically about positive and negative connotations associated with stereotypes, the people/organizations who promote stereotypes, and the political implications behind using stereotypes.

5. Students will sharpen powers of observation.

6. The teacher will establish a classroom atmosphere that encourages sharing and risk taking.

Suggested Procedures

1. Before class, place the chart in Figure 3.4 on the blackboard.

2. (5 minutes) Hold up a stack of eight different photographs of the teacher, taken at different times, in different settings. Introduce the activity by saying, "I've got amnesia and I can't remember anything about my past. The only clues that I have are these photographs. Please get into groups of three to four, and take one photograph and one worksheet for each group. As a group, try to help me regain my memory by completing the worksheet [Figure 3.5]. Some of the questions on the worksheet cannot be easily answered and require careful observation and hypothesizing. You will have approximately 20 minutes to reach consensus about your answers. After you have completed your worksheets, please select a representative to write your conclusions on the chart on the blackboard."

3. (20 minutes) While students are working in groups, the teacher should circulate and spend approximately 2–3 minutes with each group to answer questions, encourage teamwork, and remind students to write their answers on the chart on the blackboard.

4. (20 minutes) After all groups have written their answers on the chart, review the categories that seem to have the strongest agreement or contradictions across groups. Ask students to explain how they formulated their answers using evidence from the photographs or other information. If pictures were well selected, they will elicit stereotypes students use to attempt to interpret them.

5. Point out that some conclusions were founded on assumptions and that when people use stereotypes, they often rely on past experiences and information.

Homework/Assessment

Ask students to make a list of ten situations in which they observed or experienced stereotyping. Have students focus on one stereotype and research the origins of the stereotype. Ask students to present written documentation (essay or other creative format, length to be determined according to students' ability and grade) that does the following:

1. Briefly describes how the stereotype was used in the situation

2. Discusses the historical basis for this stereotype

3. Analyzes the political implications of the stereotype to the situation

	Ques. #1	Ques. #2	Ques. #3	Ques. #4	Ques. #5	Ques. #6	Ques. #7	Ques. #8	Ques. #9	Ques. #10
Group 1										
Group 2										
Group 3										
Group 4										
Group 5										
Group 6										

FIGURE 3.4   Chart for Blackboard

_____   _____
(name)   (name)

_____   _____
(name)   (name)

1. What is the setting of the photo? (city, state, country)_____

_____

2. What's taking place? _____

_____

3. What is the teacher's economic status and occupation? _____

_____

4. What is the teacher's social status and age? _____

_____

5. What is the teacher's gender orientation and marital/dating status? _____

_____

6. What is the highest educational level the teacher has achieved? _____

_____

7. How long has the teacher been in the United States? (What generation is he or she?) _____

_____

8. What messages from body language is the teacher giving? _____

_____

9. What are the teacher's personal values?_____

_____

10. What are your overall conclusions or impressions? _____

_____

FIGURE 3.5   Who Am I?

WHY THE CHANGES?

Stereotyping

Stereotypes

The "After" plan invites students to attempt to draw some hypotheses based on visual photographs of the teacher. In the process, students will get to know the teacher but will also become aware of some of their own stereotypes. The author of this lesson has used it very successfully on several occasions for this purpose. The photos she has used of herself show her in different settings during a five-year period, wearing clothing ranging from traditional Chinese dress to outdoor sportswear. The activities in which she is engaged range from petting the dog, to socializing with friends, to serving appetizers. From the photos, students have suggested a variety of assumptions about things, such as what country she is from, how well she speaks English, and even whether all the photos represent the same person. The discussion of how students answered the questions about the photos and the evidence they used has always been lively and revealing.

LESSON PLAN

BEFORE

Solving Two Equations with Two Unknowns

Subject Area: Algebra

Grade Level: 9–12

Time: Four class periods

Objective

Students will solve two equations with two unknowns using four methods (graphing, substitution, addition, and determinants).

Suggested Procedures

1. Explain to students that they will learn how to solve two equations with two unknowns using four different methods: graphing, substitution, addition, and determinants.

2. Demonstrate a detailed example of how the graphing method is used. Be sure to encourage students to ask questions if they do not understand an aspect of the method. Work through one or two more examples, allowing students to give input as to how the problem should be solved using the method. When you feel that students can apply the method, assign homework from the textbook.

3. Teach the other three methods using the process outlined in step 2.

4. Prepare a worksheet with problems involving all four methods. Distribute the worksheet for students to use as a review for the quiz.

Evaluation

1. Listen to students' input when demonstrating the examples on the board to determine if they are grasping the methods.

2. Assess students' understanding of the methods by grading their homework assignments, worksheets, and exams.

AFTER

Solving Two Equations with Two Unknowns[*]

Subject Area: Algebra

Grade Level: 9–12

Time: Four class periods

Objectives

1. Students will solve two equations with two unknowns using four methods (graphing, substitution, addition, and determinants).

2. Students will teach the methods they have studied to other students.

3. Students will interact with peers of the same and opposite sexes.

4. Students will develop attitudes and skills for cooperation.

5. Students will develop planning skills.

6. Students will realize that both sexes are equally capable of learning and teaching math.

Suggested Procedures

1. Divide students into four groups with equal numbers of girls and boys in each group. Separate the girls and the boys who associate with each other often. Separate students at the same skill levels.

2. Assign to each group one of the four methods for solving two equations with two unknowns.

3. Tell students to use their textbooks and the supplementary books to learn how to use this method. They should work together to apply the method to various problems in the books and to make sure that everyone in the group can solve the equations using the given method.

4. Once students feel confident about using the method being learned by their group, the teacher should check their problems to be sure they understand it. (Some sample problems are given in Figure 3.6.)

---

[*]*Source:* Robin White, Racine, WI.

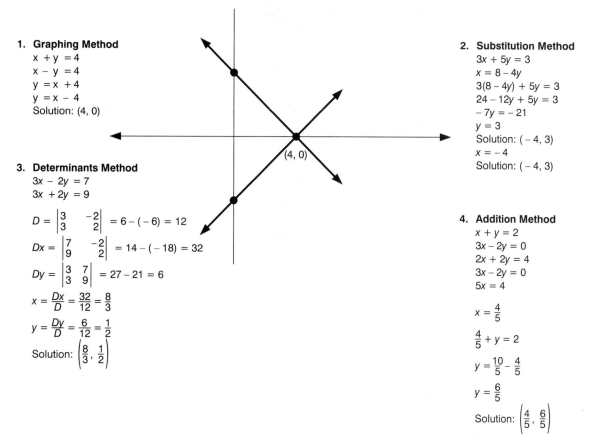

1. Graphing Method
$x + y = 4$
$x - y = 4$
$y = x + 4$
$y = x - 4$
Solution: $(4, 0)$

3. Determinants Method
$3x - 2y = 7$
$3x + 2y = 9$

$D = \begin{vmatrix} 3 & -2 \\ 3 & 2 \end{vmatrix} = 6 - (-6) = 12$

$Dx = \begin{vmatrix} 7 & -2 \\ 9 & 2 \end{vmatrix} = 14 - (-18) = 32$

$Dy = \begin{vmatrix} 3 & 7 \\ 3 & 9 \end{vmatrix} = 27 - 21 = 6$

$x = \dfrac{Dx}{D} = \dfrac{32}{12} = \dfrac{8}{3}$

$y = \dfrac{Dy}{D} = \dfrac{6}{12} = \dfrac{1}{2}$

Solution: $\left(\dfrac{8}{3}, \dfrac{1}{2} \right)$

$(4, 0)$

2. Substitution Method
$3x + 5y = 3$
$x = 8 - 4y$
$3(8 - 4y) + 5y = 3$
$24 - 12y + 5y = 3$
$-7y = -21$
$y = 3$
Solution: $(-4, 3)$
$x = -4$
Solution: $(-4, 3)$

4. Addition Method
$x + y = 2$
$3x - 2y = 0$
$2x + 2y = 4$
$3x - 2y = 0$
$5x = 4$

$x = \dfrac{4}{5}$

$\dfrac{4}{5} + y = 2$

$y = \dfrac{10}{5} - \dfrac{4}{5}$

$y = \dfrac{6}{5}$

Solution: $\left(\dfrac{4}{5}, \dfrac{6}{5} \right)$

FIGURE 3.6   Sample Problems

5. If the teacher feels that the students understand the method, the group can begin to design its mini-lesson, which they will use to teach the method to other students. The mini-lesson should have four parts—objectives, materials, procedure, and evaluation—to allow each student in the group to make some contribution to the plan. The mini-lessons can be as long or short as the group feels is necessary to teach the concept. The students may choose to explain the method and ask the other students to do problems, or they may assign homework and a quiz—the decision is to be made by the group. The students should make sure that each group member can teach the mini-lesson they have created.

6. The teacher should check each group's lesson plan to see how the methods will be taught and then make copies of the plan for each student in the group.

7. Divide students into four new groups with equal numbers of girls and boys in each group. Each group should have one or two students who can do one of

each of the four methods. Separate the girls and boys who associate with each other often. Separate students at the same skill level.

8. Each student in the group should teach his or her method for solving equations to the other group members. The students should follow their lesson plans.

9. The students should make sure that all of the members of the group can perform the four methods. When the groups feel they are confident about the methods, the game begins.

10. Each student in the group should choose a number from 1 to 4 (or up to the number of students in the group), which will serve to identify the student from each group who will be competing.

11. The teacher then chooses a number and the student from each group with that number comes to the board. The teacher reads the problem and the students must write and solve the problem. The problem must be solved by the method specified by the teacher.

12. The groups earn four, three, two, or one point for solving the problem first, second, third, or fourth, respectively. No points are given to a group that solves the problem incorrectly. All groups are required to keep score. The winning team may be given some reward, although the reward should not be overemphasized.

13. On the day after the game is played, give the students a quiz on which they must demonstrate their abilities to solve the equations.

Evaluation

1. Assess students' ability to solve the equations by correcting sample problems submitted by the initial groups and by observing their performance during the game and on the quiz.

2. Assess students' ability to teach the lessons by observing the second groupings.

3. Observe the groups to determine if interaction and cooperation are occurring.

4. Listen to group conversations to determine if boys are treating girls equally and if girls are treating boys equally.

WHY THE CHANGES?

Solving Two Equations with Two Unknowns

Cooperation

The "After" lesson plan uses the jigsaw model of cooperative learning to teach the same math concepts taught in the "Before" plan. The jigsaw model involves students interacting with a variety of peers to figure out a method of solving equations, to make sure all group members understand it, and to teach a method to other peers. Since every class member has an area of expertise in the second grouping, all students appear valuable and capable to their peers, which helps improve students' perceptions of and interactions with each other. The "After" plan also helps students learn the content better than if the teacher simply delivers it to them, in that cooperative learning actively involves them in figuring it out themselves and in helping each other to learn.

Stereotyping

At the secondary grade level, students often begin to view math more as the "male's" subject rather than as gender neutral, and many begin to doubt the competence of females in math. The "Before" lesson does not address this issue, whereas the "After" lesson does. First, all students, including females, tend to learn math better when taught using cooperative rather than competitive methods. And second, by grouping males and females equally, and by preparing each student to be an "expert" who can teach math to his or her peers, the lesson encourages both sexes to view math knowledge as something that everyone can learn equally well.

LESSON PLAN

BEFORE

Factoring Polynomials

Subject Area: Mathematics

Grade Level: 11–12

Time: One class period

Objective

Students will factor polynomials completely and accurately.

Suggested Procedures

1. Demonstrate on the board how to factor a polynomial and ask for student input while doing so. (Students should already have studied factoring previously and should be familiar with polynomials.) Do two or three more examples at the board, continuing to ask for student input.

2. Assign problems in the math textbook to be done in the class or as homework.

3. Review the problems with the class. Rework on the board those problems that students solved incorrectly.

Evaluation

Evaluate students' homework, or give each student three to five polynomials to factor independently.

AFTER ## Factoring Polynomials and Making Friends at the Same Time

Subject Area: Mathematics

Grade Level: 11–12

Time: One or two class periods

Objectives

1. Students will factor polynomials completely and accurately.

2. Students will enjoy abstract math problems.

3. Students will get along with their peers of different races and of the opposite sex.

Suggested Procedures

1. Divide students into groups of about five members each. The groups should be as race- and sex-mixed as possible, and should also mix good algebra students with those who have more difficulty in this area. Have each group select a name.

2. Demonstrate on the board how to factor a polynomial. If students do not understand, demonstrate additional examples until they do understand.

3. Write a polynomial on the board similar to those that were demonstrated. One group is to figure out how to factor it and to do so on the board. The other groups are to demonstrate whether it was done correctly and, if it wasn't, what the correct solution would be. Scoring is done as follows:

Two points are given when the group solves the problem correctly (but the points are not awarded until after the other groups have evaluated the solution).

One point is given to the evaluating groups when they evaluate correctly the solution of the group doing the problem.

No points are given to any group for incorrect solutions or evaluations.

4. Proceed to another problem; rotate the group at the board but repeat the procedure in step 3. Encourage group members to work together to figure out a solution.

5. Once students have mastered problems similar to those demonstrated by the teacher, and each group has had the same number of turns at the board, demonstrate a more complex problem and repeat the procedures in steps 3 and 4.

Evaluation

1. Give students three to five polynomials to factor independently; they should score 100 percent if the concept has been mastered.

2. Observe student–student interactions during the game and during other class activities to assess their improvement in social relationships.

WHY THE CHANGES?

Factoring Polynomials and Making Friends at the Same Time

Cooperative Learning

The "After" lesson plan uses the same problems used in the "Before" plan but presents them in a team-games cooperative lesson. If used frequently, three outcomes of this change can be expected: (1) students will make friends with teammates they might previously have ignored, (2) students will like math more, and (3) students will learn the concepts better. One of the authors used this procedure to teach grammar to high school students with learning disabilities. It worked so well that students not only learned the concepts and made new friends but also requested that the author continue teaching them more grammar than the author had planned because the process of learning it "turned them on"!

References

Allport, G. (1954). *The nature of prejudice*. Cambridge, MA: Addison-Wesley.

Banks, J. A. (1995). Multicultural education: Its effects on students' racial and gender role attitudes. In J. A. Banks & C. M. Banks (Eds.), *Handbook of research on multicultural education*, pp. 617–627. New York: Macmillan.

Johnson, D. W., Johnson, R., & Maruyama, G. (1983). Interdependence and interpersonal attraction among heterogeneous and homogeneous individuals: A theoretical formulation and meta-analysis of the research. *Review of Educational Research, 53*, 5–54.

Slavin, R. E. (1995). Cooperative learning and intergroup relations. In J. A. Banks & C. M. Banks (Eds.), *Handbook of research on multicultural education*, pp. 628–634. New York: Macmillan.

Slavin, R. E., & Madden, N. A. (1979). School practices that improve race relations. *American Educational Research Journal, 16*, 169–180.

Sleeter, C. E., & Grant, C. A. (1994). *Making choices for multicultural education: Five approaches to race, class, and gender* (2nd ed.). Upper Saddle River, NJ: Merrill/Prentice Hall.

Single-Group Studies

How much do you know about the history and contemporary culture of African American women? Mexican Americans? Asian Americans? Working-class Americans? If you are like most U.S. Americans, you probably know very little about these groups of people, able only to cite a few names and historic events. One way to enhance your knowledge about a group is to study it in some depth. The **Single-Group Studies approach** involves an in-depth study of a single group of people.

Before proceeding, you may want to analyze your own curriculum, using Action Research Activity 4.1. At first glance, your current textbooks may seem to teach about a wide variety of groups. You are aware that, prior to 1970, most school curricula concentrated on white, European American, male studies, and most curricula today represent an improvement since then. When you examine the results of your analysis, however, you will probably discover that some groups are barely included in the curricula and still others are excluded altogether. For example, in an examination of some current textbooks, one of our students discovered that three of the textbooks' coverage of Mexican Americans included only that they contributed enchiladas to U.S. American cuisine and a single poem to U.S. American literature! Single-group studies try to counterbalance this by providing an entire unit or course about Mexican Americans.

You may not be aware of omissions and distortions even when you are looking right at them if you have not studied the history, literature, and so forth of diverse groups. Your own knowledge base may reflect what is in mainstream textbooks if they have been a prime source of your own education. An eye-opening book we recommend is *Lies My Teacher Told Me* (Loewen, 1995), which critiques 12 current U.S. American history textbooks.

Single-group studies courses are usually designed for all students. However, often only women enroll in women's studies courses, only Asian Americans in Asian American studies courses, and so forth. This occurs because such courses are usually electives, and students who are not members of the group being studied view the course as unimportant or as threatening. A teacher of African American studies in a predominantly white high school told us how he works extra hard to make certain that all the students in the class feel comfortable about what he is teaching, and he encourages (through notices and displays) members of different ethnic groups to take the course.

Single-group studies can be done well, or they can be done superficially and poorly. Too often we have seen superficial attempts to teach about groups. For example, a fifth-grade teacher who normally teaches mostly about white European Americans decides to have a one-week African American studies unit during February. Knowing little about African American history and culture himself, he teaches about a smattering of famous people and events, selecting African Americans who are best known by white European Americans. When the unit is completed, the teacher returns to his regular, European American-dominated curriculum. Although teaching the unit may be better than omitting African Americans from the curriculum altogether, such a meager course may also teach stereotypes and convey to students that they have "studied" African Americans when they have only scratched the surface. As such, it is a poor example of single-group studies.

CHARACTERISTICS OF SINGLE-GROUP STUDIES

If the Single-Group Studies approach interests you, we encourage you to take the time to do it well. This means spending time first learning about the group yourself. A good single-group studies curriculum includes the following elements: perspective, history, culture, current social agenda, and other issues of particular concern.

Perspective

A single-group study takes a group's perspective about itself. This does not mean, for example, that a teacher needs to be a Chicano to teach Chicano studies, but it does mean that the teacher needs to have studied Chicanos from the perspectives of members of that group. The teacher should be able to present the points of view that are generated and receiving attention among members of the group being studied. This does not mean that the teacher is censored from presenting his or her own point of view, but the teacher should let students know that it is just another point of view. Most groups have been studied and written about by white European American male scholars; occasionally, one finds a gem (e.g., Gutman, 1977) but most often one finds distortions and stereotypes. The teacher needs to check source material to make sure the perspectives being presented are acceptable to members of the group (recognizing, of course, that no group shares a unanimous perspective on anything). A Chicana teacher we know recently expressed great frustration with the resistance of several white European American colleagues to the idea that their perspectives, when teaching about people of color, might not be the same as perspectives of people of color themselves. She used an analogy that helped get the point across: If a man were to teach women's studies, unless he was attentive to his own perspective and to those of women, most women would be upset and argue that he lacked the sensitivity to teach women's studies.

The importance of perspective has been developed in some depth by Afrocentrist scholars, who seek to uncover and use codes, paradigms, symbols, motifs, myths, and circles of discussion that reinforce the centrality of African ideals and values as a valid frame of reference (Asante, 1990, p. 6). Scholars such as Asante argue that there is no perspective free of knowledge, and that it is essential that we identify whose perspective frames our inquiry. For Afrocentrists, Africa and people of African descent center one's perspective. That certainly does not mean that there is only one Afrocentrist perspective—Afrocentrists debate each other vigorously. But they do so within a framework that acknowledges the centrality of Africa rather than Europe to organizing a perspective for understanding people of African descent.

Most of the lessons included in this chapter demonstrate the importance of perspective. There is also a growing body of texts that teachers can use that attempt to represent a specific group's perspective accurately. For example, Asante has written a history text for middle and high school students, entitled *African American History: A Journey of Liberation* (1995).

History

History is usually included in single-group studies and often has two foci. The first examines the group's historical experience and may include reference to other groups. The group's past and recent experiences are told "fairly" but from the perspectives of the group. The purpose is to document the group's history and contributions to society. Examples of lessons that focus on history include "Wheelchair Sports" (p. 127) and "Women and the Westward Movement" (p. 130).

The second focus traces and explains how the dominant group has oppressed the group being studied and how the oppressed group responded to or resisted oppression. Sometimes teachers shy away from this second focus, believing it to be controversial and detrimental to students' cross-group relationships. We believe unequal power relations between groups needs to be studied, but in a way that opens up discussion about how the future can be constructed more fairly and how everyone can participate in doing that. Young people very often are aware of various forms of inequalities between groups and wonder why things are the way they are; they are generally open to asking how they can make the world better for everyone. Examples of lessons that address oppression include "Mexican American Labor in the United States" (p. 155), "Culture in Native American Literature" (p. 151) and "Japanese Americans—U.S. Citizens" (p. 134).

Culture

The culture of a group includes the whole way of life of the group, including the group's literature, language, music, art, philosophy, and technology. Cultural contributions, which teachers often feel most comfortable emphasizing, show the group's creativity, the way the group has given meaning to its existence, and the way it has maintained and expressed its selfhood. Most students find cross-cultural sharing to be very interesting. The community can be an excellent resource for sharing culture: by exploring religious institutions, neighborhood stores, community centers, and neighborhood restaurants and by inviting students' family members to participate, teachers can design an interesting curriculum that is rooted in the perspectives and lives of real people. Lessons that discuss and illustrate cultural contributions include "Story Quilt" (p. 119), "Wheelchair Sports" (p. 127), and "Japanese Americans— U.S. Citizens" (p. 134). The lesson "Culture in Native American Literature" (p. 151) was designed to get students to consider what "culture" means and to begin to identify their own family and community culture.

Current Social Agenda

Advocates of the Single-Group Studies approach hope to use education as a means of bettering a group's current social condition. Therefore, considerable emphasis is placed on the group's current needs and experiences, the issues facing the group, and the movements involving the group. The purpose of discussing the current social agenda is to help students view themselves as active citizens who can make a positive difference in society. Sometimes teachers do not include this component of single-group studies, believing that knowledge of the group's history and contributions is sufficient. Most advocates of single-group studies view the exclusion of this component as a potential suggestion to students that the group is no longer oppressed or victimized. Teachers who are unsure of the issues that are currently on a group's social action agenda should investigate them (being aware that different subgroups may emphasize different issues). The lessons "American Indians and Institutional Racism" (p. 122), "Gay, Lesbian, and Bisexual Youth" (p. 141), "Mexican American Labor in the United States" (p. 155), and "Name-Calling" (p. 158) deal specifically with these groups' current social agendas.

Issues of Particular Concern

Most groups have particular issues that are especially important to them. For example, the study of Mexican Americans must include the issue of language; the study of

Jewish Americans must examine the Holocaust; gay and lesbian studies must examine different family structures; and women's studies must deal with the extent to which males and females differ biologically [see the lesson plan "Using the Scientific Method to Investigate Maternal Instinct" (p. 146)].

ACTION RESEARCH ACTIVITY 4.1

Textbook Analysis

Select one textbook and record the following information:

Title:

Author(s):

Publisher:

Copyright date:

Grade level (if known):

Following are guides for six kinds of analysis. Some may be appropriate to your text, some may not. Select all the analyses that can be done with your text. Go through the text page by page, completing each analysis you select. Take your time and do this carefully. Then compile your findings using the guidelines that follow and the charts shown in Figures 4.1–4.3.

Indicate here the types of analysis you completed:

	Yes	*No*
1. Picture	_____	_____
2. People to study	_____	_____
3. Anthology	_____	_____
4. Language	_____	_____
5. Storyline	_____	_____
6. Other	_____	_____

Picture Analysis.   Picture analysis is used for texts that picture U.S. American people.

1. Using the chart in Figure 4.1, tally the types of people in each picture by race and sex. The pictures may depict either individuals or groups. You will need to use your judgment on some pictures, but if a picture features one or a few individuals, tally each individual separately; if the picture features a group, tally it in the "group" row. Code each tally according to whether the individual(s) is(are) named or unnamed in a caption or in the surrounding text (N = named, U = unnamed).

		Male	Female	Both Sexes
Asian American	Individual			
	Group			
Black American	Individual			
	Group			
Hispanic American	Individual			
	Group			
American Indian	Individual			
	Group			
White American	Individual			
	Group			
Race Ambiguous	Individual			
	Group			
Mixed Race Group				
Disabled American	Individual			
	Group			

Total number of individuals depicted: _____

Total number of group scenes depicted: _____

FIGURE 4.1   Picture Tally

2. Make note of any race stereotypes.

3. Make note of any sex stereotypes/sex roles.

4. In group scenes, does any race or sex group consistently occupy the foreground? The background? Provide examples.

5. Can you tell the social-class background or setting of any of the depicted people? If so, make a note of them.

"People to Study" Analysis.   This type of analysis is used primarily for science and history texts.

In Figure 4.2, tally the race and sex of each person mentioned in the text. Distinguish between "important famous people," whose contributions are discussed in the main part of the content, and "extra people," who are added in boxes or supplementary pages at the beginning or end of the chapter.

	Main Part of Text		Supplementary	
	Male	Female	Male	Female
Asian American				
Black American				
Hispanic American				
American Indian				
White American				
Race Unknown				
Disabled American				

FIGURE 4.2   People to Study

Anthology Analysis.   This type of analysis is used for elementary readers, literature texts, music books containing works by different composers, and the like.

Across the top of the chart shown in Figure 4.3, write the name of each story, poem, essay, and song in the text (the figure has space for five titles; photocopy additional copies as needed). Complete all items that you can, using the following codes:

AM   = Asian American male   AF   = Asian American female
AAM = African American male   AAF = African American female
LM   = Latino male   LF   = Latina female
AIM = American Indian male   AIF = American Indian female
EAM = European American male   EAF = European American female
FM   = Foreign male   FF   = Foreign female
?M   = Male, race unknown   ?F   = Female, race unknown
DM   = Male with disabilities   DF   = Female with disabilities
GM   = Gay male   LF   = Lesbian female

Language Analysis.   This analysis should be recorded on a separate sheet of paper.

1. Does the textbook deliberately use nonsexist language? If not, list the male words that are used to refer to both sexes.

2. Examine the adjectives used to describe people or the contributions of people who are not white European American; list any stereotypic words, along with the group with which these words are linked.

Titles				
1. Race and sex of author				
2. Race, sex, and disability of main character				
3. Race, sex, and disability of supporting characters				
4. Are the characters all of one race? (Yes/No)				
5. Does the theme or storyline reflect the experiences of one particular group? If so, which group?				
6. Does the theme or storyline make one group look better or seem to have done more than another group? If so, which group?				
7. Is the setting rural (R), urban (U), suburban (S), or indeterminable (I)?				
8. Are there race stereotypes? If so, what are they?				
9. Are there sex stereotypes or sex roles? If so, what are they?				
10. Are there social-class stereotypes? If so, what are they?				
11. Are there disability stereotypes? If so, what are they?				

FIGURE 4.3   Anthology Analysis

3. Examine the adjectives used to describe males and females; list any that contain sex stereotypes.

4. When the word *women* is used, does it refer primarily to European American middle-class women or to all women? Look carefully, especially if you are analyzing a social studies book. Provide examples.

5. Look for words or phrases that give the actions of some groups (often European American wealthy males) an image of goodness or legitimacy in areas in which their actions might be questionable. Do this especially if you are analyzing a social studies book. Words such as *progress*, *improved*, and *successful* are commonly used in this way.

6. Look for words or phrases that give the actions of some groups (often those that live at or below the poverty level) an image of badness or trouble in areas in which there could well be another side that is not being told. Words such as *problems*, *unrest*, and *hostile* are examples.

7. Are dialects or accents portrayed? If so, what image is presented of the speaker(s)?

Storyline Analysis. This type of analysis is used for history texts, long stories in literature books, and novels. Record your answers on a separate sheet of paper.

1. What race/class/gender group receives the most sustained attention from beginning to end in the text?

2. What race/class/gender group resolves most of the problems that develop or accomplishes most of the achievements described? List the major problems and the people who resolve them. List the major accomplishments and the people who achieve them.

3. What other race/class/gender groups appear? How sustained is the attention given to each? What kinds of situations or accomplishments are associated with each?

4. How successfully and how often do the groups in item 3 resolve problems that develop? To what extent are the groups presented as causing problems? Give examples.

5. To what extent is the group in items 1 and 2 presented as a significant problem to someone else? How realistically or completely is this portrayed? Give examples.

6. What group(s) does the author intend the reader to sympathize with or to respect the most?

7. What group's experience does the reader learn most about?

8. Was the author, as nearly as you can tell, a member of the most-featured group? If not, is there anything to suggest the author is qualified to write about that group?

Miscellaneous Analyses.   If race, class, gender, and disability can be examined in any additional ways in your text, do so. For example:

1. If the text includes story problems or story examples (e.g., a math text), list who is doing what by race, sex, and disability for each problem. Then search for any race or sex stereotypes and roles.

2. Determine if the text shows an awareness of and sensitivity to the experiences of U.S. Americans of color, women, or the poor in ways not captured by previous analyses. For example, how does a health text treat pregnancy or sickle-cell anemia?

Compiling the Findings.   Compile your findings on a separate sheet of paper.

1. Compile all your data depicting the way each of the following groups is portrayed. Include how much space or attention the text devotes to each group (e.g., percentage of pictures) and to the roles and characteristics of the group.

   Asian Americans, of both sexes

   African Americans, of both sexes

   Latino Americans, of both sexes

   American Indians, of both sexes

   White European Americans, of both sexes

   Women, of various racial backgrounds

   Men, of various racial backgrounds

   The upper class

   The middle class

   People who live at or below the poverty level

   People who are gay, lesbian, or bisexual

   U.S. Americans with disabilities, of both sexes and various racial backgrounds

2. For each group in item 1, compile data on how the text depicts the concerns or experiences of the group and the group's ability to deal effectively with its concerns.

3. For each group, ask the following questions:

   a. Does the text give a student who is a member of that group much with which to identify?

   b. What kinds of roles and characteristics does the text suggest are appropriate for that student to develop or aspire to?

LESSON PLAN

BEFORE

Story-Writing

Subject Area: Language Arts

Grade Level: 3–5

Time: One week

Objectives

1. Students will demonstrate story comprehension.

2. Students will sequence events correctly.

Suggested Procedures

1. Read the story *Tar Beach* by Faith Ringgold (New York: Crown, 1991). Faith Ringgold is both an artist and a children's author, and she is noted for her quilt-making. *Tar Beach* tells a story of inner-city children creating a beach on a rooftop.

2. Have students complete a writing assignment summarizing the main idea of the story.

3. Before going to the computer lab, divide the class into groups of four students. Have each group think of a fun activity they would like to do but cannot do where they live. Have them pretend to be magicians and imagine a way of creating that activity in their own neighborhood. Tell them that good story-writers have good ideas and are able to convey them in an order that makes sense to other people.

4. In the computer lab, each group should create a short story that tells about their imaginary activity. After writing the story, they should save each sentence on a separate sheet of paper.

5. Have each group exchange stories, with the sentences scrambled. Each group should attempt to sequence the sentences into an order that makes sense. When all groups have finished, have them pass their sequenced sentences to another group, who will read the sequencing to see if the story makes sense. Then discuss the stories and the sequencing exercise.

Evaluation

1. Assess students' comprehension of the story *Tar Beach* through the writing assignment.

2. Assess students' sequencing ability through their participation in the sequencing exercise.

AFTER   ## Story Quilt*

Subject Areas: Language Arts, Art, History

Grade Level: 3–5

Time: Three weeks

Objectives

1. Students will research a historical event/period of a cultural group.

2. Students will sequence events encapsulating the information acquired.

3. Students will connect literature with the group's history.

Suggested Procedures

1. Read the story *Tar Beach* by Faith Ringgold (New York: Crown, 1991). Faith Ringgold is both an artist and a children's author, and she is noted for her quilt-making. *Tar Beach* tells a story of inner-city children creating a beach on a rooftop.

2. Tell students about Faith Ringgold's quilt-making. Two suggested resources are:

   Portfolios: African American Artists. Palo Alto, CA: Dale Seymour, 1994. (This is a book of prints of artists' works and includes a picture of Ringgold's quilt "Tar Beach.")

   Ringgold, Faith. (1996). *Talking to Faith Ringgold*. New York: Crown.

3. Tell students that they will make a quilt depicting the Civil Rights movement. Help them during the period of a week or so to find information on the movement. A useful children's book about this movement is Geoffrey Jacques, *The African-American Movement Today* (New York: Franklin Watts, 1994). If possible, use the Internet for up-to-date information. Have students make notes of the event.

4. Give each student two squares of scratch paper with which to write information about the event. Have students share one fact and tack it to a piece of butcher paper taped on a wallboard. If someone has a duplicate, use the second fact.

---

*Source: Jacquelyn King, Kenosha Unified School District, Kenosha, WI.

   Note: This lesson plan has been developed around the African American culture, but the structure of the plan lends itself to a variety of different cultural groups. A teacher would need to do a bit of research to connect literature, art, and history accurately, as this plan does.

After everyone has contributed information, the class will organize the facts in chronological order. Number the papers.

5. In journals, students will describe the event.

6. Before going to computer lab time, pass out one fact to each student. Students will type the facts, change margins if necessary so the text fits within a square. Back in the classroom, on pre-cut squares of paper, students will center and glue their typed information. (The size of the font and quilt squares will be dependent on the number of students and desired size of the finished quilt. Cut a center square for the title of the piece and signature of each student participant and whatever other information you may desire.) Students should decorate the border of their square with paper scraps, glitter, cloth scraps, beans, buttons, markers, and/or other items. Their decorations should depict events or ideas related to the Civil Rights movement.

7. To assemble the quilt, glue finished squares to large pieces of butcher paper or poster board bound together.

Evaluation

1. Assess students' research through observation and discussion as they are working and by the square each contributes to the quilt.

2. Assess students' ability to develop a sequence of events by the accuracy of their journal entry.

WHY THE CHANGES?

Story Quilt

History and Culture

The "Before" lesson disconnects Faith Ringgold's work from its cultural context. Although the story is written by a noted African American artist, very little is done with the story to develop an understanding of African American history and culture. The "After" plan develops this understanding.

The "After" plan is much more involved than the "Before" plan, but it also incorporates three different disciplines rather than one. With careful planning, this can become a thematic interdisciplinary unit that works for three different disciplines simultaneously. This interdisciplinary teaching then lends itself very well to connecting literature, art, and history to delve into a significant event in African American history.

The structure of the "After" plan lends itself well to studying different groups. For example, one could study an event in Chicano history by focusing on Chicano muralists such as Judith Baca. Students could then create a mural depicting an event such as the development of the United Farm Workers or immigration experiences. Or, students could study Asian immigration beginning with the book *The Little Weaver of Thai–Yen Village*, which is a true story of a Vietnamese immigrant girl and is written in both English and Vietnamese. In bilingual classrooms, students could then create bilingual books like this one, based on research about immigration from Asia.

Resource

Tran, K. T. (1987). *The little weaver of Thai–yen village* (*Co be tho–det lang Thai–yen*) (rev. ed.) (trans. into English by C. N. H. Jenkins & K. T. Tran). San Francisco, CA: Children's Book Press, distributed by Talman.

LESSON PLAN

BEFORE

American Indians in Our State

Subject Areas: Interdisciplinary (Social Studies, Art, Language Arts)

Grade Level: 5–8

Time: Three or four class periods

Objectives

1. Students will identify American Indian reservations on a state map and name tribes in the state.

2. Students will list towns, cities, rivers, and other geographic features in the states that have American Indian names.

3. Students will appreciate local American Indian art and literature.

Suggested Procedures

1. Ask students if they know what American Indian tribes live in the state. List the tribes on the board and teach students how to pronounce each one correctly.

2. On a large wall map, show where American Indian reservations are located in the state and where the majority of each tribe lives. (If a tribe lives on more than one reservation, or if more than one tribe lives on a reservation, clarify this; also point out where most American Indians live who are not on the reservation.) Pass out individual maps of the state; have students label and color the reservations and other places where the tribes live.

3. Ask students if they are aware of any American Indian names for places in the state. Start a list on the board. Supply American Indian names that students do

not offer. Help students to see that one cultural legacy of the American Indians is names. Point out which tribes contributed which names. Discuss any history behind the names of places.

4. Bring to class samples and pictures of American Indian art work. Point out the particular skills involved in creating them and any symbols in the designs. Also point out the uses that artifacts have in American Indian culture.

5. Select a few folktales, poems, or songs produced by local American Indian tribes. Have students read them and discuss their meaning and significance.

Evaluation

1. Evaluate students' appreciation of American Indian art and literature through their reactions to them.

2. Evaluate students' knowledge of American Indian reservations, tribe names, and American Indian names for geographic locations through a quiz.

AFTER

American Indians and Institutional Racism[*]

Subject Areas: Interdisciplinary (Social Studies, Math, Composition)

Grade Level: 5–8

Time: Three or four class periods

Objectives

1. Students will identify areas of good and poor agricultural land on a map.

2. Students will analyze the distribution of agricultural land to European Americans and American Indians and the consequences of land distribution.

3. Students will construct bar graphs from numerical data.

4. Students will distinguish between institutional racism and individual prejudice.

5. Students will appreciate the potential of their own actions for changing institutional racism.

---

[*]*Source:* Lynette Selkurt Zimmer, Kenosha, WI.

Note: Students often think of racism only as the individual prejudice that one person displays toward another (e.g., calling someone by a racist name). The concept of **institutional racism** is usually more difficult to grasp because it involves questioning institutional practices that many of us take for granted. This lesson plan uses examples from one state to help students understand institutional racism. Similar lessons can be developed in other states, drawing on the particulars of how oppression of a group is maintained.

Suggested Procedures

1. Ask students what **racism** means. They will probably define the term or give examples in terms of individual prejudice; accept their definitions for the time being. Ask how they would describe racism today toward American Indians.

2. Pass out a soil map and a growing season map (see Figure 4.4). Discuss with students which land they would like to own if they were farmers and why.

3. Pass out the Wisconsin reservations map (see Figure 4.4) or a similar map of your own state. Ask students to compare the locations of American Indian reservations with the most and least desirable farmland.

4. Provide information on Wisconsin's and the federal government's treatment of American Indians, including the following:

   a. The six distinct tribes, each with its own language and culture (Chippewa, Menominee, Oneida, Potawatomi, Stockbridge, and Winnebago [later, the Hochunk Nation])

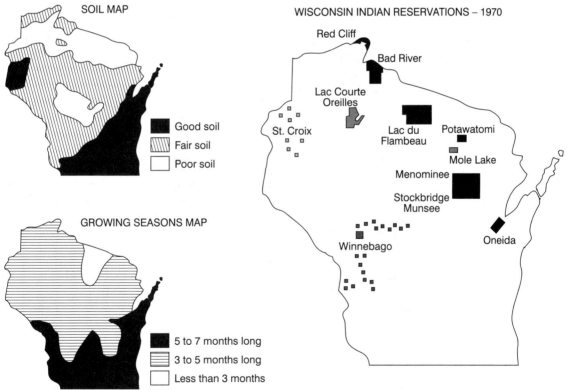

FIGURE 4.4

Source: Adapted from *Tiller's Guide to Indian Country* by Veronica E. Tiller & Velarde Tiller, 1996, Albuquerque, NM: BowArrow.

b. The "hands-off" policy, which forced Indians onto reservations and made them fend for themselves

c. The "Americanize" policy, in which tribal governments were undermined, religions suppressed, native arts discouraged, and family life hurt by government boarding schools

d. The year 1924, when American Indians became full U.S. citizens

e. The Indian Restoration Act of 1934, which did away with severe Americanization programs

5. Divide the class into small groups and distribute a sheet like the one shown in Table 4.1. Have each group locate data using the Internet; two suggested URLs include:

> INDIANnet Census Information Center
> http://seal.monterey.edu/academic/faculty-staff-projects/indian-net/indian-net.html
>
> NativeWeb Home Page
> http://www.maxwell.syr.edu/nativeweb/

Then have them construct a bar graph using data they located. For example, one group could construct a bar graph depicting, for American Indians and all races, the following data:

> Percentage of families living in poverty
>
> Percentage of families living in poverty headed by a female
>
> Percentage of total persons living in poverty

6. Have students present their bar graphs and explain them to the class.

7. Discuss the relationship between the information on students' bar graphs and the arability of soil on the reservations. Explain that this is an example of institutional racism, in which American Indians today suffer the adverse effects of land distribution, compounded by past government policies.

8. Ask students to suggest ways that Wisconsin citizens and the federal government could help solve these unequal conditions. From students' suggestions, select targets for a letter-writing campaign. Have students write letters (e.g., to members of Congress) expressing their feelings and proposing their suggestions.

Evaluation

1. Assess students' understanding of land distribution through class discussion.

2. Assess students' understanding of the consequences of land distribution through their presentations and discussion of small-group bar graphs.

3. Assess students' understanding of institutional racism through class discussion and their suggestions for helping undo racism.

TABLE 4.1   Worksheet for Gathering Information About Wisconsin Indians' Access to Resources

	Wisconsin Indians	All Races
Resource: Housing		
Number of year-round housing units		
Percentage lacking some or all plumbing facilities		
Median number of rooms per unit		
Number of occupied units		
Median number of persons per unit		
Resource: Education		
Median number of school years completed		
Resource: Income, jobs		
Percentage of families living in poverty		
Percentage of families living in poverty headed by a female		
Percentage of total persons living in poverty		
Percentage of unemployed persons		
Percentage of civilian labor force employed in manufacturing		

4. Assess students' appreciation of themselves as social actors through the content and quality of their letters.

WHY THE CHANGES?

American Indians and Institutional Racism

Perspective and Current Social Agenda

The "Before" lesson probably seems more familiar than the "After" lesson. The "Before" lesson teaches mainly about the contributions that American Indians have made to European Americans, which often is the main perspective used by teachers. The "Before" lesson teaches the names that American Indians contributed for geographic locations and their artistic and literary contributions. Often when selecting these, we choose historic rather than contemporary contributions. Although it is acceptable to teach this information, to focus on it makes American Indians' cultural contributions seem more important than the people themselves. It also makes the contributions used and appreciated by white

European Americans seem more valuable than those used and appreciated mainly by American Indians, and it makes historic American Indian culture seem more worthy of study than the status of the American Indian people today.

The "After" lesson shifts the perspective, and in so doing it shifts the focus of the entire lesson. It is oriented around the perspective that institutional racism is a major problem continuing to thwart the chances of American Indian people today, and that this is at least as important for students to understand as is American Indian culture.

Cultural Contributions

At a later point, students can and should learn more about American Indian culture. But they should learn what American Indians today are saying about themselves and their lives through such media as literature and art. Contemporary art and literary forms can certainly be linked with historic art forms, but contemporary culture should be focused on itself.

LESSON PLAN

BEFORE

Wheelchair Basketball

Subject Area: Physical Education

Grade Level: 5–8

Time: One-half hour

Objectives

1. Students will learn how basketball can be modified to accommodate wheelchair athletes.

2. Students will become aware that there is a local wheelchair basketball league.

Suggested Procedures

1. In the context of teaching a unit on basketball, ask students if they have ever watched wheelchair basketball. Explain how the game is modified for wheelchairs. Have available some wheelchairs and demonstrate or walk students through some of the moves and plays used in wheelchair basketball.

2. Tell students about any local wheelchair basketball leagues that exist. Provide students with a schedule in case they wish to attend any games.

Evaluation

Include two or three questions on wheelchair basketball on a quiz at the end of the basketball unit.

AFTER

Wheelchair Sports

Subject Areas: Interdisciplinary (Physical Education, Social Studies, Reading)

Grade Level: 5–8

Time: One week

Objectives

1. Students will appreciate the struggle that people with physical disabilities have had in developing programs and options in athletics.

2. Students will name several athletes with physical disabilities and appreciate their strength, determination, and skill.

3. Students will attend or participate in local wheelchair athletics.

4. Students will actively support the work of people with disabilities today directed toward taking control of their own lives.

Suggested Procedures

1. Have students read the trade book *Winning* by Robin Brancato (1978), a story about an adolescent boy who is injured playing football and becomes a quadriplegic. Have students discuss what they know about future life options for such a person and how they could deal with life if such an accident happened to them. It is likely that students will see little hope for a rich and satisfying life as a quadriplegic and will know little about the range of activities open to such a person.

2. Have students study the history and development of wheelchair sports. One way this can be done is by having them read *Wheelchair Basketball* by Brad Hedrick (1994) or *Wheelchair Champions* by May Savitz (1978) and/or view the videotape *The Wheelchair Basketball Video*. This can also be done through lecture and supplemented by guest speakers who have helped develop wheelchair sports locally. Wheelchair sports began in the United States during the 1940s, as soldiers with permanent disabilities returned from the war. Since then, athletes with disabilities have developed organized sports in many different areas of athletics and have made great achievements. Spend time providing information on the developments in different sports and on the achievements of athletes—there is a rich history to be told.

3. Attend a local athletic competition for people with physical disabilities. If possible, arrange for one of the athletes or coaches to visit the class first and explain

to students what they will be seeing, including how the sport has been modified, how people train for it, and how local competitions are organized.

4. In physical education, teach students the rudiments of a sport such as wheelchair basketball or wheelchair floor hockey. Allow students to practice until they begin to gain some degree of competence; their biggest first challenge will be learning to drive a wheelchair. The students may not develop much skill, but the experience will help them appreciate the skill that a wheelchair athlete must develop.

5. Invite a speaker from a local organization for people with physical disabilities to describe current problems and issues that these people are addressing in athletics and other areas of life.

6. Start a bulletin board on which students may place newspaper and magazine articles about the current issues and needs that people with physical disabilities face. As articles are added, have students discuss how they as citizens, whether they have physical disabilities or not, can actively support work by people with disabilities to control their own lives and to open up options for productive living. (An excellent resource is *The Ragged Edge*, Box 145, Louisville, KY 40201.)

Evaluation

1. Assess students' knowledge of the history of wheelchair sports and of athletes with disabilities through a quiz.

2. Assess students' appreciation of wheelchair sports through their reactions to attending a wheelchair athletic competition and to practicing a wheelchair sport.

3. Assess students' support of the current struggles of people with physical disabilities through the articles they choose and their discussion of them.

Resources

Brancato, Robin. (1978). *Winning*. New York: Alfred A. Knopf.

Hedrick, Brad. (1994). *Wheelchair basketball* (2nd ed.). Washington, DC: Paralyzed Veterans of America.

Savitz, May. (1978). *Wheelchair champions*. New York: Thomas Y. Crowell.

The wheelchair basketball video. (1989). Washington, DC: Paralyzed Veterans of America, Sports and Recreation Department.

WHY THE CHANGES?

Wheelchair Sports

History and Culture

The "Before" plan incorporates as much or more attention to wheelchair sports as one would normally find in lessons for students who are not physically impaired by acknowledging that wheelchair basketball exists. The "After" plan draws on materials written for students in different subject areas to develop an interdisciplinary unit on wheelchair sports. Both books can be read by students in the fifth- to eighth-grade range. *Wheelchair Champions* could also be used as a resource book by the teacher in the event that the school cannot acquire multiple copies. The "After" plan teaches students about an area most people know virtually nothing about and sensitizes them to the needs and abilities of people with physical disabilities. It also alerts students to the fact that all of us could one day have a physical disability and that concern for the quality of life of people with disabilities can be selfishly motivated as well as humanitarian.

Studying the history of wheelchair sports can reinforce students' understanding of political and social history. For example, wheelchair sports did not start by accident in the 1940s; rather, it was directly related to the war experience as well as to medical and technological developments of the time.

Students tend to find this area of study quite interesting, partly because it is new to them and partly because students usually know individuals who have disabilities. The topic can, in many cases, be motivating to students.

LESSON PLAN

BEFORE

Pioneers

Subject Area: Social Studies
Grade Level: 6–8
Time: Five days

Objectives

1. Students will describe the problems that the pioneers faced as they moved westward.
2. Students will describe why the early settlers moved westward.
3. Students will identify the supplies the pioneers took west and explain why they needed them.
4. Students will name the time period when the westward movement took place.
5. Students will identify the routes that most wagon trains took west.

Suggested Procedures

1. Have students read about the westward movement in their textbook.
2. Ask the school librarian to provide students with a list of books on the westward movement. Encourage each student to read a book and to do a short oral report in class.

TABLE 4.2 Wagon Train Supply Record: What Supplies Did Pioneers Carry on Wagon Trains?

Supplies	Amount	Date Opened	Date Used
Coffee	Ten 2-lb. bags	May 16, 1839, bag 1	May 31, 1839, bag 1

3. Provide students with a "supply record" guide sheet that they can complete as they read. An example is shown in Table 4.2.

4. If available in your area, have students watch the television series "Wagon Train."

Evaluation

1. Quiz the major points of the lesson.

2. Assess students' successful completion of the wagon train checklist.

AFTER

Women and the Westward Movement

Subject Area: Social Studies

Grade Level: 6–8

Time: Five to eight days

Objectives

1. Students will describe the important role that women of different races played in the movement west.

2. Students will describe and analyze why many European American and African American women wanted to move west and why many Native American women and Mexican women tried to resist the movement.

3. Students will describe and evaluate differences in the life changes and opportunities for pioneer men and women.

4. Students will identify evidence of sexism during the time of the westward movement and compare it with evidence of sexism in society today.

5. Students will identify, analyze, and discuss differences in the culture and roles of pioneer women and Plains Indian women.

Suggested Procedures

1. As a pre-activity, discuss the life conditions of, and society's expectations for, African American and European American women in U.S. society during the time of the wagon trains.

2. Have students read and examine the chapter on the westward movement in their social studies textbook. They should ascertain how the textbook treats women (e.g., How much is the pioneer women's role in the westward movement discussed? Are African American women included in the discussion? Are Native American women or Mexican women discussed and described as resistors to the movement?).

3. If students discover that women—African Americans, Native Americans, Mexicans, and European Americans—are not sufficiently addressed in the chapter, they should write a letter to the publisher to ask why this is so.

4. Organize students into sex-mixed groups. Each group is to research a topic related to women and the westward movement (e.g., the reasons women moved west; the life and duties on the wagon train for men and women; family roles once the pioneers reached their destinations).

5. Ask the school librarian to provide students with a list of trade books about women and the westward movement. Suggested books include D. Levenson's *Women of the West,* F. Lockley's *Conversations with Pioneer Women,* and I. L. Bird's *A Lady's Life in the Rocky Mountains.* Have the librarian point out which books include information about Native American, Mexican, and African American women. Tell each member of each group to read one book and to take notes on the treatment of women of all races in the book. The data students collect allow them to analyze and discuss with group members the treatment of women during the westward movement.

6. During class discussion, ask students to compare gender prejudices during the days of the wagon train with gender prejudices that exist today. Remind students that gender prejudice is directed toward both sexes (e.g., in the past, women were considered weak and timid and men were considered unable to raise children and run a household). Encourage some students to prepare the information for the school newspaper.

7. Ask students to examine the customs, roles, and regulations of the school to determine if gender biases are present. Have some students develop the findings into an article for the school newspaper.

8. Have students view western films to determine how they portray women—African Americans, European Americans, Mexicans, and Native Americans.

Evaluation

1. Students' written reports can serve as a source of evaluation.

2. Observe students' attitudes and behavior toward sex bias.

3. Observe students' understanding and attitudes about the gender biases toward white European American women and women of color.

4. Give an essay examination of the main points in the activity.

Resources

Bird, I. L. (1960). *A lady's life in the Rocky Mountains*. Norman, OK: University of Oklahoma Press.

Levenson, D. (1973). *Women of the west*. New York: Franklin Watts.

Lockley, F. (1981). *Conversations with pioneer women*. Eugene, OR: Rainy Day Press.

WHY THE CHANGES?

Women and the Westward Movement

Perspective on History

Many social studies textbooks do not give equal treatment to the roles of men and women in U.S. American history. The "Before" lesson plan accepts the lesser treatment that women usually receive. In contrast, the "After" lesson plan provides an opportunity to examine how women worked side by side with men during the movement west and points out the hidden biases that often appear in instructional materials. The "After" plan explicitly asks students to learn about African American, Mexican, and Native American women in addition to European American women (often when lessons focus on women, they focus on European American women). In attending to Native American and Mexican women, students are asked to consider not only the perspective of the pioneers moving west but also that of the people whose land was being invaded by the pioneers. The "After" plan allows students to work in sex-mixed groups that encourage them to eliminate sex-role stereotyping as they examine the ideas, attitudes, and behaviors in the instructional materials.

Current Social Agenda

The "Before" plan deals with only historic events. In contrast, the "After" plan asks students to compare the role of women in the 1850s with the role of women today, encouraging them to think about contemporary issues of sexism. The lesson also promotes students' own analysis and evaluation of curriculum materials, whereas the "Before" plan asks students to describe events and to accept what they have read.

BEFORE

LESSON PLAN

Back Home During World War II

Subject Area: Social Studies

Grade Level: 7–12

Time: Two class periods

Objectives

1. Students will describe the mobilization efforts of the U.S. government and the experiences of citizens on the home front during World War II.

2. Students will describe the national security efforts of the U.S. government and of its citizens on the home front during World War II.

Suggested Procedures

1. Ask students to read in their text about victory gardens, rationing, and the way war bond sales and taxation helped finance World War II.

2. Have students ask their grandparents or elders in their community about salvage collections of rubber, metal, and grease for the war effort.

3. Ask students to read in their text about the relocation of Japanese Americans. Have them discuss why the relocation occurred and whether the government had a right to relocate Japanese Americans.

Evaluation

On the next quiz, ask students to describe the mobilization and national security efforts on the home front during World War II.

| AFTER |

Japanese Americans—U.S. Citizens

Subject Area: Social Studies

Grade Level: 7–12

Time: Two weeks

Objectives

1. Students will identify many Japanese people as long-time American citizens born in this country.

2. Students will appreciate the loyalty and contributions of Japanese Americans to their homeland, the United States.

3. Students will describe the immigration story of the Japanese to the United States.

4. Students will learn how prejudice, racism, and ethnocentrism can lead people to act unfairly and unjustly toward other people.

Suggested Procedures

1. Ask students to describe what they know about Japanese American history and contemporary life. Pay attention to the extent to which students associate Japan-

ese Americans with the Japanese from Japan (e.g., do they associate televisions and automobiles made in Japan with Japanese Americans?).

2. Divide students into groups of four or five and ask each group to prepare a report on the Japanese immigration to the United States. Provide some groups with information written by Japanese American authors and other groups with school textbooks from different publishing companies. Have students compare the quality of information as each group presents its report to the class.

3. Ask students to compare why the Japanese and the British settled in this country. Have them examine why the Japanese Exclusion Act of 1924 was passed and enforced.

4. Ask students to read about Hikozo Hamada (who later changed his name to Joseph Heco), the first Japanese to become an American citizen.

5. In groups, have students prepare a report on Japanese American loyalty to this country during their forced internment in concentration camps during World War II. If possible, invite Japanese American guests to speak on these topics. Also, have students examine the role of the Nisei soldiers during World War II.

6. Discuss with the class how racism and ethnocentrism can lead to unjust treatment of a group of people. Ask students to describe other examples of mistreatment caused by racism, prejudice, and ethnocentrism.

7. Invite to class a Japanese American speaker to discuss the problems and issues facing Japanese Americans today. Ask students to compare and contrast these problems and issues with those that occurred during World War II. Have them determine whether racism still exists and, if so, why.

8. Discuss the major similarities and differences between contemporary Japanese and Japanese Americans. Make sure students appreciate that the two groups are not the same.

Evaluation

1. Assess students' appreciation of Japanese Americans' loyalty and contributions through small-group reports.

2. Assess students' knowledge of the Japanese immigration story and of prejudice, racism, and ethnocentrism through oral discussion and a quiz.

WHY THE CHANGES?

Japanese Americans—U.S. Citizens

History

The "Before" plan covers a number of events and activities related to World War II but in a somewhat more limited manner than the "After" plan. Also, the

"Before" plan is not directly connected to present-day events and experiences. In contrast, the "After" lesson plan focuses on and examines the past and present treatment of Japanese Americans. It also helps students to identify and describe how racism, prejudice, and ethnocentrism can lead to the unjust mistreatment of groups of people. The "After" plan makes clear the distinction between Japanese Americans and the Japanese; that is, the former are American citizens.

Cultural Contributions

The "After" plan discusses the loyalty of and the contributions that Japanese Americans have made to the United States. Further, by using different sources of information, the lesson provides students with an opportunity to discover how Japanese Americans overcame racism and prejudice in a nonviolent manner, demonstrated patriotism during World War II, and continue to fight racial prejudices today.

Current Social Agenda

The guest speaker and discussion of current issues of racism help focus students' attention on problems that still exist today, problems directly connected with the history being studied.

UNIT PLAN: GAY, LESBIAN, AND BISEXUAL ISSUES[*]

Schools and teachers can do a great deal to develop a school culture that says that any type of discrimination and invisibility of any student is not acceptable. It is safe to say that most of us believe that all students have a right to an education that meets their needs and is reflective of themselves and their families. This means that teachers cannot ignore issues of importance to gays, lesbians, and bisexuals if we advocate being inclusive of difference in our classrooms. When we exclude these issues in our schools and classrooms, we are saying a great deal about what is legitimate and what is not.

Yet, when discussing this issue with heterosexual teachers, we are often met with fear and apprehension. However, it is vital that heterosexually identified teachers be among the first to eradicate homophobia (the irrational fear of gays, lesbians, and bisexuals and those perceived to be gay, lesbian, or bisexual) and heterosexism (the individual and institutional belief that all people are heterosexual). If they address these issues it will do much to erase the notion that the only people who care to talk about heterosexism and homophobia are gays, lesbians, and bisexuals. Heterosexual

---

Source: Lisa W. Loutzenheiser, University of Wisconsin–Madison, Madison, WI.

educators must also speak out because their very heterosexuality gives them a measure of privacy and protection that gay, lesbian, and bisexual teachers do not have.

Educators can begin with small steps. First and foremost, as with an area of cultural difference, teachers must educate themselves about diverse gay, lesbian, and bisexual communities and explore their own attitudes and feelings before attempting to teach. There are many excellent resources available, among them Ann Heron (ed.), *Two Teenagers in Twenty: Writings by Gay and Lesbian Youth* (Boston: Alyson Publications, 1994); Lea Due, *Joining the Tribe* (New York: Anchor Books, 1995); Kurt Chandler, *Passages of Pride* (New York: Times Books, 1995); and Dan Woog, *School's Out* (Boston: Alyson Publications, 1995) (this has an excellent resource list in the back).

Teachers can do things as simple as acknowledge that homophobic comments, just as racist or sexist comments, are not acceptable in the classroom, and define homophobia if students do not understand it. Each and every time a student calls another student a name, or remarks that something is *gay* (meaning bad), address the issue, reminding students that all discriminatory remarks are unacceptable. This will begin to ingrain in students the concept that this is an issue of equality and human rights.

Another small step that can be made by instructors is not assuming their own students' heterosexuality. One exercise to try is to place yourself in your gay, lesbian, or bisexual student's chair, and imagine a typical class in your room. How might he or she feel invisible, or *less than*? Then rewrite the lesson or the lecture with this student in mind. By making gays, lesbians, and bisexuals an everyday part of the classroom curriculum and pedagogy, the discomfort and apprehension about discussing it begin to fade into the rest of classroom culture. For example, when assigning research topics, include issues of interest and importance to gay, lesbian, and bisexual youth. Or in biology class, challenge students to explore the myths surrounding the transmission of AIDS or to explore the genetic theories about homosexuality. Mixing these examples in with all the other topics demonstrates to students that gay, lesbian, and bisexual issues are not *special*, only to be brought up during particular (and often uncomfortable) classes, but that they are *everyday* issues, and can be discussed alongside any other.

Teachers can also alter the curriculum so that the contributions of gays, lesbians, and bisexuals can be acknowledged. For example, when discussing James Baldwin's contribution to literature, also consider that he was gay and the way this might have influenced his writings. The same can be done with the art of Michelangelo, the music of Tchaikovsky, and the scientific method of Francis Bacon. In these ways gay, lesbian, and bisexual students begin to see and hear themselves in the classroom not as odd or bad, but part of the discussion.

The lessons that follow can be used as a mini-unit for introducing students to gay, lesbian, and bisexual issues, or they can be used individually. They offer preliminary examples of how to approach discussing these issues by beginning with the abstract historical experiences of gays, lesbians, and bisexuals; moving the discussion to the more immediate by viewing a video about gay youth; and last, making it more personal by asking students to explore their own views, reactions, and opinions.

LESSON PLAN

The Legacies of the African American Civil Rights Movement

Subject Area: U.S. History

Grade Level: 9–12

Time: Three to four class periods, as part of a larger unit on civil rights

Objectives

1. Students will identify how the women's, American Indian, Chicano/Latino, and disability rights movements were influenced by the push for civil rights among African Americans in the south.

2. Students will compare and contrast the social, political, and economic issues and development of the women's, American Indian, Chicano/Latino, and disability rights movements.

3. Students will appreciate the importance of the early African American Civil Rights movement for other subordinated groups such as women, people of color, and people with disabilities.

4. Students will gain experience with analyzing primary documents.

Suggested Procedures

1. Read the appropriate sections of the textbook for information about how the social, political, and economic issues of the times affected these civil rights movements.

2. Over the course of a number of days, students will read, analyze, and discuss a number of first-person accounts and other primary documents on each particular movement. This work is to be accomplished in small groups and full class discussions.

3. Small groups will be formed and asked to develop a short classroom presentation on a different aspect of one of the movements and compare it with the early Civil Rights movement of African Americans.

4. Keep a daily response journal.

Evaluation

1. Assess students' ability to compare and contrast the women's, American Indian, Chicano/Latino, and disability rights movements with each other and with the earlier civil rights movements through classroom and small-group discussion.

2. Evaluate the students' understanding of the legacies of the African American Civil Rights movement through discussion, group presentation, and written exam/essay.

3. Assess students' ability to analyze primary documents through small-group discussion and daily response journals.

AFTER

The Legacies of the African American Civil Rights Movement

Subject Area: Social Studies

Grade Level: 7–12

*Time: Four to five class periods as part of a larger civil rights unit; one to one and
a half class periods if this lesson is presented by itself, without unit*

Objectives

1. Students will appreciate the influence of the African American Civil Rights
   movement on other human rights struggles, including gay liberation, women's,
   Chicano/Latino, Native American, and disability rights.

2. Students will explain why Stonewall was seen as the beginning of the modern
   gay, lesbian, and bisexual rights movement and why it should be included in
   studying the struggles of the sixties.

3. Students will appreciate the impact of the early African American Civil Rights
   movement on other subordinated groups such as women, people of color, people with disabilities, and gays, lesbians, and bisexuals.

4. Students will gain experience in analyzing primary documents.

Suggested Procedures

(Following the procedures outlined in the "Before" plan, include Stonewall as
follows.)

1. Ask students to brainstorm about the conditions for gays, lesbians, and bisexuals
   in the late 1950s and early 1960s. If not raised, point out that there were gays,
   lesbians, and bisexuals who were of color and/or had disabilities.

   Ask students what kind of public establishments they like to hang out in and
   with whom. Point out that they spend time with people who are like them in
   some way. Tell students of the laws that make it illegal to run bars or restaurants
   that catered to homosexuals. Draw comparisons with Jim Crow laws.

   Ask students to look at the clothes they are wearing and count how many articles they have on that could be labeled as unisex (like boxers and jeans). How
   many (like a bra) are considered for one sex only? Inform the students that gay
   men and lesbians could and were arrested if they did not have at least three articles of clothing on that the police department deemed *male* or *female*. Ask the

students to compare this with the harassment of other subordinated groups they have studied.

2. Remind students of the changing culture of the cities in the late 1960s. Review the riots of 1968, the change in the war movements, and so on. Read chapter 13 of *Becoming Visible* (or something similar) on the Stonewall riots and the *New York Daily News* article of July 6, 1969.

3. As a class, discuss the content of the articles and compare and contrast the views of the authors. Ask the students: What do you learn from one and not the other? Is either objective? What do you think happened at Stonewall? Why would this have been a catalyst for the gay liberation movement? It is important to note that some of those arrested were people of color and to discuss how gays and lesbians come from diverse racial, class, and ethnic backgrounds.

4. Ask the students to write journal entries on how and why the reasons for the gay rights movement were similar to and different from those of other movements. How have rights of gays, lesbians, and bisexuals moved as far or farther than other groups? Why?

5. On the following day, ask for a volunteer or two to read her or his entry out loud and ask the class for responses.

Evaluation

1. Assess students' ability to compare and contrast the women's, American Indian, Chicano/Latino, and disability rights movements and the gay liberation movement with each other and the earlier civil rights movements through classroom and small-group discussion.

2. Evaluate the students' understanding of the legacies of the African American Civil Rights movement through discussion, group presentation, and written exam/essay.

3. Assess students' ability to analyze primary documents through small-group discussion and daily response journals.

WHY THE CHANGES?

The Legacies of the African American Civil Rights Movement

Content

While the structure and content of the "Before" plan is retained, including the gay rights movement presents a positive model of gay liberation in the context of other civil rights movements. Modeling in this manner gives gay, lesbian, and bisexual students a sense of inclusion. It also encourages all students to realize how gays, lesbians, and bisexuals have faced oppression and how they have responded.

Perspective

Using primary documents and encouraging discussion that includes the perspectives of gays, lesbians, and bisexuals, along with those of people with disabilities and people of color, the school is developing a broad spectrum of opinions and voices, reflecting the diversity of our schools and society.

Comparing and contrasting the civil rights movements, including the gay liberation movement, and encouraging debate about the gay movement's place there, pushes students to develop the ability to see issues from multiple points of view and multiple perspectives of which movement had what impact on the others.

Resources

Jennings, K. (Ed.). (1994). *Becoming visible: A reader in gay and lesbian history for high school and college students*. Boston: Alyson Publications.

Lisker, J. (1969, July 6). Homo nest raided, queen bees are stinging mad. *New York Daily News*.

LESSON PLAN

BEFORE   ## Gays, Lesbians, and Bisexuals

Subject Areas: Social Studies, Health, Human Sexuality

Grade Level: 9–12

Time: One-half class period

Objectives

1. Students will understand that homosexuality exists.

2. Students will explore the debates surrounding the causes of homosexuality.

Suggested Procedures

1. Read the relevant section in the textbook (for instance, a health book).

2. As part of discussing an introduction to sexuality, explain that homosexuality is part of the spectrum.

3. Explain the nature versus nurture debates as they relate to the cause of homosexuality. Ask the students to state their opinions.

Evaluation

Students will correctly answer multiple-choice test questions.

AFTER

Gay, Lesbian, and Bisexual Youth*

Lesson 1—Gay, Lesbian, and Bisexual Youth

Subject Areas: Social Studies, Health, Human Sexuality

Grade Level: 7–12

Time: Two class periods

Objectives

1. Students will identify and analyze stereotypes of gays, lesbians, and bisexuals.

2. Students will discuss the experiences of gay and lesbian youth.

3. Students will consider viewpoints about gays, lesbians, and bisexuals that may differ from their own.

4. Students will recognize the ways stereotypes can lay the foundation for intolerance.

5. Students will gain the opportunity to openly discuss issues surrounding gays, lesbians, and bisexuals.

6. Students will draw comparisons between the experiences of gay and lesbian youth seen in the video and those of gay, lesbian, and bisexual students at school.

Suggested Procedures

1. It is very important that ground rules about insults, interrupting, and the ability to speak are set up with students before the lesson begins. It is vital that students be reminded that comments can be honest without being disrespectful toward any group or individual.

2. Show the video *Gay Youth* (40 minutes).

3. Break the students up into preplanned groups of four to five. (When forming groups, keep in mind the nature of the discussion, and attempt to balance the amount of trust needed to have such a discussion with the need not to form groups around friendship groups.)

---

*Note: These two lesson plans can be done in either order, or pieces of each can be used in a different order depending upon the instructor's desires and comfort level. For example, instructors could do parts 1–4 of lesson 2, then do lesson 1, and then return to the last activity of lesson 2.

4. Give each group a discussion question, asking each to appoint a spokesperson and a scribe. Tell them they have 15 minutes to discuss the question and will be asked to report to the class.

Examples of questions:

a. Many of the teens in the video talk about their parents. Bobby Griffith's mother discusses his suicide, and Gina is seen with her parents. Why might parental reactions be important? Is it fair that Gina's parents might have different rules for her sister than for her?

b. Based on what you heard in the video, why might it be difficult to be a gay, lesbian, or bisexual teen today? What kinds of issues do they face, and how might they be different than their heterosexual peers? Why do you believe teens are, as Gina says, insensitive to other teens?

c. Why would Bobby Griffith's mother think it is important to speak out now? Many of the young people in the video spoke of self-destructive behavior; what drives them to the point of alcohol/drug abuse, depression, or self-mutilation? How might schools respond to help these students?

d. One of the parents in the video stated that "being different is harder." Is this still true? What kind of a reception would a student like Chris be expected to get at this school? Why would Gina be able or not able to do her monologue or go to the prom at this school? Are these responses proper for the school? Should they be changed?

e. What purposes do you think Pam Walton (the director) had in making this video? That is, why do you think she made it? Does the video fulfill its purposes? What makes this a "good" or "bad" video, and would you suggest it be used in other classes?

5. Have each group read the question and report their discussion. Invite other class members to respond also.

Evaluation

1. Assess students' ability to apply the abstract images to their own lives and those of their peers through small and large group discussion.

2. Assess students' understanding of their own perspectives of gay, lesbian, and bisexual youth through classroom discussion.

3. Assess students' ability to reflect on others' points of view through their willingness to listen and engage in discussion.

Resource

Walton, Pam. (1991). *Two in twenty: Writings by gay and lesbian youth* (three-tape series). Wolfe Video, P. O. Box 64, New Almaden, CA 95042, Tel. (408) 268-6782; or BANGLE (Bay Area Network of Gay and Lesbian Educators), Tel. (415) 648-8488. A similar unit can be built around the articles in the book.

Lesson 2—The Experiences of Gays, Lesbians, and Bisexuals

Subject Areas: Social Studies, Health, Human Sexuality

Grade Level: 7–12

Time: Two class periods

Objectives

1. Students will name several gays, lesbians, and bisexuals in history and current affairs.

2. Students will identify and analyze stereotypes of gays, lesbians, and bisexuals.

3. Students will recognize and discuss their own perspectives about gays, lesbians, and bisexuals.

4. Students will consider viewpoints about gays, lesbians, and bisexuals that differ from their own.

5. Students will recognize the ways stereotypes can lay the foundation for intolerance.

6. Students will gain the opportunity to openly discuss issues surrounding gays, lesbians, and bisexuals.

Suggested Procedures

1. It is very important that ground rules about insults, interrupting, and the ability to speak be set up with students before the lesson begins. It is vital that students be reminded that comments can be honest without being disrespectful toward any group or individual.

2. Prior to students' entry into the class, list ten to fifteen gays, lesbians, and bisexuals on the board (e.g., James Baldwin, Leonardo da Vinci, Janis Joplin, James Dean, J. Edgar Hoover, Angela Davis, Alexander the Great). Ask the students what these people have in common.

3. After someone has guessed gay or lesbian, make sure, if not addressed, that the issue of bisexuality is included. Remind the students that it is important to be respectful of differences as they discuss a topic that can bring up strong emotions. Ask students to add to the list. Use this as an opportunity to ask how they know that the person is gay, lesbian, or bisexual. Discuss gender-based stereotypes of masculinity and femininity. If students state, "Well, everyone knows that person is gay," again ask how they know or why they think it, but this time ask why it might be a negative thing to be called gay, lesbian, or bisexual.

4. Erase the board and ask the students to brainstorm all of the pejorative names for gays, lesbians, and bisexuals. If they have difficulty getting started, write *faggot* and *dyke* on the board. Allow a limited amount of time for this activity. Ask

the students how these words might affect gays, lesbians, or bisexuals who hear them. Ask them if they have heard these words around the school and how they might affect students. Make sure to include gay, lesbian, and bisexual students *and* heterosexual students with gay, lesbian, or bisexual family members.

5. Pass out index cards. Tell the students not to sign the cards, and let them know they will not read their own cards. Without further discussion, ask the students to write down the answer to the following question: "What would you say and how do you think you would react if your brother/sister or best friend told you that she or he were gay, lesbian, or bisexual?" Collect the cards, mix them up, and hand them back out to the students. Have students read each card in succession, saving discussion until all the cards are read.

6. Solicit student responses to what was written on the cards. During the discussion, encourage students to analyze their own reactions and suppositions about gays, lesbians, and bisexuals.

7. Ask students to complete a 10- to 15-minute free write or journal entry and give them a choice of expanding on what they said on the cards and classroom discussion or how and why the classroom discussion might affect how they feel about gays, lesbians, and bisexuals.

Evaluation

1. Assess students' skills analyzing stereotypes and their impact through classroom discussion.

2. Assess students' understanding of their own perspectives of gays, lesbians, and bisexuals through classroom discussion and the follow-up journal entries/free writes.

3. Assess students' ability to reflect on others' points of view through their willingness to listen and engage in discussion.

WHY THE CHANGES?

Gay, Lesbian, and Bisexual Youth

Perspective/Issues of Particular Concern

Issues concerning gays, lesbians, and bisexuals are rarely discussed in the classroom. In reality, even lessons as basic as that detailed in the "Before" plans rarely occur.

The "After" plans above allow all youth, regardless of their sexual orientation, to see adults modeling positive discussions about homosexuality. Students are given visual representations of the experiences of a wide variety of gay, lesbian, and bisexual youth, which along with follow-up activities allow and encourage students to compare these experiences with their own and their experiences in school.

History

By listing gay men, lesbians, and bisexuals in history, students are able to realize that homosexuality is not a modern phenomenon, as well as gain a better understanding of the many contributions that gays, lesbians, and bisexuals have made to a wide variety of areas.

Current Social Agenda

Since there are few forums to discuss issues surrounding gays, lesbians, and bisexuals in school, students do not have the chance to deal with their questions and curiosities, as well as their own intolerance. Within these plans, gay, lesbian, and bisexual students, and students with gay, lesbian, or bisexual family members, have an opportunity to gain positive images of themselves in the school setting. Heterosexual students are able to gain an awareness and understanding of the discrimination faced by gays, lesbians, and bisexuals.

LESSON PLAN

BEFORE

The Scientific Method and Animal Instincts

Subject Area: Biology

Grade Level: 9–12

Time: Two separate days

Lesson 1 (early in the school year)

Objectives

1. Students will describe the scientific method.

2. Students will apply the scientific method to a hypothetical problem.

Suggested Procedures

1. Ask students to imagine that they want to discover why trees lose their leaves in the fall. Ask them to suggest ways to investigate this.

2. Have students read pages in the textbook on the scientific method.

3. When they have completed the reading, return to the problem of why trees lose their leaves. Help the class to formulate a hypothesis, identify variables, and design a procedure for testing the hypothesis and formulating a conclusion.

Evaluation

On the next quiz, present a problem and have students state a hypothesis and suggest a procedure for testing it.

Lesson 2 (later in the school year)

Objective

Students will distinguish between innate and learned behavior and provide examples of each.

Suggested Procedures

1. Have students read pages in the textbook on innate and learned behavior. Review the main ideas and vocabulary terms.

2. Show a film on instinctual behavior.

3. Ask students if humans have any instincts. Encourage students to base their beliefs on their observations of human behavior and to determine carefully if the examples they provide could have resulted from learning.

Evaluation

Assess students' understanding of innate and learned behavior through class discussion and a quiz.

AFTER

Using the Scientific Method to Investigate Maternal Instinct

Subject Area: Biology

Grade Level: 9–12

Time: Five to eight class periods

Objectives

1. Students will distinguish between innate and learned behavior.

2. Students will describe the scientific method.

3. Students will use the scientific method to investigate a real problem.

4. Students will realize that both sexes are equally capable of learning to parent.

5. Students will critique text materials for relevance to a real-life concern.

Suggested Procedures

1. Ask students if they believe males and females to be equally capable of caring for babies. Encourage them to voice what they have heard about **maternal instinct** (the term may not yet be a part of their vocabulary, so watch for the idea).

2. Have students read pages in the textbook on innate and learned behavior. Ask them to describe the extent to which the reading helped illuminate human behavior commonly classified as instinctual (most likely, the text will provide only a brief passage).

3. Divide the class into small groups of about four students each. Give each group a short description of an experiment investigating maternal behavior (see the Resources on page 148). Have each group critique how well their experiment informs of the existence of maternal instinct in the species studied and of the capability of males to raise the young. Ask each group to give a brief report.

4. Ask students how they might design a study to investigate whether human females, more than males, instinctively know how to care for infants. Lead them to design an investigation they can actually carry out. For example, students could interview new parents about their own behavior, knowledge, and prior learning about infant care; the class could visit a hospital maternity ward and interview a nurse who works with new parents about what is known instinctively and what parents must be taught; or students who have siblings who are parents can interview them. Help the class design any interview questions and arrange interviews. Questions that could be asked of both parents include the following:

    a. Did you know what to do when your baby cried during the first few days? If so, where did this knowledge come from?

    b. Did you know how to hold the baby when he or she was born? If so, how did you know?

    c. Did you know how to change the baby's diapers? How much practice did it take until you became proficient?

    In selecting the parents to be interviewed, try to include those of various cultural and social-class backgrounds.

5. Monitor students' data collection. When the studies are completed, divide the class into small groups to compile and analyze their findings. One way to organize this is for one group to compile data for question a, another for question b, and so on. Have the class examine the data for any cultural patterns.

6. The class should come to the conclusion that human parental behavior is learned. Students may also discover that infant care is learned fairly quickly by necessity, and if one parent practices it more than the other, the practiced parent often assumes much of the responsibility for child care. Although this may appear to be instinctive, it is a result of learning, and some variation in learning

may occur among different cultural groups. Discuss with the class why the myth of maternal instinct exists and who benefits and in what ways from its existence. Lead students to realize that the myth tends to maintain that child care is a female rather than a shared parental responsibility.

7. Based on their investigation, have students write an addition to or revision of their textbook discussion of innate and learned behavior. Ask students to select the best description, which should be duplicated and used with future classes.

Evaluation

1. Assess students' understanding of innate versus learned behavior through class discussion and through their textbook "additions" and "revisions."

2. Assess students' ability to design and conduct an experiment by monitoring their activities and by observing how they analyze data in small-group situations.

3. Assess students' understanding of the research on maternal instinct through class discussion and their textbook "additions" and "revisions."

Resources

Mitchell, G., Redican, W. K., & Gomber, J. (1974). Lesson from a primate: Males can raise babies. *Psychology Today*, *7*(11), 63–68.

Moltz, H., Lubin, M., Leon, M., & Numan, M. (1970). Hormonal induction of maternal behavior in the ovariectomized rat. *Physiology and Behavior*, *5*, 1373–1377.

Rosenblatt, J. S. (1967). Nonhormonal basis of maternal behavior in the rat. *Science*, *156*, 1512–1514.

Rosenblatt, J. S. (1969). The development of maternal responsiveness in the rat. *American Journal of Orthopsychiatry*, *39*, 36–56.

WHY THE CHANGES?

Using the Scientific Method to Investigate Maternal Instinct

Issues of Particular Concern

In the "Before" plan, the scientific method and animal instinct are studied with little or no relationship to human issues or to issues of particular interest to adolescents. The "After" lesson uses concepts normally studied in biology to examine a topic of particular concern to women's studies: whether one sex is naturally more predisposed than the other to parenting. The topic is likely to generate student interest, in that students are probably thinking about it as they consider their own futures, and they are likely to hold different opinions about it.

The research conducted in the "After" plan is more of a survey study than an experimental one. The teacher needs to decide how much emphasis to give to scientific research over the school year; many teachers will probably find neither plan adequate in this regard. It is quite possible to introduce the scientific method at the beginning of the year, as the "Before" plan does, but to involve students in using it only minimally throughout the year. On the other hand, if students are involved in using it to investigate a number of different issues throughout the year, they can be exposed to a variety of research strategies such as the survey research used here.

The "After" plan encourages students to think critically about what they read, which the Single-Group Studies approach often encourages. The plan asks students to examine the extent to which their biology textbook teaches them about human instinctual behavior, and at the conclusion of the lesson students write a new passage to be used along with the textbook by future students. This places students in a role of questioning knowledge produced by others—not rejecting it, but seeing its limitations—and producing knowledge themselves. The teacher of the "After" plan has supplemented the textbook with research studies, exposing students to these as a source of knowledge. Students work in groups on them; published research studies tend to be difficult to read and understand, and group work allows students to help each other.

The "After" plan can stand alone as an isolated single-group studies lesson, but it is richer if linked with other women's studies lessons either in science or in other subject areas. In science, for example, students can investigate other sex differences to determine whether they are real or imagined, innate or learned. In other subject areas, students can study, for example, the domestic division of labor and how this affects division of labor in the workforce or female mental health.

LESSON PLAN

BEFORE

Identifying Themes in Literature[*]

Subject Area: English

Grade Level: 9–12

Time: Six to eight days

Objectives

1. Students will identify main themes in short stories.

---

[*]*Source:* Anne Fairbrother, Salinas Union High School District, Salinas, CA.

2. Students will identify common themes shared by three different stories.

3. Students will write a formal essay that is organized, contains an introduction and conclusion, and uses evidence appropriately.

Suggested Procedures

1. Explain to the students what a **theme** is. Have them give you examples of themes from the core works they read the previous year in their English class.

2. Read "If I Forget Thee, Oh Earth" by Arthur C. Clark. (This story contains many possible themes, including those of hope, remorse, and responsibility. As fantasy, it can also be seen as an analogy.) After reading, have students do a quiz or discussion questions. Then have students brainstorm possible themes, list them on the board, discuss them, and write notes. Students should keep their notes until they have read all three stories.

3. Read "The Enchanted Bluff" by Willa Cather. (This story contains analogy and addresses many themes, including those of dreams, hopes, and growing up.) After reading, have students do a quiz or discussion questions. Then have students brainstorm possible themes, list them on the board, discuss them, and take notes.

4. Read "Uncle Einar" by Ray Bradbury. (This story addresses many themes, including those of dreams and fulfillment of dreams, being true to one's nature, and maturity. It also can be seen as an analogy.) After reading, have students do a quiz or discussion questions. Then have students brainstorm possible themes, list them on the board, and discuss them.

5. Have students meet again with their groups, brainstorming from their notes on each story and the themes the three stories have in common.

6. Each student may choose their own theme from the group's choices and should complete the following thesis statement for him- or herself: "The major theme that all three stories have in common is _____ ."

7. Help students start to write an essay with an introduction and thesis statement, with one paragraph for each story, showing that the theme is indeed in that story, supported with interpreted evidence, and a conclusion. Set a date when the first draft is due, to be shared in response groups, and set a date when the final draft is due.

Evaluation

1. Evaluate students' ability to identify main themes in short stories through participation in class and group discussions and/or through quizzes.

2. Evaluate students' ability to identify common themes shared by three different stories through participation in group discussions and development of a thesis statement.

3. Students will receive one grade for the first draft of their essay, one for the quality of their response to a partner's essay, and two for the final essay—one for content and one for form.

Resources

Bradbury, Ray. (1980). Uncle Einar. In Ray Bradbury, *The stories of Ray Bradbury*. New York: Knopf.

Cather, Willa. (1956). The enchanted bluff. In Willa Cather, *Five stories*. New York: Random House.

Clark, Arthur C. (1985). If I forget thee, oh earth. In W. M. Miller & M. H. Greenberg (Eds.), *Beyond armageddon*. New York: D. I. Fine.

AFTER

Culture in Native American Literature

Subject Area: English

Grade Level: 9–12

Time: Eight to ten days

Objectives

1. Students will identify main themes in short stories.

2. Students will identify common themes shared by three different short stories that reflect the boarding school experience of Native Americans over two generations.

3. Students will examine what constitutes culture, how education relates to culture, and the concept of assimilation.

4. Students will write a formal essay that is organized, contains an introduction and conclusion, and uses evidence appropriately.

Suggested Procedures

1. Write on the board as you ask the questions: What is culture? How is it transmitted? Can it be destroyed? Introduce the idea of cultural assimilation.

2. Show the movie *Where the Spirit Lives*, which is about a Canadian Indian girl taken to a boarding school where she and her brother experience enforced cultural assimilation. After the movie, have students look at all the things they identified as making up culture (probably including language, religion, customs, food, music, clothes, history, stories, and values) and ask them what was hap-

pening to the students at the boarding school. Students will see that there was a conscious attempt to replace the children's American Indian culture with the European American culture.

3. Explain the historical events and political and religious rationale behind the establishment of the boarding school policy in the United States (starting with Pratt establishing Carlisle in 1879).

4. Read "Canassatego Gives an Offer of Help" (from *The National Experience—A History of the United States to 1877*). (Any statement of American Indian resistance to the forced attendance of boarding schools could be used, with appropriate questions.) In groups, have students answer these questions:

   a. Why doesn't the American Indian want the white man's education?

   b. Judging from this statement, how does education relate to culture?

   c. What is the tone of the passage? What is implied in the closing sentences?

   On the board, have students discuss how education relates to culture. Brainstorm what education is for and how education is a socializing agency—that is, a method of transmitting culture to each generation.

5. Students will now read three stories by Native American authors that deal with the boarding school experience:

   a. "Charlie," by Lee Maracle (from *Voices Under One Sky*, edited by Trish Fox Roman). Read it aloud in class, and have students make notes on what happens in the story.

   b. An excerpt from chapter 2 in *Lame Deer—Seeker of Visions*, by Lame Deer and Richard Erdoes (as excerpted in *Growing Up Native American*, edited by Patricia Riley). Read it aloud in class, and have students make notes on what happens in the story.

   c. "Civilize Them with a Stick" (chapter 3 from *Lakota Woman*, by Mary Crow Dog (delete sections as needed). Read it aloud in class, and have students make notes on what happens in the story.

6. After reading all three stories, let students work in groups. Using a Venn diagram (with three intersecting circles), students will show what each piece has in common with one or both of the other pieces and what is peculiar to each story.

7. When students have filled up all the parts of the diagram, show them that in the center of the diagram they have identified what themes the pieces have in common. On the back of their papers, have them write out the three major themes they all share, as part of a thesis statement: "Three themes that these stories have in common are (1) _____ , (2) _____ , and (3) _____ ."

8. Help students start to write an essay with an introduction and thesis statement, with one paragraph for each theme, supported with interpreted evidence to

show that that theme does appear in each story, and a conclusion. Set a date when the first draft is due, to be shared in response groups, and set a date when the final draft is due.

9. An appropriate movie at the end would be the TNT production of the book *Lakota Woman*. It will facilitate discussions about the Battle of Wounded Knee in 1890, the Occupation of Wounded Knee in 1973, the American Indian movement, and the issue of the Black Hills for the Sioux Nations. You could also show *The Spirit of Crazy Horse* for an excellent overview of Sioux history, experience, and issues; or *In the White Man's Image*, an excellent documentary of the boarding school "experiment."

Evaluation

1. Evaluate students' ability to identify main themes in short stories through participation in class and group discussions.

2. Evaluate students' ability to identify common themes shared by three different stories through participation in group discussions and through the group work.

3. Evaluate students' understanding of the concepts of culture and cultural assimilation through participation in class discussions and a written essay.

4. Students will receive one grade for the first draft of their essay, one for the quality of their response to a partner's essay, and two grades for the final essay—one for content and one for form.

Resources

Print

Crow Dog, M. (1990). *Lakota woman.* New York: Harper Perennial.

Fire, J., & Erdoes, R. (1972). *Lame Deer—Seeker of visions.* New York: Simon & Schuster.

The national experience—Part one: A history of the United States to 1877 (8th ed.). (1993). Ft. Worth: Harcourt Brace Jovanovich.

Riley, P. (Ed.). (1993). *Growing up Native American.* New York: Morrow.

Roman, T. F. (Ed.). (1994). *Voices under one sky.* Freedom, CA: Crossing Press.

Video

Lakota woman: Siege at Wounded Knee. (1994). Turner Pictures, Inc., Turner Home Entertainment, One CNN Center, Atlanta, GA 30303.

The spirit of crazy horse. (1990). Pacific Arts Video Publishing, 50 N. La Cienego Blvd., Beverly Hills, CA 90211.

Where the spirit lives. (1989). Studio Entertainment, 386 Park Avenue So., New York, NY 10016.

In the white man's image. (1991). WGBH-TV, Boston; WNET-TV, New York; and KCET-TV, Los Angeles.

LESSON PLAN

BEFORE

Mexican Americans

Subject Area: Social Studies

Grade Level: 10–12

Time: Three separate days over the course of seven months

Lesson 1 (in November)

Objectives

1. Students will identify reasons why Texas and California declared independence from Mexico.

2. Students will describe how the United States acquired territory in the southwest.

Suggested Procedures

1. Discuss the idea of Manifest Destiny. On a wall map, point out the territory owned by Mexico in the early 1800s and the territory claimed by both Mexico and the United States.

2. Have students read pages in the textbook about the war with Mexico.

3. Ask students to discuss whether the war was justified.

Evaluation

Include questions on a test regarding how and why the United States acquired territory from Mexico.

Lesson 2 (in January)

Objectives

1. Students will explain why immigrants came to the United States between 1880 and 1920.

2. Students will describe how U.S. Americans reacted to the influx of immigrants and why they reacted that way.

Suggested Procedures

1. Ask students to brainstorm, from previous lessons, a list of the various industries that expanded during the late 1800s. Have them suggest sources of workers, from the perspectives of business owners, and discuss which sources might be best and why.

2. Ask students to read pages in the textbook about industrial expansion during this time period.

Evaluation

Include questions on a test about what industrial expansion involved, where immigrants came from, and why they came.

Lesson 3 (in May)

Objectives

1. Students will describe issues of concern to Latinos during the 1960s and 1970s.

2. Students will name and describe prominent Latino leaders from that time period.

Suggested Procedures

1. Have students read pages in the text about the Chicano movement.

2. Discuss the similarities and differences among issues of concern to Latinos, African Americans, and American Indians during the Civil Rights movement.

Evaluation

On a test, present a civil rights issue and ask students to describe the relevant concerns and actions of Latinos, African Americans, or American Indians.

AFTER	Mexican American Labor in the United States

Subject Area: Social Studies

Grade Level: 10–12

Time: One week

Objectives

1. Students will describe how the United States historically has shifted its policies toward Mexican and Mexican American laborers to acquire cheap, temporary labor.

2. Students will appreciate different perspectives on the history of Mexican labor in the United States, particularly the perspective of Mexican and Mexican American laborers.

3. Students will locate information, particularly information about subordinate groups.

4. Students will develop a personal perspective on current debates about the United States–Mexico border and illegal Mexican immigrants.

Suggested Procedures

1. Ask students to describe what they know or have heard about the issue of illegal Mexican workers in the United States. Ask for their opinions, based on what they know, regarding whether Mexican immigration should be restricted and border controls tightened. Point out that the perspective the public most often hears is that of white European American business owners; other groups' perspectives may be downplayed, distorted, or omitted altogether.

2. Divide students into six groups. Explain that they will research the history of this issue from the perspectives of the following different role groups (make sure students distinguish between Mexicans—citizens of Mexico—and Mexican Americans—citizens of the United States):

   a. Mexican business owners

   b. Mexican Americans living at or below the poverty line

   c. European American business owners

   d. U.S. government

   e. Mexican American workers

   f. European working-class Americans

   g. Mexican people who are searching for work

   Explain that students are to locate the answers for their role group to the following questions:

   a. What were your group's economic needs?

   b. How did your group view each of the other groups?

   c. What was your group doing during the time periods of 1845–1850; 1850–1900; 1900–1924; 1924–1930; 1930–1947; 1947–1965; 1965–1980; and 1980–present?

   Discuss sources of information; you may wish to locate sources yourself and make them available to students.

3. Assist students as needed while they complete their research.

4. Construct a large wall mural from butcher paper on which the time periods noted in item 2 appear across the top at intervals of 2 to 3 feet. On the left-hand side of the mural, each of the six groups should be listed. With the whole class,

and starting with the first time period (1845–1850), each group should report on and chart the history of this issue. Have one student (or yourself) write key points and events on the chart for each time period. Encourage students to discover and explain the relationships among the groups' needs and desires and how they responded to each other and to historical events.

5. Have the class debate the following question: Should the United States further restrict immigration of Mexican workers into the country? Students should first debate the question from the perspective of the group they represent and then from their own perspectives.

6. Ask students which groups' perspectives and experiences were most difficult to locate and least publicized and whose were easiest to locate and best publicized. Lead them to recognize that the control of information can influence public opinion and distort the average person's understanding of history.

Evaluation

1. Assess each student's understanding of the role group that he or she represented through oral contributions to the mural.

2. Assess students' understanding of U.S. history and policy and of the actions and perspectives of different groups through a quiz.

3. Assess students' skill at locating information through their oral contributions to the mural.

4. Assess students' development of personal perspectives through the class debate.

**WHY THE
CHANGES?**

Mexican American Labor in the United States

Perspective on History

The "Before" plan presents only one racial group and does so in a fragmented way—it gives little information about the group and in disconnected pieces, making it difficult to get a coherent sense of the group's experience. Further, the information presented is not connected to current issues related to the group's experiences. The story being told is European American, with the perspective that Mexican Americans have occasionally interacted with and contributed to European American history.

In contrast, the "After" plan shifts the perspectives of the lesson to those of Mexican Americans. This helps students to recognize the diversity within the Mexican American population and the multiple viewpoints that have existed, to connect a viewpoint they hear with a group who shares that viewpoint, and to appreciate debates and conflict that surround history and policy.

The "After" plan asks students to compile research on their own (although the teacher must make the materials available to them). This activity encourages students to construct the story of what happened, which enhances their understanding more than if they are told of the events. It also helps them to realize that some groups' viewpoints are better preserved and publicized than others, providing a basis for examining how control over knowledge can help a group control public opinion and social policy. For example, students will find that locating information about white European American business owners' needs and views is easier than obtaining the same information about Mexicans and Mexican Americans who live at or below the poverty level. From this discovery, students learn that a lack of knowledge of Mexicans and Mexican Americans who live at or below the poverty level can cause the average student or person to misunderstand this group of people.

Current Social Agenda

The purpose of the "After" plan is to help students understand the problems faced by Mexican Americans today and that their success in this country is greatly influenced by others. That is, battles over the group's status are still being fought, and all citizens have a say in how their struggles are resolved. The plan does this by concentrating on a current issue—how open the United States–Mexico border should be. Students come to understand that studying history is valuable not only for its own sake but also because it helps us understand current issues.

Finally, the cooperative learning and role-playing devices used in the "After" lesson are more enjoyable and conducive to learning than the textbook reading and large-group discussion and recitation strategies employed in the "Before" plan.

LESSON PLAN

BEFORE

Name-Calling

Subject Area: Language Arts

Grade Level: 10–12

Time: One class period

Objectives

1. Students will stop name-calling.

2. Students will realize the personal negative impact involved in name-calling and racial slurs.

3. Students will select carefully the words they use to refer to people.

Suggested Procedures

1. Have students discuss how they feel when called a name.

2. Have students discuss why people are usually called names and the results of name-calling and racial slurs.

3. Divide students into small groups and have them discuss how they can prevent name-calling.

Evaluation

1. Observe students' behavior in the lunchroom and other less-supervised areas of the campus to ascertain the frequency and kind of name-calling or racial slurs that occur.

2. Ask students to write a short essay about their feelings on name-calling or racial slurs.

AFTER

Name-Calling

Subject Area: Language Arts

Grade Level: 10–12

Time: One week

Objectives

1. Students will not use derogatory names.

2. Students will understand that name-calling and racial slurs are sometimes used to obtain economic gains and social acceptance.

3. Students will select carefully the words they use to refer to people with whom they may have a problem or conflict.

Suggested Procedures

1. Movies are often made with the advanced teenager and young adult in mind, and in many movies racial slurs are used. Divide the class into groups and make each group responsible for reviewing one or two movies (e.g., *The River, Saturday Night Fever, Roots, Taxi Driver, Escape from Alcatraz, Trading Places, Blade Runner,* and *After Hours*) to determine which racial slurs are used and why students think they are used. (Make certain the ratings of movies selected are in keeping with students' ages.) Ask students to consider such questions as who

gains economically from such sensationalism and whether other words could have been used. Have the groups prepare essays on their conclusions.

2. Ask the same groups of students to be participant observers in their leisure setting and to record the racial slurs and racial jokes that occur. Have them tabulate who is the butt of the jokes and why they think this is so.

3. Have some students report on Richard Pryor's use of racial slurs before and after his trip to Africa. Question the use of racial slurs in Pryor's routine to aid his success with European American audiences, or the racial jokes used by Eddie Murphy to help him have a wider appeal to European American audiences.

4. Have students discuss the reasons why members of a racial group may sometimes refer to each other by using a racial name or tell each other a racial joke that puts down their own ethnic group. Have students examine where these actions often lead. Discuss when such an action represents laughing at oneself in a healthy sense and when it represents a put-down.

Evaluation

1. Assess students' sensitivity to name-calling through each group's essay and record of racial slurs and racial jokes.

2. Evaluate students' discussion of in-group use of racial slurs and name-calling.

WHY THE CHANGES?

Name-Calling

Perspective

The "Before" plan approaches a sometimes common problem in a routine manner, which may stop the current problem but go no further. The "After" plan argues that there is more to name-calling and racial slurs than just a need for "human relations." It encourages students to examine their own behaviors, the behaviors of their classmates, the media's perspective in regards to name-calling, and racial slurs as a means of accepted communication among racial groups.

Current Social Agenda

The "Before" plan does not consider the current social agenda of African Americans. The "After" plan actively promotes racial pride by having students examine why some of the most derogatory words in the English language are often used in different settings for profit and social acceptance.

References

Asante, M. K. (1990). *Kemet, Afrocentricity and knowledge*. Trenton, NJ: Africa World Press.

Asante, M. K. (1995). *African American history: A journey of liberation*. Maywood, NJ: Peoples Publishing Group.

Gutman, H. G. (1977). The black family in slavery and freedom, *1750–1925*. New York: Random House.

Loewen, J. W. (1995). *Lies my teacher told me*. New York: New Press.

5

Multicultural Education

Some of you probably like most of the ideas in the three approaches discussed in this text so far (Teaching the Exceptional and Culturally Different approach, the Human Relations approach, and the Single-Group Studies approach) and are wondering how they can be combined. You may be asking yourself questions such as the following:

Should the perspectives and experiences of a wide range of cultural groups, different sexual orientations and disabilities, and of both sexes be included in the curriculum regardless of students' backgrounds?

Should teachers help students to discover and examine inequities in society, especially those that are influencing the students' life chances?

Should teachers always try to capitalize on the learning styles and interests of their students?

Should teachers evaluate and group students in ways that do not label individuals and groups as losers or winners?

Should school staffing patterns as well as the curriculum provide students with a variety of role models, including those with nontraditional roles, those of various cultural and economic backgrounds and sexual orientations, those of both sexes, and those with disabilities?

Should the classroom and school climate in general celebrate diversity, equal opportunity, and equity?

The **Multicultural Education approach** addresses these kinds of questions. It calls for the reform of the entire classroom and the school itself, and it is for all students.

The approach rests on two ideals: equal opportunity and cultural pluralism. The ideal of **equal opportunity** holds that each student should be given equal opportunity to learn, succeed, and become what he or she would like, with full affirmation of his or her sex, race, social class background, sexual orientation, and disability, if any. But equal opportunity does not just happen by will or by declaring it policy—one must work deliberately and consistently to implement it. For example, a student who is behind his or her peers in reading does not have equal opportunity to learn science when science is taught through reading material beyond the student's level. A Latina does not have equal opportunity to succeed if the curriculum portrays Latinas as invisible, unimportant, or not U.S. American. Equal opportunity does not mean ignoring differences or pretending that they do not exist. On the contrary, it means viewing differences as normal and desirable and supporting them in such a way that they do not hinder a person's ability to dream and reach his or her goals.

Also, to achieve equal opportunity it may be important to explore issues of power and privilege. Sometimes power and privilege are accepted as invisible norms (rights) of the dominant group (e.g., for males), and this marginalizes the opportunity of other groups.

Equal opportunity supports the second ideal of the Multicultural Education approach: cultural pluralism. Essentially, **cultural pluralism** means that there is no one best way to be U.S. American. An "all-American" child does not necessarily have blond hair and light skin and eat toast and cereal for breakfast; one who is dark, lives in an extended family, and eats rice or tortillas for breakfast is also a U.S. American. Cultural pluralism is not separatism. Rather, it includes a sharing and blending of different ethnic cultures and other forms of culture that constitute the shared mainstream U.S. American culture, and it also supports ethnic, gender, disability, and other groups as they enjoy and continue to develop distinctive group cultures. U.S. Americans should not have to give up their families' identities, sense of group solidarity, or cultural beliefs and traditions to be accepted as U.S. American or to participate fully in U.S. society.

MEETING THE GOALS OF THE MULTICULTURAL EDUCATION APPROACH

Based on its two ideals—equal opportunity and cultural pluralism—the Multicultural Education approach includes the following goals:

1. To promote an understanding and appreciation of cultural diversity in the United States.

2. To promote alternative choices for people, with full affirmation of their race, gender, disability, language, sexual orientation, and social class background.

3. To help all children achieve academic success.

4. To promote awareness of social issues involving the unequal distribution of power and privilege that limits the opportunity of those not in the dominant group.

This approach advocates transformation of the school as a whole. Action Research Activity 5.2 helps you examine your school as a whole, as well as your own classroom. What can the classroom teacher do to accomplish these goals?

Curriculum Materials

Many teachers begin to use this approach with materials for the curriculum. Materials should portray the contributions and perspectives of a variety of U.S. American cultural groups; gays, lesbians, and bisexuals; people with disabilities; and both sexes, and they should do so in a manner that does not reinforce and promote stereotypes or exoticize cultural groups. This material should also, when relevant to the concept being taught, include discussions about who has power and privilege and whose interest is being served and at what cost. Diverse groups should be included substantively; adding a few names or pictures of Asian Americans, Latinos, Native Americans, and people with disabilities is not sufficient. Groups should be presented relatively equally; white European American males should not dominate the roles or space in the text. Language should be gender inclusive. You may feel that your materials already do this because great improvements in curricular materials have been made over the past 20 years. You should examine them closely—materials that seem balanced at first glance often are not on closer examination. The lesson plan "Folk and Fairy Tales" (p. 191) illustrates how you can use biased materials.

There is a rapidly growing body of alternative multicultural curriculum materials. Many of these are published by small local presses, although they are becoming more widely distributed than previously through multicultural catalogues and displays at conferences. Teachers can create rich, exciting multicultural curricula by collecting and drawing on these materials. The plans for "HyperMedia History" (p. 222) and "Literature on Migrant Workers and Exploitation" (p. 227) illustrate ways of doing this.

Curriculum Content

Curriculum content is a broader term than *materials,* but the same considerations apply. Examine the content you plan to teach in a given area over a period of time to determine whether it reflects multiple and divergent perspectives (most of the lessons in this chapter deal explicitly with this issue), engages all students in learning the different subject areas, and considers gender issues. Also, look at your curriculum to see how well it connects with the social context of your students' interests and experiential backgrounds and with the types of information they would want to learn more about. A lesson such as "Our National Anthems" (page 217) connects content with students' everyday interests and concerns. Similarly, lessons such as "Estimation" (p. 180) and "Self-Interest" (p. 243) connect with students' life circumstances and help students to deal with issues of bias, power, and privilege. The focus of these lessons involves tapping into students' interests and drawing on a culturally expanded pool of knowledge for selecting academic content. The lessons also extend students' knowledge about the experiences and contributions of both sexes and various cultural groups and inform them how gender and other biases are manifested in society.

You may wish to investigate how much you and your students already know about various groups and the issues and concerns of these groups to determine your starting points. Action Research Activity 5.3 is useful with younger students. Action Research Activity 5.1 is appropriate for students in grades 6–12 as well as for adults. Making your curriculum content multicultural requires work, and you may become frustrated. Most of us have not been educated multiculturally and do not know where to go for information. Following are some helpful places to start:

1. Curriculum specialists and resource centers in many school districts have material to help teachers in this area; often it goes unused simply because people do not know to ask for it.

2. Librarians can be an excellent resource; for example, a reference librarian at the public library may be able to provide a wide range of literature or music in a short period of time to a teacher who is not sure what to look for.

3. Students, parents, and local community members can be excellent resources for content on locally represented cultures; most people are receptive to teachers who genuinely want to learn more about their culture and customs.

4. Discuss your ideas with one or two of your colleagues. You may find that they have excellent ideas and suggestions and are also interested in multicultural education.

5. Many cities and larger towns have multicultural bookstores. If there is one in your vicinity, it is well worth spending time (and money) there.

6. The new magazine *Multicultural Education* contains curriculum ideas and materials reviews in each issue.

There are also many commercially produced bibliographies. Once a teacher has gotten started, these can be helpful sources of materials.

Multiple Perspectives

It is a reality of life that on virtually every issue there are multiple points of view. Yet, historically schools have tended to teach children to seek "the right answer." One important way the Multicultural Education approach affirms cultural pluralism is by helping students appreciate multiple perspectives or interpretations. Whenever possible, try to help students recognize that there is more than one way to view an issue, more than one side to a story, more than one "right" cultural practice; and help them discern the standpoints from which other people's perspectives make sense. By doing this, you can help students develop flexible thinking, an expectation that other viewpoints exist, and an appreciation of the similarities and differences among people. The lesson plans "Introduction to Native American Literature" (p. 235) and "HyperMedia History" (p. 222) concentrate on these goals.

Instructional Strategies

Earlier in the chapter we noted the importance of adapting to students' learning styles and skill levels; these recommendations are especially valuable here as well. Essentially, to help your students achieve, you need to be willing to test the various approaches to teaching to identify those that result in achievement. A good deal of patience is often required when trying out new ideas. Students may need a period of adjustment. Usually, the more information students receive about an idea (including why they are doing it), the more they will work with you. Lessons that use various learning and teaching styles include "Alaska" (p. 182), "Fables" (p. 206), and "Our National Anthems" (p. 217).

Language Diversity

The Multicultural Education approach values language diversity and language resources available in the United States, specifically the millions of students who use another language (including sign language) in addition to English. Ideally, all U.S. Americans should be bilingual, mastering English and at least one other language. Some schools offer content instruction (such as history or mathematics) in languages other than English, a practice that dates back more than a century. For example, one of the authors teaches at a university in which several courses outside the Languages Institute are taught in Spanish.

The regular classroom teacher usually is not trained as a language teacher, but with the United States becoming more of a global society, teachers (as well as students) need to develop an interest in second language learning. Resource people can teach conversational phrases or songs in another language. The concept of multilingualism can be presented in a positive manner, and the limitations of knowing one language can be discussed. This is illustrated in the lesson "Our National Anthems" (p. 217). The languages students bring with them should also be used as a teaching resource, as the lesson "An Inspirational Glimpse of Aztec Mythology" (p. 196) illustrates.

Student Evaluation

In the process of evaluating students, we often do so in terms of "winners" and "losers," especially if we expect some students to do better than others. Standardized norm-referenced tests, designed to compare and rank-order students and based on a conception of normalcy that usually favors the European American middle- or upper-middle-class child, often evaluate students in the same way. A more productive way to evaluate, from the perspective of the Multicultural Education approach, is to determine which students need further instruction and in what areas and then to implement that instruction and to reevaluate. By using evaluation to guide instruction, it should be possible for all children to be successful.

Further, multiple forms of assessment that are respectful of diversity should be used to evaluate mastery of multicultural content. The materials used should not penalize students who have low skill levels in areas other than those the teacher has taught. For example, students should be given ample time and not be penalized if they work slowly; they should be encouraged to spell correctly but not be penalized for spelling on a test (unless it is a spelling test); and oral evaluation should be offered to those who do not write well. Although some of these suggestions may conflict with the teaching procedures of some readers, it is important to remember that our primary goal as teachers is to "turn on" learning.

Grouping Students

Grouping students for instruction is a complex practice that often institutionalizes biases and stereotypes. We become so used to grouping patterns that we assume the groups reflect characteristics of students rather than our own beliefs and expectations. Grouping practices that permanently define some students as inferior (e.g., tracking and ability grouping) or superior (e.g., gifted programs) are strongly discouraged. Once students are labeled and tracked, their chances of moving up a group are fairly slim, and the groups become more and more different each year students are in them. Similarly, grouping students in ways that reflect stereotypes, such as enrolling girls in sewing and boys in autoshop, is also discouraged.

The Multicultural Education approach values small-group activities that allow students to get to know each other and to express their individuality. Thus, heterogeneous groups (in terms of race, gender, social class, and academic skill level), in which students work cooperatively, work well in many situations. Such groups are used in the lessons "Tie-Dyeing" (p. 186), "Alaska" (p. 182), and "Our National Anthems" (p. 217). Interest groups, such as students interested in animal stories, are another alternative, as are temporary skill-level groups for working on specific skills. At the same time, homogenous groups are useful in some circumstances. In bilingual or multilingual classrooms, it is often helpful for students to work with others who speak the same language; talking over material in their first language helps them to learn. Sometimes girls work better in single–sex groups, where they do not defer to the boys. Grouping practices should be flexible, and multiple groupings should be used. Students need to learn to relate to their peers and not to categorize people on the basis of a permanent instructional group. At the same time, they also need the most optimal opportunity for learning.

Visuals

What does your classroom look like when you enter it? What do the halls look like? Whose pictures are displayed, what do the visuals tell about the students, and do they say clearly that this is the school of all the students enrolled? A school using the Multicultural Education approach radiates life and diversity in visual displays. Posters depict people of different races, both sexes, and with disabilities, as well as extended and gay and lesbian families. Languages used by students and the community are used. Student work is displayed. The school and classroom look warm, friendly, and inviting. Quotations and statements on posters that encourage critical thinking about problems and issues students are facing are displayed as well.

Some high school teachers tell us that at the secondary level less attention is given to visuals because the students are older, and a teacher may have to share the classroom with several other teachers. Therefore, they argue that they should not be too concerned about visuals. Although we recognize these issues, we also think that every student in that school should believe that it is his or her school, and this should not be left to chance. To do nothing may suggest to students that "business as usual" is OK.

Role Models

A school using the Multicultural Education approach provides students with a diversity of role models filling both traditional and nontraditional roles. For example, the principal may be a female of color. Teachers may include both men and women of various ethnic backgrounds, including some who are openly gay, lesbian, or bisexual, and they are not confined to sex-stereotypic subjects. There may be male secretaries and cafeteria workers and female custodians, and there may be a teacher who is hearing impaired or in a wheelchair. Role models are also provided through guests and speakers, and a conscious effort is made to provide models with whom students can identify, having a variety of careers and interests. Role models are involved throughout the school year, not only for special occasions. Role models should also encourage students to aspire highly, to think creatively about their own futures. Lessons that deal with role models include "Division" (p. 202) and "The Importance of Math to Everyday Life" (Chapter 2, p. 27).

Home and Community Relationships

Normally, parents occupy a spectator role in regards to their child's education, and parents living at or below the poverty line or from minority backgrounds may be excluded from the school in a number of ways. The Multicultural Education approach builds a partnership among the home, school, and community. This partnership seeks to include parents in school activities and on decision making and policy formation committees. Also, this approach encourages communication in the parents' home language. It argues for meetings to be scheduled at convenient times and held in nonthreatening locations. For example, one of our colleagues who is an urban administrator holds family dinners in a church to discuss school issues, and his approach has been highly successful.

Teachers using this approach learn about the community in a methodical manner. For example, they learn the community's history, become familiar with the housing patterns, introduce themselves to the community leaders, and visit organizations, associations, and religious institutions. They read the community newspapers and/or neighborhood bulletins. They communicate personally with parents, providing them with progress reports on their children. This approach sees the school as just one of the institutions of the community and seeks to build communication with the other institutions to maximize the effectiveness of each one. For example, schools work closely with social service agencies and youth clubs to see that students receive the best care possible both during and after school hours. The lesson plan "An Inspirational Glimpse of Aztec Mythology" includes parents as teachers and fosters home–school partnerships (p. 196).

Extracurricular Activities

This approach encourages a wide variety of extracurricular activities. It sees these activities as a way to stimulate greater interest in school and to appeal to students' special and unique talents. By using clubs, sports, dramatics, and school events as a vehicle, students can be given increased opportunities to demonstrate leadership skills and deal with social problems and issues facing society on their own terms. These activities are designed to avoid the perpetuation of stereotypes and categorization of students into stereotypic roles (e.g., boys as athletes and girls as onlookers cheering the boys). Students can join the activities of their choice but are encouraged to cross boundaries and participate in activities that challenge the way they have previously thought about things (e.g., girls joining the mechanics club and boys joining the cooking club).

The names and logos used to identify extracurricular activities (e.g., sport teams) should avoid using terms that may be offensive, such as a team using the name of a racial group (e.g., the Mohawks). We have been in situations in which teachers have debated the merits of school clubs that cater to one group, such as MEChA (Movimiento Estudiantil Chicano de Aztlán), which caters to Chicano students. Our own view is that such clubs may be exactly what a school needs to make its students feel welcome and provide a time and place to be with "their own." We endorse mixing students as much as possible but also recognize value in being with others with whom one shares a special bond. Opportunities for both kinds of interaction should be plentiful.

The preceding recommendations of the Multicultural Education approach span the entire school environment. Use Action Research Activity 5.2 to examine your own school.

ACTION RESEARCH ACTIVITY 5.1*

How Culturally Literate Are You?

True/False

_____ **1.** The first clock in the United States was made by an African American mathematician.

_____ **2.** Charles Drew was an African American surgeon who performed the first successful heart operation.

_____ **3.** Just one hundred years ago, during the decade of the 1890s, the U.S. government took over Puerto Rico and the Philippines through war, legalized racial segregation in the United States, overthrew the government of Hawaii, consolidated the subjugation of Native American nations, and opened its gates to European immigrants.

_____ **4.** The forced migration of the Sioux people from their homeland in Georgia to Oklahoma, during which one-fourth of them died of starvation, disease, and exposure, is known as the "Trail of Tears."

_____ **5.** During World War II, the United States placed many innocent citizens in concentration camps and confiscated their property.

_____ **6.** There was no federal ruling protecting U.S. citizens' rights to marry a person of another race until 1970.

_____ **7.** Mong people began to immigrate to the United States after their Southeast Asian country was destroyed in their defeat by the United States.

_____ **8.** During the Renaissance, the status of women (especially creative and independent women) in Europe rose fairly significantly.

_____ **9.** Mexican women have never been involved in political or labor struggles because their place has traditionally been in the home.

_____ **10.** During the 15th and 16th centuries, Timbuktu in the African kingdom of Songhay was one of the world's greatest cities, renowned as an intellectual and cultural center.

Multiple Choice

1. The "Yellow Rose of Texas" was written to refer to:

    a.   a flower.

    b.   a poor African American woman.

Sources: Bob H. Suzuki, California Polytechnical University, and Christine E. Sleeter. ©1989 Merrill/Prentice Hall Publishing Company. Permission is granted for noncommercial reproduction.

    c.   a European American southern belle.

    d.   a cow.

2. LULAC is a:

    a.   name of a song.

    b.   type of American Indian poetry.

    c.   Filipino club.

    d.   Latino American political organization.

3. The League of Six Nations was:

    a.   a political alliance of African states established in the 1600s for mutual protection against European encroachment.

    b.   an organization of European countries formed in the 1700s.

    c.   a sophisticated network of political alliances among the Iroquois, who lived in the northeastern part of the United States.

    d.   an organization of the six major world powers formed after World War I.

4. The National Women's party first introduced the Equal Rights Amendment in Congress in:

    a.   1923.

    b.   1949.

    c.   1963.

    d.   1972.

5. America was discovered by:

    a.   African explorers in 1252 A.D.

    b.   Hwui Shan, a Chinese Buddhist priest, in 458 A.D.

    c.   Christopher Columbus in 1492 A.D.

    d.   Japanese fishermen around 3000 B.C.

    e.   Leif Ericson in the 11th century.

    f.   none of the above.

6. The following statement was made by which of the following?

I am not, nor ever have been, in favor of bringing about in any way the social and political equality of the white and black races; I am not, nor ever have been, in favor of making voters or jurors of Negroes, nor qualifying them to hold office. . . . I will say in addition to this that there is a physical difference between the white and black races which I believe will ever forbid the two races living together on terms of social and political equality

    a.   Herbert Spencer, a leading exponent of Social Darwinism in the late 1800s

    b.   Jefferson Davis, president of the Confederacy

    c.   Abraham Lincoln, sixteenth president of the United States

    d.   The Know-Nothing Party's presidential candidate in 1852

    e.   none of the above

7. *Akwesanse Notes* is currently the national newspaper of:

    a.   the Mohawk Nation.

    b.   Puerto Rico.

    c.   Japanese Americans in California.

    d.   Bolivia.

8. The 11 persons who were murdered in a mass lynching in New Orleans in 1891 were members of which of the following ethnic groups?

    a.   Chinese

    b.   African Americans

    c.   Italians

    d.   French Indians

9. A man and his son were involved in a car accident in which the father was killed instantly and the son seriously injured. The son was rushed to the hospital and taken immediately into surgery. The surgeon entered the operating room, looked at the patient, and exclaimed, "Oh my god! I can't operate. That's my son!" The explanation for this situation is that:

    a.   it was a case of mistaken identity.

    b.   the surgeon was the boy's stepfather.

    c.   the surgeon was the ghost of the boy's father.

    d.   none of the above.

10. If you are a *sansei,* you are:

    a.   a master in karate.

    b.   a respected grandparent.

    c.   a third-generation Japanese American.

    d.   a foreigner in an Asian American community.

Matching

_____	**1.** Richard Wright	a. Mexican American labor leader
_____	**2.** Mary McLeod Bethune	b. African American psychiatrist on Harvard faculty
_____	**3.** Emma Tenayuca	c. opera singer
_____	**4.** Patsy Takemoto Mink	d. founder and former president of a college
_____	**5.** Marian Anderson	e. first Native American woman to direct the Bureau of Indian Affairs

_____	**6.** Judy Baca	f.	Mexican American historian
_____	**7.** Larry Itliong	g.	African American male novelist
_____	**8.** Leslie Silko	h.	Filipino American labor leader
_____	**9.** Reies Lopez Tijerina	i.	internationally known Chicana muralist
_____	**10.** Lerone Bennett	j.	Mexican American political leader
_____	**11.** Ada Deer	k.	author of children's books
_____	**12.** Alvin Pouissaint	l.	American Indian novelist
_____	**13.** Lucy Stone	m.	African American female novelist
_____	**14.** Yoshiko Uchida	n.	former member of the U.S. Congress
_____	**15.** Zora Neale Hurston	o.	African American historian
_____	**16.** Rudolfo Acuña	p.	worked actively for abolition and for women's suffrage

ANSWERS: How Culturally Literate Are You?

True/False

T   **1.** His name was Benjamin Banneker.

F   **2.** The surgeon was Daniel H. Williams; Charles Drew pioneered research on blood plasma. Both were African Americans.

T   **3.** The revolutionary movements of Puerto Rico and the Philippines were betrayed by the United States when it forced both countries to become its protectorates and replaced Spanish with U.S. American colonial rule. This was the period of "Manifest Destiny" and the beginning of U.S. American imperialism. The last decade of the nineteenth century could be considered the most aggressively racist and imperialist of U.S. history. Effects of that decade are still very real: the United States still occupies Puerto Rico and Hawaii; Puerto Ricans and Filipinos live and work on the U.S. mainland but experience highly disproportionate poverty rates; segregation was not legally undermined in the United States until 1954, and its effects are still felt; American Indian nations and Hawaiian people are still attempting to reclaim land, treaty rights, and legal recognition; and the economic status of European Americans is considerably higher than that of other groups partly because of their legalized access to jobs over several decades.

F   **4.** It was the Cherokee who were moved, not the Sioux. This action was actually taken against a U.S. Supreme Court ruling.

___T___   **5.** The victims of this action were Japanese American citizens; Italian Americans also experienced confiscation of property.

___T___   **6.** Many states protected this right, but some did not, and the federal government did not until 1970.

___F___   **7.** Mong people had migrated to Laos before the Vietnam War; they had no country of their own. They sided with the United States during the war and lost many people then. Because they were allied with the United States, thousands were driven out of Laos to refugee camps in Thailand, and they subsequently immigrated to the United States.

___F___   **8.** Paradoxically, although creativity flourished among European men during this time, the status of women fell as women in large numbers were persecuted and burned as witches. Creative and independent women were especially vulnerable; women's power was suppressed and maligned to such an extent that today "witches" are laughed at and ridiculed and the persecution of women is barely remembered.

___F___   **9.** Mexican and Mexican American women traditionally have occupied an important place in the home but may have also been involved in political and labor struggles. (A good source of information on this subject is Adelaida R. Del Castillo [Ed.], *Between Borders: Essays on Mexicana/Chicana History* [Encino, CA: Floricanto Press, 1990].)

___T___ **10.** Songhay was one of a number of highly advanced empires in Africa, a fact rarely developed in textbooks. Some books still perpetuate the myth of Africa as the "dark continent," despite increasing archeological evidence that it may have been the "seat of civilization" where the human species originated.

Multiple Choice

___b___   **1.** This is an example of how some European Americans have appropriated a song created by another racial group and passed it off as their own. This has happened over and over again, particularly with music created by African Americans.

___d___   **2.** The acronym stands for League of United Latin American Citizens.

___c___   **3.** In fact, Benjamin Franklin is said to have obtained many of his ideas for the Federation of States from this organization.

___a___   **4.** It has been introduced every year since then.

___f___   **5.** While there is evidence ranging from well established to speculative that all of the people mentioned in *a* through *e* arrived in the Americas on about the dates indicated, the best answer is probably *f*, inasmuch as millions of Native Americans were present long before any of these others arrived. In fact, to speak of the "discovery of America" is an insult to Native Americans, as it seems to imply that the Americas had no significance until someone who was not Native American arrived and "discovered" them.

   c   **6.** It is interesting that despite this attitude toward African Americans, Lincoln later became known as the "Great Emancipator." His position on slavery was probably dictated more by politics than by moral concerns.

   a   **7.** As semisovereign nations, several Native American nations have their own newspapers. Some, such as the Menominee, produce their own license plates. Many maps of the United States still do not recognize American Indian reservations, which perpetuates the invisibility of these governmental units among the non–American Indian population.

   c   **8.** There were also many other incidents of violence against Italians in the late 1800s.

   d   **9.** A more plausible answer is, of course, that the surgeon was the boy's mother.

   c   **10.** A first-generation Japanese American is called *issei,* and a second-generation Japanese American is called *nisei*. These are Japanese terms that Japanese Americans use to describe themselves in the United States.

Matching

   g   **1.** His most well-known novel is *Native Son*.

   d   **2.** The college was called the Daytona Educational and Industrial School; it was for African American girls.

   a   **3.** She was jailed for her actions in the Pecan Shellers' strike in 1937.

   n   **4.** She was a representative from Hawaii and the only Asian American woman to serve in Congress.

   c   **5.** She was the first African American to sing at Carnegie Hall; African Americans had previously been prohibited from singing there (as well as many other places).

   i   **6.** She is currently on the faculty in art at the University of California, Los Angeles, and also at California State University, Monterey Bay.

   h   **7.** He helped organize the grape boycott with César Chavez.

   l   **8.** She is best known for her novel *Ceremony*.

   j   **9.** He fought state and federal authorities for land grants to Latinos that were legally protected by the Treaty of Guadalupe.

   o   **10.** He is best known for his book *Before the Mayflower*.

   e   **11.** A member of the Menominee Nation, she has also taught at the University of Wisconsin–Madison.

   b   **12.** He publishes widely in both scholarly and popular literature, such as *Ebony*.

   p   **13.** She was one of several European American women who first became politically active fighting against slavery, then channeled that activism into fighting for women's right to vote. Unlike many European American feminists, however, she was not troubled by the possibility that African American men might become enfranchised before women.

___k___ **14.** A former Japanese American internment camp prisoner, she has published numerous stories.

___m___ **15.** Her most well-known novel is *Their Eyes Were Watching God*.

___f___ **16.** His best-known book is *Occupied America*.

Resources

Mirande, A., & Enriquez, E. (1979). *La Chicana*. Chicago: University of Chicago Press.

Sertima, I. V. (1977). *They came before Columbus: The African presence in ancient America*. New York: Random House.

ACTION RESEARCH ACTIVITY 5.2

Classroom and School Assessment

Activity 5.2 is designed for the teacher or administrator interested in assessing his or her own workplace. Student teachers can use this instrument as well, substituting a specific teacher's name for reference to "you" and "your classroom" where appropriate. Indicate in the blank: to a great extent; somewhat; very little; or not at all.

Classroom Level

_____ **1.** To what extent do you consider affirming human diversity a top priority for your teaching?

_____ **2.** To what extent do visuals (charts, pictures, and so on) reflect race, gender, sexual orientation, and disability diversity in a nonstereotypic manner?

_____ **3.** To what extent do your regular instructional materials include people who differ by race, sex, class, language, sexual orientation, and disability in a nonstereotypic manner?

_____ **4.** To what extent do resource materials include people who differ by race, sex, class, language, sexual orientation, and disability in a nonstereotypic manner?

_____ **5.** To what extent does your plan for selecting materials include multicultural education criteria?

_____ **6.** To what extent do your daily lessons reflect human diversity?

_____ **7.** To what extent do your long-range curriculum plans promote multiculturalism and multilingualism?

_____ **8.** Other than on special occasions, to what extent do you use resource people with various racial and social class backgrounds, those of both sexes, those of different sexual orientations, and those with disabilities?

_____ **9.** To what extent do you use different strategies to teach students with different learning styles and skill levels?

_____ **10.** To what extent do your teaching strategies promote active learning and critical thinking?

_____ **11.** To what extent do you set and maintain high expectations for all your students?

_____ **12.** To what extent is nonsexist and nonheterosexist language used?

_____ **13.** To what extent do grading and grouping practices encourage and reward success for all students equally?

_____ **14.** To what extent do your tests reflect sensitivity to multicultural education?

_____ **15.** To what extent do plans for "special event" celebrations reflect diversity based on race, ethnicity, religion, or gender?

_____ **16.** To what extent do you try actively to communicate with parents, especially those who live at or below the poverty level, are minorities, or speak a language other than English?

_____ **17.** To what extent are notices sent home in the parents' language?

School Level

_____ **1.** To what extent does the school philosophy explicitly address multicultural education?

_____ **2.** To what extent do visuals in the hall or office (pictures, bulletin boards, and so on) reflect race, gender, disability, sexual orientation, and language diversity in a nonstereotypic manner?

_____ **3.** To what extent is there a plan to ensure that curriculum and classroom materials schoolwide reflect multicultural education?

_____ **4.** To what extent does the plan for selecting materials include multicultural education criteria?

_____ **5.** To what extent do library materials reflect cultural and language diversity, both sexes, gays, lesbians, bisexuals, and people with disabilities in a nonstereotypic manner?

_____ **6.** To what extent are resources, in-service, and planning time made available to help the staff work with multicultural and bilingual education?

_____ 7. To what extent are cooperative working relationships between special education and regular education staff supported and encouraged?

_____ 8. To what extent do policies and practices for assigning students to instructional groups and courses facilitate equal opportunity and equal access to a strong education?

_____ 9. To what extent are both sexes offered the same education?

_____ 10. To what extent does the school support and encourage bilingualism or multilingualism for all students?

_____ 11. To what extent are notices sent home in the parents' language?

_____ 12. To what extent does the school staffing pattern provide students with diverse role models in nonstereotypic roles?

_____ 13. To what extent do plans for "special event" celebrations reflect diversity based on race, ethnicity, religion, gender, or disability?

_____ 14. To what extent do discipline policies and procedures treat all students and student groups equally and equitably?

_____ 15. To what extent are testing procedures nonbiased and used to help teach rather than categorize students?

_____ 16. To what extent is there a plan to involve actively all parents, especially those who live at or below the poverty level or minority background?

_____ 17. To what extent is instruction available in the language of linguistic minorities, including American Sign Language?

_____ 18. To what extent are facilities accessible to students and parents with physical and visual disabilities?

_____ 19. To what extent do school lunch menus reflect the culturally diverse tastes of students?

_____ 20. To what extent do extracurricular activities provide for the diverse interests, cultural backgrounds, and physical capabilities of students?

_____ 21. To what extent are students actively invited to participate in extracurricular activities, regardless of race, sex, social class, sexual orientation, or disability?

ACTION RESEARCH ACTIVITY 5.3

What Do Kids Already Know? (and Where Did They Learn It?)

This is an interview to find out what knowledge (which may be inaccurate) kids bring to school with them about different groups and where they got that knowledge. The idea is that multicultural education of a sort is already going on in kids' daily lives. The issue for teachers often is not whether kids should learn about other groups but what the school should do to develop or even correct what kids are learning elsewhere.

When interviewing, ask about several groups, such as the following; select any group(s) except the one(s) the student is a member of.

African American males	European American	Mexican American
African American	females living at the	females
females	poverty level	Puerto Ricans
American Indians	European American	Southeast Asians
Arab Americans	males living at the	People who are blind
Chinese Americans	poverty level	or deaf
Cuban Americans	Filipino Americans	People in wheelchairs
European American	Japanese Americans	
middle-class	Jewish Americans	
females	Mexican American males	

For each of the groups listed, ask the following questions:

1. Have you had any personal contact with [group]? If not, have you heard that term or do you know who they are? (You may have to give some equivalent terms or an example; if the student still does not know, select another group.)

2. If I were a visitor from outer space trying to find out more about the United States, how would you describe [group] to me?
   a. What have you heard about them?
   b. What have you seen?
   c. What has your own personal experience taught you?

3. How certain do you feel the information you have is accurate?

4. Where did you learn most of your information? (After the student has responded, probe to find out what was learned from each of the sources below.)
   a. parents, family
   b. TV
   c. movies
   d. books
   e. magazines, comics
   f. school
   g. personal experience
   h. the computer
   i. music

LESSON PLAN

BEFORE

Estimation

Subject Area: Mathematics

Grade Level: 2–4

Time: One or two days

Objectives

1. Students will explain what estimation is and how it differs from guessing.

2. Students will make reasonable estimates.

3. Students will check their estimates by comparing them with real measurements.

Suggested Procedures

1. Show students a glass bowl full of jelly beans, which you have counted previously. Ask how many jelly beans are in the jar. Someone will suggest that we count them. Ask students first to give their best guess as to how many jelly beans are in the bowl.

2. Ask students to estimate the number of boys or girls in the classroom; then have them count to check their estimates. Discuss with them questions such as the following:
    a.   How did you go about selecting your estimate?
    b.   What clues can you use to help make an estimate?

3. Ask students to estimate the distance between two objects. Compare true measurement (tm) and estimate (e).

4. Ask students to observe and record estimates of different measuring units and to select appropriate measuring units to check estimates.

5. Have students discuss their experience with estimation in terms of the following questions:
    a.   How accurate were your estimates?
    b.   Which estimates seemed easier? more difficult? Why?
    c.   What clues were you able to use?
    d.   In what situations might you want to estimate?

Evaluation

Give students a quantity to estimate, have them explain why they think the estimate is reasonable, and then check it.

AFTER

Estimation

Subject Area: Mathematics

Grade Level: 2–4

Time: Two days

Objectives

1. Students will explain what estimation is and how it differs from guessing.

2. Students will make reasonable estimates.

3. Students will check their estimates by comparing them with real measurements.

4. Students will recognize race and gender biases in various aspects of their lives.

Suggested Procedures

1. Show students a large picture or poster that portrays a great number of people. Ask students how many people are in the picture. Students will probably start to count; ask them first to give their best guess. Explain the word *estimate* and the difference between estimation and guessing. Then count the number of people in the picture; ask students how accurate their estimates were.

2. Have students estimate the number of males, females, Asian Americans, blond-haired people, and so on, in the picture. Then have them count to check their estimates. Discuss with them questions such as the following:

    a.   How did you go about selecting your estimate?

    b.   What clues can you use to help make an estimate?

3. Ask students to estimate the number of male teachers and female teachers in the school (teachers should have this information available). Ask them also to estimate other staffing patterns, such as the number of custodians and teachers of color, female secretaries, and so on. Then use this to discuss the following questions:

    a.   Which estimates were more accurate and why?

    b.   Did stereotypes or expectations influence their estimates?

    c.   Was the race or gender of different staff members relevant?

4. Have students estimate the number of each of the following groups represented in pictures in one of their textbooks: European American males, European

American females, African American males, African American females, Latino males, Latino females, American Indian males, American Indian females, Asian American males, Asian American females, and persons with disabilities. Then have them count to check their estimates. Use this to discuss questions similar to those in item 3.

5. Ask students to estimate the number of female physicians in the local hospital in comparison with the number of male physicians. Ask them to estimate the number of physicians of color in comparison with the total number of physicians. Have this information available. Discuss with students questions similar to those in item 3.

Evaluation

1. Assess the reasonableness of the estimations that students make in class and their understanding of estimation through class discussion.

2. Assess students' awareness of race and gender biases through class discussion.

WHY THE CHANGES?

Estimation

Curriculum Content

This lesson applies the content of a subject area that is often viewed as impossible to make multicultural—math—to a social concern without sacrificing the mathematical operations we are teaching. In math, we often give more attention to the mathematical operations we are teaching than to the content of the problems we ask students to solve. The problems are treated as a vehicle for practicing the mathematical operation more than as worthwhile areas of investigation in themselves. The "After" plan applies the mathematical concept of estimation to a social issue involving race and gender bias. It then asks students to consider not only the accuracy of their estimates but also the significance of their findings.

BEFORE

LESSON PLAN

Alaska

Subject Area: Social Studies

Grade Level: 4–6

Time: One week

Objectives

1. Students will locate geographic features of Alaska on a map.

2. Students will explain how Alaska's climate influences life there.

3. Students will describe the main features of Alaska's economy.

4. Students will compare an Eskimo family with a U.S. American family.

Suggested Procedures

1. Pass out blank maps of Alaska. Using a large wall map, have students locate the following on their maps: Alaska, the Arctic Ocean, the Pacific Ocean, Juneau, Anchorage, Fairbanks, Nome, Barrow, and the Yukon River.

2. Show pictures of Alaska in summer and winter. Discuss Alaska's climate. Compare the summer and winter temperatures in Alaska with the temperatures in your own state. Have children think of the problems that the climate of Alaska may cause for people living there; list the problems on the board.

3. Read about how people make a living in Alaska. Show pictures of people fishing, working in a cannery, working on the pipeline, working in an office. Have the class make a collage depicting Alaska's economy. With the class, develop a list of the kinds of trade that exist between Alaska and the rest of the United States.

4. Show pictures of an Eskimo family. On the board, make a chart on which students list the similarities and differences they see between an Eskimo family and their own family. Read a story, if available, about an Eskimo family.

Evaluation

Test students on their skills in locating places on a blank map and on their knowledge of Alaska's climate, Alaska's economy, and facts about Eskimo families.

| **AFTER** | Alaska |

Subject Area: Social Studies

Grade Level: 4–6

Time: One week

Objectives

1. Students will appreciate Alaska's size and its geographic and cultural diversity.

2. Students will explain the way environment influences culture.

3. Students will analyze the economic patterns of Alaska and the economic base of different groups of Alaskans.

4. Students will develop respect for the culture and life-style of an Alaskan family.

5. Students will make and test hypotheses based on available information.

Suggested Procedures

1. Have students describe what they think Alaska's geography and topography are like. Locate Alaska on a large wall map. Using a cut-out of your home state, compare the sizes of the two states, then show pictures of different regions of Alaska, stressing Alaska's topographical diversity. Help students analyze their own stereotypes of Alaska.

2. Show pictures depicting winter and summer in both Anchorage and Barrow. Point out similarities and differences between the climates of these two cities and their climates compared with your home city or town.

3. Divide the class into three groups. Provide pictures of the land and animals around Anchorage, Barrow, and Sitka. Also provide written descriptions of each, detailing their climate and natural resources. (At this time, do not include pictures or descriptions of the peoples of these areas.) Explain to students that each group will pretend they live in one of these three areas. Using the information provided, they are to decide how they would live in regard to the following: housing, food, clothes, employment, transportation, and recreation. Students may develop their ideas in writing, in pictures, or both.

4. When groups have completed their work, have them share the life-styles they have created.

5. Show pictures of and/or have students read about people actually living in these areas. For Barrow, be sure to include both native Alaskan and white European Americans. For Anchorage, include American Indians, "pioneer-like" European Americans, professional European Americans and African Americans, Mexican Americans, and Asian Americans. For Sitka, include whites of Russian ancestry, newer white Americans, and coastal Indians. Be sure both men and women are portrayed. Point out that as an airway crossroads, a former gold rush site, and currently a major oil source, Alaska has attracted a mixed population. Have students compare their versions of how they thought people would live with pictures and descriptions of how different Alaskans actually live. Through discussion, help them to see that different life-styles are developed by people in different parts of Alaska (in this case) as viable adaptations to the environment. Have students form hypotheses about the extent to which differences among Alaskan life-styles seem to be due more to ethnicity, geographic location, degree of urbanization, economic circumstances, or some combination. Help students think of ways they can test their hypotheses.

6. Locate families representing each of the groups in item 5 with whom the class can correspond. You can do this through schools in different regions of Alaska.

Evaluation

1. Assess students' reasonableness of hypothesized life-styles based on their group reports.

2. Assess students' understanding of the extent and roots of cultural diversity in Alaska based on class discussion and a written or oral quiz.

3. Assess students' enjoyment of corresponding with an Alaskan family.

WHY THE CHANGES?

Alaska

Curriculum Materials

Materials in the "After" lesson have been selected to represent Alaska's rich cultural diversity; in the "Before" plan, they are not. The "After" plan specifies not only that the materials depict racial and gender diversity but that they accurately reflect groups in different regions of Alaska as well. For example, rather than grouping all Alaskan natives together, materials should distinguish between Inuit and coastal Indians. Rather than grouping all whites together, materials should depict whites of different social classes and distinguish between whites from the United States and those of recent Russian ancestry. The lesson attempts to convey to students as accurately as possible the diverse population of the state and to challenge stereotypes they may have about groups.

Curriculum Content

The content of the "After" plan is quite different from that of the "Before" plan in a number of ways. The "Before" plan stresses acquisition of facts while presenting Alaska as a fairly homogeneous place. It teaches stereotypes by reducing Alaska to a series of facts to be memorized.

The "After" plan stresses concepts and uses examples of diverse people and places in Alaska to help students develop concepts. For example, rather than looking superficially at the geography of the whole state, students compare the geography of three different areas and use this to suggest relationships between environment and life-style.

The "Before" plan also presents native Alaskans as stereotypic, different, and non–U.S. American. The "After" plan retains the idea of studying Alaskan families but broadens this to include diverse families.

Multiple Perspectives

The "Before" plan does not teach multiple perspectives. The "After" plan teaches this by having groups of students analyze the reasonableness of different life-styles of three different regions and the reasons people develop different life-styles. In addition, the pen-pals activity invites real families to share their perspectives in the form of letters.

Instructional Strategies

The "After" plan uses a variety of teaching strategies and places students in a more active and participatory role than the "Before" plan. In the "After" plan, students view visuals, discuss, write, draw, and read. Part of the work is done as a whole class and part as small groups. The "After" lesson has not been adapted specifically to the learning styles of a particular class of students; the teacher may wish to modify the teaching style of this purpose. The "After" plan also gives students more interesting and challenging work to do than the "Before" plan by asking them to think critically and to participate actively.

Evaluation

The "Before" plan evaluates students by giving them a test asking recall questions. The "After" plan broadens evaluation to include also the results of students' group work, which gives the assignment more importance. The "After" plan also provides for oral evaluation of students whose writing skills are poor.

LESSON PLAN

BEFORE   ## Tie-Dyeing

Subject Area: Art

Grade Level: 4–6

Time: Two class periods

Objectives

1. Students will identify primary and secondary colors.
2. Students will produce patterns through tie-dyeing.

Suggested Procedures

1. Show the color chart. Explain the meaning of primary and secondary colors.

a. *Primary colors*—red, yellow, blue—are so called because they cannot be made by mixing any other colors.

b. *Secondary colors*—orange, green, violet—are colors that come about from mixing the primary colors:

Red + Yellow = Orange

Yellow + Blue = Green

Blue + Red = Violet

2. Explain to the class that they will be mixing secondary colors from primary colors. Pass out bowls of dye (one red, one yellow, one blue) and three empty bowls to each student. Have each student mix each of the three secondary colors.

3. Pass out 12-x-12-inch cloth and several pieces of string to each student.

4. Explain the concept of pattern. **Pattern** is the repetition of lines or shapes. The chief purpose of pattern is to provide a decorative quality to enrich the surface of the cloth.

5. Explain the principles of tie-dyeing. Cloth is wrapped in various ways with the pieces of string to make a pattern. The cloth is then put in the dye bath. The cloth underneath the string resists the dye and stays white while the rest of the cloth turns the color of the dye, thus making a pattern.

6. Have each student wrap his or her cloth in the pattern desired; then dip all or sections of it in the dye.

7. When the cloth is dry, have each student unwrap his or her own piece, compare it with others in the group, and discuss how the pattern was obtained.

Evaluation

Assess students' understanding of the concepts of color and pattern and of the process of tie-dyeing through the quality of their tie-dyed products.

AFTER

Tie-Dyeing*

Subject Area: Art

Grade Level: 4–6

Time: Two or three class periods

Objectives

1. Students will identify primary and secondary colors.

---

*Sources: P. Lloyd Kollman, Kenosha, WI, and Debra Owens, Racine, WI.

2. Students will appreciate the traditional Native American use of natural dyes to obtain various primary and secondary colors.

3. Students will produce patterns through tie-dyeing.

4. Students will appreciate the traditional Black/African use of pattern in clothing.

5. Students will work with peers of different races and gender.

Suggested Procedures

1. Divide the class into groups of six students each. Groups should be as race- and gender-mixed as possible.

2. Show the color chart. Explain the meaning of primary and secondary colors.

   a. *Primary colors*—red, yellow, blue—are so called because they cannot be made by mixing any other colors.

   b. *Secondary colors*—orange, green, violet—are colors that come about from mixing the primary colors:

   Red + Yellow = Orange

   Yellow + Blue = Green

   Blue + Red = Violet

3. Explain that art for the Native American Indian was not separate from life; rather, it was a balance of tradition and spirituality. Color to the Native American Indian had energy and spiritual qualities. Read examples of American Indian poetry and traditional stories involving color, such as the following:

   Prayer After Singing Gahe Songs (Chiricahua)

   Big Blue Mountain Spirit,
   The home made of blue clouds,
   The cross made of the blue mirage,
   There, you have begun to live,
   There, is the life of goodness,
   I am grateful for that made of goodness there.
   Big Yellow Mountain Spirit in the south,
   Your spiritually hale body is made of yellow clouds;
   Leader of the Mountain Spirits, holy Mountain Spirit,
   You live by means of the good of this life.
   Big White Mountain Spirit in the west,
   Your spiritually hale body is made of the white mirage;
   Holy Mountain Spirit, leader of the Mountain Spirits,
   I am happy over your words,
   You are happy over my words.

   Big Black Mountain Spirit in the north,
   Your spiritually hale body is made of black clouds;

In that way, Big Black Mountain Spirit,
Holy Mountain Spirit, leader of the Mountain Spirits,
I am happy over your words,
You are happy over my words,
Now it is good.

(Hoijer, 1938, p. 69)

Song of the Sky Loom (Tewa Indian Weaving Song)

Oh our Mother the Earth, oh our Father the Sky,
Your children are we, and with tired backs
We bring you the gifts that you love.
Then weave for us a garment of brightness;
May the warp be the white light of morning,
May the weft be the red light of evening,
May the fringes be the falling rain,
May the border be the standing rainbow.
Thus weave for us a garment of brightness
That we may walk fittingly where birds sing,
That we may walk fittingly where the grass is green,
Oh our Mother the Earth, oh our Father the Sky!

(Spinden, 1933, p. 94)

4. Explain that many Native American nations got the colors used in dyeing wool from natural plants. Give examples:

    Red—Juniper Ash (tree): bark of the root *cercocarpus parvifolius*

    Blue—Indigo (plant): blue corn, blue clay

    Yellow—Rabbit Weed (flower): Chamizo blossoms and twigs

5. Explain to students that they will mix secondary colors from the primary colors. Pass out three buckets of dye (one red, one yellow, one blue) and three empty buckets to each group. Have each group of six pair up (two–two–two). Each pair of students will mix a secondary color for their group (orange, green, violet).

6. Pass out 12-x-12-inch cloth to each student and several pieces of string.

7. Explain the concept of pattern. **Pattern** is the repetition of lines or shapes. The chief purpose of pattern is to provide a decorative quality to enrich the surface of the cloth.

8. Explain the principles of tie-dyeing. Cloth is wrapped in various ways with the pieces of string to make a pattern. The cloth underneath the string resists the dye and stays white while the rest of the cloth turns the color of the dye, thus making a pattern.

9. Explain to the class that in many Black/African cultures pattern and tie-dyeing are a way to decorate clothing. Show a sample of the loose-fitting garment

called the dashiki, which probably originated in West Africa. Show examples of African animals as well.

10. Have each student wrap his or her cloth in the pattern desired; then dip all or sections of it in the dyes in the group.

11. When the cloth is dry, have each student unwrap his or her own piece, compare it with others in the group, and discuss how the pattern was achieved.

12. Pass out one 48×32-inch burlap piece and some glue to each group. Explain that each student in the group will contribute his or her tie-dyed cloth to make a large wall hanging for the class. It is up to the group members to decide on the design for the wall hanging. Figure 5.1 shows an illustration of a wall hanging made by one group. While the students are working on their wall hanging, play West African music.

13. When the wall hangings are finished, display one on each wall.

Evaluation

1. Assess students' understanding of the concepts of color and pattern and the process of tie-dyeing through the quality of their tie-dyed products.

2. Assess students' appreciation of other cultures (Native American, Black/African) through class discussion.

3. Assess students' ability to work cooperatively and to contribute to the class through observation.

FIGURE 5.1   Wall Hanging

Resources

Hoijer, H. (1938). *Chiricahua and Mescalero Apache texts*. Chicago: University of Chicago Publications in Anthropology, Linguistic Series.

Spinden, H. J. (1933). *Songs of the Tewa*. New York: Exposition of Indian Tribal Arts.

WHY THE CHANGES?

Tie-Dyeing

Curriculum Content

The "After" plan explores the cultural uses and origins of the concepts in the "Before" plan for the purpose of enhancing students' understanding of them and their knowledge and appreciation of other cultural groups. Content about how American Indians mixed color teaches students how colors can be achieved in ways other than using purchased dyes, as well as how color is derived from nature. The American Indian poetry teaches students to view color aesthetically and symbolically. Content about African use of tie-dyeing teaches students about the origins of this art form, as well as about the technique and thought behind one kind of African textile.

Grouping of Students

In the "Before" plan, each student works alone. The "After" plan encourages cooperation for reasons similar to those in the Human Relations approach: to encourage the appreciation of peers and the development of skills and attitudes for cooperating.

LESSON PLAN

BEFORE

Folk and Fairy Tales

Subject Area: Language Arts

Grade Level: 4–6

Time: Three days

Objectives

1. Students will appreciate lesser-known fairy tales.

2. Students will explain the origins of fairy tales.

3. Students will develop dramatization skills.

Suggested Procedures

1. Ask students what fairy tales they are familiar with (such as "Cinderella" and "Snow White").

2. Introduce some lesser-known folk and fairy tales (such as "Stone Soup"). Explain to students what is known about the historical origin of these and the more popular fairy tales. Have students suggest reasons why the popularity of folk and fairy tales often persists.

3. Divide students into three groups. Have each group read one folk/fairy tale. Then have them work out a dramatization for it. Help students improvise costumes and props. Have students perform for each other.

Evaluation

1. Assess students' appreciation and dramatization skills through their group presentations.

2. Assess students' understanding of the origins of fairy tales through a test at the end of the unit.

AFTER   ## Folk and Fairy Tales[*]

Subject Area: Language Arts

Grade Level: 4–6

Time: Four days

Objectives

1. Students will analyze folk and fairy tales for racism, ageism, sexism, ablism, heterosexism, and classism.

2. Students will recognize stereotypic representations in folk and fairy tales.

3. Students will understand that literature often reflects the times in which it was written.

4. Students will develop small-group interaction skills and group relations.

5. Students will avoid stereotypes and stereotypic language in their writing and thinking.

6. Students will write folk and fairy tales from multicultural points of view.

---

[*]*Source:* Linda Roberts, Salem, WI.

7. Students will appreciate viewpoints other than their own and other than those presented in folk and fairy tales.

8. Students will learn that they can search on their own for books with gender, sexuality, ethnic, class, disability, and age stereotypes.

Suggested Procedures

1. Introduce some popular folk and fairy tales (such as "Cinderella" and "Snow White"). Ask students if they are familiar with these tales and to name others. Select one story for analysis. Have students brainstorm how the story depicts the "perfect Prince," "perfect Princess," "perfect witch," and so on; record the findings on the board. Then ask the class to brainstorm the "imperfect Prince," and so on, for comparing and contrasting. The lists will probably show that the story depicts "perfect" women primarily in passive roles, working in the kitchen, or following rather than leading. Most often, they are concerned with beauty, clothes, jewelry, and finding "Prince Charming." Other females are depicted as "little old" women and wicked witches, with an occasional fairy godmother. Men are depicted as young, virile, handsome, solving problems, going on quests, slaying dragons, and rescuing maidens. Infrequently, a "little old" man is shown. Men are most often portrayed as strong and forceful, rarely displaying unmanly emotions. European fairy tales rarely have main characters that are not white, except an occasional stereotyped member of a European minority group.

2. For the next day's assignment, ask students to bring in their own copies of folk and fairy tales to analyze (or they may use copies you have provided).

3. Form cooperative groups based on students' interest in particular books to analyze. Have each group role-play their book as it is originally written.

4. Remind students of the discussion in procedure 1. Ask the groups to rewrite their fairy tales from a nonstereotypic point of view, including groups that are often omitted. Ask them also to explore nontraditional roles for men as well as women.

5. Have students role-play (in groups) their new version of the fairy tales. Discuss ways that the new versions are more egalitarian than the old ones and the ways students feel about both versions.

6. Have the class produce a booklet of their new fairy tales. They may be handwritten or produced on a word processor and should be illustrated. The booklet can be put in the library (complete with its own call number and card in the card catalog) and reproduced for each class member.

7. Introduce folk and fairy tales from cultures other than white and European, such as African American, Native American, Latino American, and Asian American. Also read folk tales from other countries, including those in Asia, Africa, and others, pointing out literary style and story structure.

8. At the end of the unit, ask students to discuss how stereotypes can affect people's feelings and lives. Students should have the awareness needed to analyze literature for stereotypes on their own.

Evaluation

1. Assess students' ability to analyze folk and fairy tales for racism, sexism, ageism, ablism, heterosexism, and classism through class discussion and the groups' analyses of the folk tales.

2. Assess students' small-group interaction skills through observation.

3. Assess students' skill in writing and thinking multiculturally through their rewritten fairy tales.

4. Assess students' appreciation of other viewpoints through observation of their interaction and through the presence of diverse viewpoints in their rewritten fairy tales.

WHY THE CHANGES?

Folk and Fairy Tales

Curriculum Materials

Folk and fairy tales often contain sexist and racist stereotypes and negative images of people with disabilities. The "Before" plan uses them without examining for stereotypes. The teacher can deliberately select some to be stereotype-free, but it is more useful to teach students to recognize the stereotypes present within traditional folk and fairy tales. The "After" plan encourages students to examine materials for biases and stereotypes and to rewrite literature to make it fairer to diverse groups.

Curriculum Content

The "Before" plan does not specify the culture from which folk and fairy tales are drawn; most often they are from northern and western Europe. The "After" plan directs the teacher to teach folk and fairy tales from a variety of cultural groups.

Multiple Perspectives

In the "Before" plan, students share perspectives only when they suggest reasons fairy tales are popular. In the "After" plan, students share their perspectives about the fairy tales and their views about stereotypes. Students are also exposed to perspectives from various cultural groups on what constitutes a folk or fairy tale.

Grouping of Students

Both plans use cooperative learning. However, in the "After" plan, students not only plan and present a skit but also analyze and rewrite fairy tales.

LESSON PLAN*

BEFORE

Hidden Mythologies

Subject Area: Language Arts (English Language Development)

Grade Level: 4–8

Time: Three or four weeks

Objectives

1. Students will read and write a summary of a creation myth by identifying/sequencing the main ideas in the story.

2. Students will increase acquisition of English through discussion and carefully organized comprehension of questions in English.

Suggested Procedures

1. Discuss with students the definition of the term *myth* since they will be reading a myth. According to the *Macmillan Dictionary for Students*, edited by William D. Halsey, a myth is a "traditional story of unknown authorship that expresses a belief of a particular people usually involving gods and heroes. A myth is an attempt to explain a phenomenon of nature, an event in history, or the origin of a particular custom, practice, or religious belief."

   This discussion will be in English. Tell students that the myth they will be reading is an Aztec myth. In the discussion, the question will be raised on the validity of myths—are myths true? Students may be told that myths are beliefs and beliefs cannot be proven. Myths and beliefs must be distinguished from fact. Facts can be proven. The Aztecs used these myths to explain their beliefs. The Aztecs were a civilization that was still developing in the sixteenth century.

2. Tell students to follow along in their own copies of the bilingual myth, while the teacher reads the English version of *How We Came to the Fifth World/ Como vinimos al quinto mundo.* As an introduction, tell students that the Aztecs believed the world was destroyed four times, each time by a natural element and/or gods

---

*Source: Gloria Nájera, Alisal Union School District, Salinas, CA.

   Note: This lesson plan is written for Latino students who are learning English as a second language.

because of the "evil" or the imbalance the people caused. After the destruction of each world, one good couple survived. According to this story and Aztec mythology, the "fifth" world is the present world.

3. Since this story is divided into five parts, or five worlds, discuss the story with students to identify each world and state verbally in English how each world was destroyed. This activity is necessary to give students a general sense of the sequence of events.

4. Ask students to take turns reading about the first world aloud, while the teacher asks questions that have been prepared in advance to elicit comprehension of the storyline and increase the acquisition of English.

5. Ask students to write a summary about the first world in English. Ask them to reread and edit their own summaries. Next, ask students recopy their summaries neatly and turn these in for further editing and corrections.

6. The teacher will edit and correct students' versions of the first world and will return these to students. Ask students to rewrite stories neatly on binder paper with mistakes corrected. Also ask students to illustrate their stories, since each student will make his or her own book.

7. Ask students to repeat steps 4–6 to write about each world; each student will then have a copy of his or her own book.

Evaluation

1. Assess students' understanding of the myth by giving them a quiz each time they write their own version of each world of the myth. The questions on this quiz will have been carefully written in English by the teacher to gain an accurate assessment of the students' comprehension of the story in English.

2. Assess students' understanding of sequence by giving students a quiz with sequential statements out of the order in which these occur in the story. The students' task is to arrange these statements in the proper order of sequence as these occurred in the story.

AFTER   # An Inspirational Glimpse of Aztec Mythology

Subject Area: Language Arts (English Language Development)

Grade Level: 4–8

Time: Three or four weeks

Objectives

1. Students will read and write a creation myth by identifying/sequencing the main ideas in the story.

2. Students will increase acquisition of English through discussion and carefully organized comprehension questions in English.

3. Students' identities will be validated by interviewing/recording parents' mythologies.

4. Students' histories will be validated by researching mythologies of their own ethnic ancestry.

Suggested Procedures

Lesson 1

1. Discuss with students the definition of the term *myth* since they will be reading a myth. According to the *Macmillan Dictionary for Students*, edited by William D. Halsey, a myth is a "traditional story of unknown authorship that expresses a belief of a particular people usually involving gods and heroes. A myth is an attempt to explain a phenomenon of nature, an event in history, or the origin of a particular custom, practice, or religious belief."

   This discussion will be in Spanish to make sure students acquire adequate knowledge of the topic, especially since this is academic information being presented for the first time. (Kathleen Kenfield [1992] discusses Stephen Krashen's theories specifically, providing "comprehensible input" in the form of "knowledge of the topic.") Tell students that the myth they will be reading is an Aztec creation myth taken and deciphered from the Aztec calendar. In the discussion, the question will be raised on validity of myths—are myths true? Do not take a position, but do give information on Western and Meso-American views on mythology. As a follow-up lesson, the next day, the teacher may want to show students the Aztec calendar and present the creation myth as shown on the face of the calendar.

2. Tell students to follow along in their own copies of the bilingual myth, while the teacher reads the Spanish version of *How We Came to the Fifth World/Como vinimos al quinto mundo*. The myth is read in Spanish to give students "comprehensible input." As an introduction to the story, tell students that the Aztecs believed the world was destroyed four times, each time by a natural element and/or gods because of the "evil" or the imbalance the people caused. After the destruction of each world, one good couple survived. According to this story and Aztec mythology, the "fifth" world is the present world.

3. Since this story is divided into five parts, or five worlds, discuss the story with students, in Spanish ("comprehensible input"), having them briefly identify each world and state how each world was destroyed. This activity is necessary to give students a general sense of the sequence of events.

4. Ask students to read about the first world silently in English. Give a reasonable amount of time for most students to finish reading. On an overhead projector or

on the blackboard, do a "webbing" activity. The way to do this activity is to put the central character (in this case a god) in the center of a circle and write the main ideas in the form of sentences or phrases around the circle. Have the whole class participate with you on this activity. This is done in English. Ask students to copy this information in journals, since students will use this information to write summaries in English with a partner about the first world as a next step. Tell students that these summaries will be made into books after corrections are made.

5. In advance, identify students with advanced English acquisition and students with less language acquisition. Divide students into two groups and let students select a partner. Let students know that in the future you will identify and divide students into groups according to Spanish dominance. Stress the idea of the equitable value of both languages and the value of working cooperatively. Tell students that they will help each other edit their stories. In addition, they will be expected to illustrate their stories.

6. The following steps are taken from Kathleen Kenfield's manual "Planning for Success," based on Katherine Davies Samway's *Writers' Workshop and Children Acquiring English as a Non-Native Language.* Ask students to write a summary about the first world in English. Ask them to reread and edit their own summaries.

7. Ask students to pair off with their partners and edit each other's summaries based on a rubric the class has worked on together. One student reads his or her essay, while the other gives positive feedback and points out errors. (The student rubric is based on the district rubric for language arts–writing.)

8. Ask students to combine both summaries to create one version of the first world. This needs to be recopied neatly after corrections have been made. While one partner is recopying the story, the other partner will be drawing the illustration for the first world. Ask partners to decide which task each of them will do. They must take turns when writing subsequent versions of the other four worlds. Ask students to turn in recopied and corrected versions.

9. Request a conference with both partners to give positive feedback and point out errors, usually for areas students need to work on. Ask the students to make corrections on their papers as you point out errors. Ask them to rewrite their story and redo a final draft of drawings for publication.

10. Request students to repeat steps 4-9 to write about each world.

11. Ask students to write their own ending to this creation myth by analyzing what changes we would need to make to save our world and keep it from being destroyed.

12. Show students how to make Aztec codices (folded fanlike books made with grocery bag paper).

Evaluation

1. Assess students' understanding of sequencing by reading written summaries of myths when conferencing with students.

2. Assess students' acquisition of English by comparing each student's written rough drafts of the first world and the fifth world and doing holistic scoring according to the student-written rubric.

Lesson 2

1. Review and discuss the definition of *myth* in Spanish (refer to objectives 1 and 2 for a rationale of this discussion in the students' primary language). According to the *Macmillan Dictionary for Students*, edited by William D. Halsey, a myth is a "traditional story of unknown authorship that expresses a belief of a particular people usually involving gods and heroes. A myth is an attempt to explain a phenomenon of nature, an event in history, or the origin of a particular custom, practice, or religious belief." It is important that students truly have an understanding of this definition; therefore, discuss the following words that are a part of the definition: *heroes, natural phenomenon, event in history, custom, practice, belief, religious belief,* and other pertinent words that come up in the discussion.

2. Have students reread the Aztec myth, *How We Came to the Fifth World*, and discuss and apply the particulars of this definition to this myth. This discussion is in Spanish (rationale stated in objectives 1 and 2).

3. Have students read other myths and apply the particulars or categories of the definition while doing a thorough analysis (critical, contextual, literary, historical, etc.) of myths. It is very important to select myths that are about the students' ethnic and cultural backgrounds and then include myths about other ethnic and cultural groups. This is crucial not only because it will validate students' identities but because it will also increase their understanding of the definition of *myth*, since you are building on the students' own previous background knowledge (culture and possibly history). It is also important to select powerful and meaningful myths (are these myths worthy of reading and writing about?).

4. Have students select myths from the school or city library to share with peers. This will ensure students' participation and responsibility in their own learning. Tell students to choose myths from their own cultural backgrounds to share with the class. This will give students an opportunity to build background knowledge of their own culture and ensure that all ethnic groups have been included and respected. In addition, this activity will offer a demonstration and an informal assessment of students' understanding of *myth* through their respectively selected stories. This offers the class a learning opportunity to decide whether the student-selected stories are really myths or another literary genre. It is important to share stories in the students' primary language and some in English.

5. Teach students interviewing strategies and techniques, since they will be interviewing parents, grandparents, extended-family members, or respected elder friends of the family. Students should plan on interviewing at least three or four people—either one or both parents and grandparents and one or two extended-family members or friends, preferably elders. Together with students, brainstorm what information and/or questions should be in the interview on myths, and then work on a draft. Students should also receive training in tape-recording techniques if this is to be part of the interviewing process.

6. Give students an opportunity to practice the interviewing process before they conduct their interviews. They can interview each other using the draft of the interview on myths. This may be followed by a discussion to decide what information and/or questions are necessary, what should be deleted, what areas need clarification, and so on. A final draft of the interview may then be written and formulated to be used in the actual interviews. Make sure students also have practice time using a tape player when interviewing their peers. Borrow several tape players from other teachers, and do this activity in a cooperative center. Videotape students' interactions as they interview each other.

7. Draft a letter together with students that will be given to all interviewees explaining the interviewing process. Decide what information, steps, and/or procedures are necessary so that interviewees have an understanding of myths and the procedure students will follow to carry out the interview. Explain in the letter that students will do the following: explain the definition of the term *myth,* read one or two myths to interviewees (to promote an understanding of what a myth is), tape record and/or videotape a myth interviewees would like to share. In the letter, emphasize the preference for myths that are generational, but indicate that it is fine to share myths that have been heard outside the family or that have been read. Also stress the importance of sharing powerful myths, worthy of learning, reading, and writing. Emphasize that the interviewees' participation is crucial for the students' fulfillment of the assignment and for the completion of this project.

8. Meet with the whole class to discuss any problems that surfaced when students were conducting their interviews. Make any necessary adjustments, and have students continue their interviews.

9. Have students work in pairs (one dominant English/bilingual proficient student with one student who has less English proficiency) so that they can verbally share their favorite myth bilingually. To do this, students will have to help each other translate their favorite myths. Students can also work in their "language" pairs to type their myths on the computer either in class or in the computer lab.

10. When all mythologies have been typed, compile them into a book and invite interviewees and students to a special program, preferably in the evening when most parents are not working. Have interviewees or students read their recorded myths bilingually. Videotape the program, keeping in mind the way students interact with each other and with interviewees.

Evaluation

1. Assess students' understanding of myths by listening to the myths that students selected from the library.

2. Assess students' understanding of myths by having students identify and label actual myths from teacher-selected pieces of different types of literary genres.

3. Assess students' acquisition of English by conferencing with "language"-paired students and comparing myths recorded in the primary language and the same English translated myths.

4. Assess students' interactions on videotaped copies of student/peer interviews and compare them with videotaped student/interviewee oral presentations.

Resources

Kenfield, K. (1992). "Planning for success." Pacific Grove, CA. (Web site: kkenfield@aol.com.)

Kenfield, K. (1993). "Basics of the classroom where children are writers." Pacific Grove, CA. (Web site: kkenfield@aol.com.)

Rohmer, H., & Anchondo, H. (1976). *How we came to the fifth world/ Como vinimos al quinto mundo*. San Francisco, CA: Children's Book Press.

Samway, K. D. (1992). *Writers' workshop and children acquiring English as a non-native language*. Washington, DC: National Clearinghouse for Bilingual Education.

WHY THE CHANGES?

An Inspirational Glimpse of Aztec Mythologies

Curriculum Content

The "Before" lesson includes content from the cultural tradition of the students, but it is not well developed. The "After" lesson develops children's sense of cultural identity and personal history, which empowers students. If you teach them about their culture, their identity, and their personal histories, this strengthens their sense of who they are, their sense of their own importance. As a consequence, the teacher raises their motivation, self-confidence, rate of learning, and efficiency of learning. Students can take this experience and apply it to other learning situations, becoming more self-directed learners. The "Before" lesson simply lacks this grounding.

Further, the "Before" lesson implies that Aztec mythology lacks truth. The "After" plan encourages students to seek truth in mythology and in the stories passed down through generations in their families.

Instructional Strategies

In the "Before" lesson, the teacher is more in control of learning than are the students. The teacher gives assignments and the students do them. In the "After" lesson, the students are more responsible for their own learning. The "After" lesson uses a writer's workshop, in which students read each other's writing and give feedback. The "After" lesson also has students gather information from their families and teach that to other students. The students act as a teacher to other students, teaching something they learned through the interviewing process.

Many more instructional strategies are used in the "After" plan than in the "Before" plan. The "Before" plan doesn't use technology; the "After" plan uses both computers and videotape recorders.

Home and Community Relationships

In the "Before" lesson, the role of parents is absent. In the "After" lesson, the parent is a participant, involved in education, a teacher. Passing on information from parent or grandparent to child is a powerful learning experience for the child and the family as a whole. This reinforces self-empowerment, self-identity, and the value of knowledge.

Language Use

In the "After" plan there is a more equalized status of the Spanish language. Bilingualism is used—the students' language is used for instruction, and bilingual students' expertise in two languages is used to help those who are not as bilingually proficient.

LESSON PLAN*

BEFORE   Division

Subject Area: Mathematics

Grade Level: 4–8

Time: One class period

---

*Note: This plan can be used to teach various math operations, with or without the aid of a calculator. For example, some teachers do not drill students in long division but instead teach the concept of division and how to compute it on a calculator. The worksheet can be redesigned to reflect this alternative approach.

FIGURE 5.2   Division Worksheet

Work all of the following problems using long division. Show your work!

1. 14)784   2. 23)1702   3. 33)693

4. 56)2352   5. 21)1386   6. 10)320

7. 18)486   8. 30)1350   9. 17)1224

10. 61)1098   11. 25)1275   12. 42)2520

Objective

Students will divide whole numbers using long division.

Suggested Procedures

1. After having demonstrated long division with two-digit divisors the day before, distribute the worksheet shown in Figure 5.2. Have students practice computing long division.

2. Review students' answers in class. Work any problems on the board that students found difficult.

Evaluation

Assess students' mastery of long division by evaluating their worksheets individually.

AFTER

Division: You Too Can Be a Mathematician!

Subject Area: Mathematics

Grade Level: 4–8

Time: One class period

Objectives

1. Students will divide whole numbers using long division.

2. Students will appreciate the contributions made by mathematicians and scientists of various racial backgrounds and both sexes.

3. Students will enjoy practicing mathematics skills.

Suggested Procedures

1. After having demonstrated long division with two-digit divisors the day before, distribute the worksheet shown in Figure 5.3. Explain that it contains a puzzle—a person's name—that they should solve by computing the division problems.

2. When students have completed the exercise, have them tell you the name. On the worksheet, it is Kovalevskaya. Tell students who Sonya Kovalevskaya was, using resource material like those shown in Figure 5.4. Discuss the difficulties she faced because people did not believe a woman should be an excellent mathematician or a university professor.

3. Review the math problems in class. Work any problems on the board that students found difficult.

Evaluation

1. Assess students' mastery of long division by evaluating their worksheets individually.

FIGURE 5.3   Who's the Mathematician?

Work all of the following problems using long division. Show your work! Locate the alphabet letter that corresponds to the correct answer for each problem. Arrange the letters in the order in which problems are numbered to spell the mathematician's name.

1. $14\overline{)784}$ 2. $23\overline{)1702}$ 3. $33\overline{)693}$

4. $56\overline{)2352}$ 5. $21\overline{)1386}$ 6. $10\overline{)320}$

7. $18\overline{)486}$ 8. $30\overline{)1350}$ 9. $17\overline{)1224}$

10. $61\overline{)1098}$ 11. $25\overline{)1275}$ 12. $42\overline{)2520}$

A	B	K	S	L	M	A	Y	O	Q	C	B	T	V	U	K	D	G	O
18	12	56	45	28	37	60	51	43	52	19	39	40	21	54	72	47	45	74

P	Z	O	J	E	S	N	A	G	L	N	E	B	M	C	H	S	O	T
34	22	26	38	32	55	58	42	16	66	73	17	33	76	49	63	75	61	23

I	Y	V	R
44	51	27	29

She is: ___ ___ ___ ___ ___ ___ ___ ___ ___ ___ ___ ___
          1.   2.   3.   4.   5.   6.   7.   8.   9.   10. 11. 12.

Answer Key

1. 56 = K   7. 27 = V
2. 74 = O   8. 45 = S
3. 21 = V   9. 72 = K
4. 42 = A   10. 18 = A
5. 66 = L   11. 51 = Y
6. 32 = E   12. 60 = A

Caroline V. Still Anderson, M.D. (1849–1919). An African American pioneer in medicine. She was refused internship at the Boston New England Hospital for Women and Children the first time she applied because she was Black but was later accepted unanimously. She also helped organize the first Colored Young Women's Christian Association.

Benjamin Banneker (1731–1806). The first African American to publish scientific material. He taught himself math and astronomy and helped survey and draw plans for the site on which Washington, D.C., was built.

F. Chin Chu, Ph.D. (1919–   ) A professor of chemical engineering at Polytech Institute of Brooklyn and one of the foremost chemical engineers in the United States. He has represented the United States at NATO conferences on propulsion and specialized in research on various aspects of propulsion technology.

Charles Alexander Eastman, M.D. (1858–1939). A Sioux physician who received his M.D. from Boston University's School of Medicine in 1890. He practiced at Pine Ridge, South Dakota; St. Paul, Minnesota; and Crow Creek, South Dakota. He also represented the Sioux people in Washington, D.C.

Sir William Rowan Hamilton (1805–1865). One of the greatest mathematicians and scientists to have come from Ireland. He published extensively during the 1800s on optic rays and his theory of quaternions.

Sonya Kovalevskaya, Ph.D. (1850–1891). A Russian woman who became one of the most notable European mathematics researchers in the late 1800s, specializing in mathematical analysis and infinite series. She was unable to attain a teaching position in a Russian university because of her sex but was hired as a lecturer at the University of Stockholm.

Seki Shinsuke Kowa (1642–1708). Considered the greatest mathematician in Japan during the seventeenth century. He was largely self-taught in math and mechanics. He developed theories in calculus and in solving higher equations and used determinants in solving simultaneous equations.

David Sanchez, Ph.D. (1933–   ). A professor of mathematics at the University of New Mexico. He conducts research on direct methods in the calculus of variations and nonlinear ordinary differential equations.

Chien Shiung Wu, Ph.D. (1929–   ). A Chinese American woman who is one of the world's leading physicists and a professor of physics at Columbia University. She conducted important research on particles of the nucleus of an atom.

Grace Chisholm Young, Ph.D. (1868–1944). An English mathematician and a productive researcher in number theory and geometry. She collaborated with her husband on several books, including books on how to teach math to children.

FIGURE 5.4   Resource Material: Mathematicians and Scientists

Sources: Bell, E. T. (1965). *Men of mathematics.* New York: Simon & Schuster; Olson, L. M. (1974). *Women in mathematics.* Cambridge, MA: M.I.T. Press; Perl, T. (1978). *Math equals.* Menlo Park, CA: Addison-Wesley; and Smith, D. E. (1958). *History of mathematics,* vols. I and II. New York: Dover.

2. Assess students' enjoyment and appreciation of math through their participation in the activity.

Division: You Too Can Be a Mathematician

Curriculum Content

The "Before" plan stresses only practice in a mathematical skill. The addition of the puzzle to the worksheet in the "After" plan does at least two things. First, it makes the drill worksheet more fun. Second, it allows the teacher to teach about people who have contributed to the fields of math and science, particularly women and men of color. Students often do not connect math with people, particularly with people who are not white men.

LESSON PLAN

Fables

Subject Area: Language Arts

Grade Level: 4–8

Time: Two class periods

Objectives

1. Students will explain that fables are used as a literary device to teach about human behavior, using animals to represent humans.

2. Students will appreciate and enjoy fables.

3. Students will create a fable to express a concern about human behavior.

Suggested Procedures

1. Using the fable "The Lion and the Mouse" by Aesop, first ask students to predict what the fable is about from its title. After reading the fable, help students to discover the lesson of the story and to apply it to human behavior.

2. Discuss the purpose of fables. Ask students to suggest how this literary device can be effective.

3. Have students read additional fables, such as "The Hare and the Tortoise" by Aesop. Discuss the lesson in each fable and the human characteristics represented by the animals.

4. Instruct students to write their own fables, using animals to represent human behavior. Encourage them to use this exercise as a device for illustrating behavior they would like to see people change.

Evaluation

1. Assess students' understanding of the use of fables through class discussion and the fables they write.

2. Assess students' enjoyment of fables through class discussion.

AFTER

Fables

Subject Area: Language Arts

Grade Level: 4–8

Time: Two or three class periods

Objectives

1. Students will explain that fables are used by different cultures as a literary device to teach about human behavior, using animals to represent humans.

2. Students will appreciate and enjoy the fables of various cultures.

3. Students will create a fable to express a concern about human behavior.

Suggested Procedures

1. Using the fable "The Lion and the Mouse" by Aesop, first ask students to predict what the fable is about from its title. After reading the fable, help students to discover the lesson of the story and to apply it to human behavior.

2. Discuss the purpose of fables; show students books and records of fables from various cultures, pointing out that many different peoples have used fables. Ask students to suggest how this literary device can be effective and how it is used by different cultural groups.

3. Also, to help students see that what is appropriate behavior in one culture may not be the same in another culture, lead them in a discussion of how fables from different cultures may be similar to or different from each other. Encourage them to compare and contrast the lessons about human behavior that are being taught through the fables.

4. Read "The Partridge and the Crow," an Asian Indian fable from the book *The Panchatantra* (1964). Discuss the implications of the fable, which tells of a crow who tried to imitate the gait of the partridge; the crow forgot her own walk and never learned that of the partridge.

5. Point out to students that some cultures have taught children appropriate behavior through stories told orally. Play the recording of "The Light in the House" (1970), an Ethiopian oral fable. Discuss the lesson that the fable teaches about greed. As another example of an oral fable, play the recording of "Mockingbird Sings Many Songs" (1970), a Navajo fable. Point out how the Navajo used lessons observed in nature to remind people how to behave, as the mockingbird was rewarded with a gift of many songs for his generosity in supplying the birds with a song.

6. Instruct students to write or tape record a fable, using animals to represent human behavior. Encourage students to use this exercise as a device for illustrating behavior they would like to see people change.

Evaluation

1. Assess students' understanding of the use of fables through class discussion and the fables they create.

2. Assess students' enjoyment of fables through class discussion.

Resources

Aesop. (1975). "The lion and the grateful mouse." In P. Gregory & J. Gregory (trans.), *The fables of Aesop*. Boston: Gambit.

"The light in the house." (1970). In *African village folktales*, vol. 3. New York: Caedmon Records.

"Mockingbird sings many songs." (1970). In *Navajo bird tales*. Wheaton, IL: Theosophical Publishing House.

Ryder, A. W. (Trans.). (1964). The partridge and the crow. In *The Panchatantra*. Chicago: University of Chicago Press.

WHY THE CHANGES?

Fables

Curriculum Content

The "Before" plan presents examples of fables from only one cultural source, yet many cultural groups have used this literary form. In contrast, the "After" plan uses fables from a variety of cultural groups, which helps students to develop an understanding of more than one cultural tradition. It also enriches the concept of fable by providing a variety of examples and shows that people of different cultural groups share many of the same concerns about human behavior. Further, the Asian Indian fable teaches a lesson about diversity—that one should be proud of who one is and not try to imitate someone else.

Instructional Strategies

The "Before" plan includes only written fables, whereas the "After" plan presents both written and oral fables. The use of oral fables teaches students that cultures without writing systems did have a form of sophisticated literature, one requiring acute listening and memory skills. Further, oral fables are particularly meaningful to students with low reading levels.

The "After" plan allows students to write or tape record their own fables (the option of tape recording is not provided in the "Before" plan). Another alternative is to permit students to work in small cooperative groups of two or three to create the fables.

LESSON PLAN

BEFORE

Wholesale and Retail

Subject Area: Math

Grade Levels: 5–8

Time: Four days

Objectives

1. Students will define the terms *wholesale, retail, mark-up, mark-down,* and *supply and demand.*

2. Students will describe how these concepts influence shopping.

Suggested Procedures

1. Explain to students the meanings of the concepts *wholesale, retail, mark-up, mark-down,* and *supply and demand.*

2. Have students clip advertisements that are examples of the these concepts.

3. Have students compute price changes, using percentages and decimals, based on story problems from newspaper advertisements about pricing of various items.

4. Invite proprietors from local stores to the class and have them give examples of how supply and demand of merchandise will influence the mark-up and/or mark-down of the goods.

Evaluation

Assess students' understanding of the meanings of *wholesale, retail, mark-up, mark-down,* and *supply and demand* through discussion and written exam.

AFTER

Carpets and Rugs from Asia

Subject Areas: Math, Economics, Social Studies, Art

Grade Level: 5–8

Time: Two weeks

Objectives

1. Students will discover how money and tradition often serve as excuses for some in power to argue against making constructive changes.

2. Students will identify the term *oriental rug* as one that many Asian Americans find offensive, although it is commonly used to refer to carpets made in Asia.

3. Students will define the terms *wholesale, retail, mark-up, mark-down,* and *supply and demand*.

4. Students will examine carpets and rugs from Asia for different mathematical designs and artistic beauty.

5. Students will distinguish between hand-knotted Asian rugs and machine-made Asian rugs and between their prices and artistic value.

6. Students will identify countries where hand-knotted Asian rugs are made, the people who make them (e.g., race, class, gender), and the way they are made.

7. Students will discover who makes the most money from the sale of hand-knotted Asian rugs: the maker, the dealer, or the owner of the store where they are sold.

Suggested Procedures

1. Have students discuss why the use of some words and phrases that have been a part of U.S. folkways is considered insensitive to certain groups (e.g., *paddy wagon, oriental, noble savage, blacklisted, lame*). Remember, many of these terms were developed by European Americans at a time when the United States was not as aware of and/or concerned about racial and other issues regarding marginalized groups as we are now. Therefore, the origin and history of these taken-for-granted terms need to be discussed and challenged.

2. Ask students why some people are against changing and/or eliminating the use of certain words and phrases, (e.g., *Cleveland Indians, Chicago Blackhawks, ori-*

ental rug) to describe a team or a product. Have students conduct interviews to collect responses to the question. Next, have students analyze the responses to determine whether there are categories of reasons (e.g., tradition, financial market image).

3. Explain to students the meanings of the words *wholesale, retail, overhead,* and *supply and demand.*

4. Take the students on a field trip to a store that specializes in the selling of carpets made in Asia, and/or invite a dealer/seller of Asian rugs to visit the class. Have the dealer/seller bring along several examples of hand-knotted and machine-made Asian rugs so he or she can explain the difference between the two (e.g., how they are made, how the design and style of hand-knotted rugs give specific information on where they are made, how the colors of the rugs look different when examined from different angles).

5. Invite a home decorator from a department store and have him or her provide a cost comparison between the hand-knotted and the machine-made Asian rugs, and have him or her explain the difference between wholesale and retail cost.

6. Set up an Asian rugs center, including color pictures of different sizes of Asian rugs from different locations. Also have several picture books that provide historical information on Asian rugs.

7. Have students consult the World Wide Web for information on where Asian rugs are made, the people who make them, and these people's way of life.

8. Explain that rugs, like other commodities, pass through several hands in the process of economic exchange: the laborers, the factory owners, wholesalers, and retailers, such as local store owners. Help students to conduct research on the amount of money from the sale of rugs that goes to each person or role group (i.e., from production to final sale). If possible, find out whether there is a gender distinction in this chain of work and profit. Invite students to question who profits most from the production and sale of Asian carpets and rugs.

9. Ask students to compare and contrast how various individuals they encountered during this unit talked about Asian rugs, and formulate hypotheses as to how one's relationship to the rug production and selling process affects one's viewpoint.

10. Using census data on annual income, have students identify which families can most likely afford to purchase hand-knotted Asian rugs.

Evaluation

1. Assess students' understanding of why the term *oriental* is seen by many people as a negative or inappropriate term through class discussion.

2. Assess students' understanding of the terms *wholesale, retail, mark-up, markdown,* and *supply and demand* in a written essay or exam.

3. Assess students' ability to tell the difference between machine-made rugs and hand-knotted rugs in small-group discussions.

4. Students will create an art project in which they represent visually what they learned from this unit about Asian rugs and economics.

5. Assess students' understanding of where Asian carpets are made, who makes them, and how these people live through a written essay.

WHY THE CHANGES?

Carpets and Rugs from Asia

Curriculum Content

The "After" plan helps students to see that materials that come out of non-Western areas can serve as a primary source to gain knowledge. In the "Before" plan, the concepts are presented almost in isolation of anything else, although they are connected to advertising that students might encounter. The "After" plan connects several disciplines to provide students with a richer experience and with a more in-depth examination of key concepts. It is longer than the "Before" lesson because it is interdisciplinary and connects several subject areas. This would require some planning across subject areas.

Also, the "After" plan prompts students to begin to think about social and economic inequities by examining who profits the most from the sale of the rugs. Often we romanticize imported commodities without questioning social class relationships. Students are also encouraged to question traditions and commonly accepted terms that are not respectful of cultural groups of color and other marginalized groups and to consider the reasons for the maintenance of and allegiance to these traditions.

Multiple Perspectives

The "After" plan encourages students to examine the opinions of the home decorator and the dealer/seller and to compare and contrast the information they collect. Here students will have to analyze and critique the information they receive. Also, the "After" plan encourages students to examine the positions of the various people involved in the production and sale of the rugs. Here they judge whether they would rather be a rug maker, wholesaler, or retailer and how these positions influence the way people living in these different roles live. Students examine the amount of weight that these different people assign to the artistic versus the economic value of the rugs.

Visuals

The "After" plan presents the students with curriculum material (rugs) that comes from different countries and regions in Asia.

LESSON PLAN

Techniques of Painting

Subject Area: Art

Grade Level: 7–9

Time: Two weeks

Objective

Students will express emotion through sketching and painting, using at least two of the techniques of color, contrast, perspective, form, line, subject matter, and texture to give meaning to an art form.

Suggested Procedures

1. Review with students the following techniques of painting, asking them to take notes during your review:

    Color

    Contrast

    Perspective or space

    Form or relationship of the shapes

    Line

    Meaning or subject matter

    Texture

2. Show slides of paintings by the U.S. American artists John Copley, Gilbert Stuart, George Caleb Bingham, Thomas Cole, and James A.McNeill Whistler. Review each technique thoroughly as you discuss the paintings with the class, making sure that students write down important information related to technique (e.g., sharp lines, dull colors, smooth textures). Ask students how each painting makes them feel (e.g., happy, sad, bored, angry, mixed up) and record their answers. Point out the elements in each painting that convey an emotional response and how these elements work together to convey the meaning of the work.

3. Over the remaining days of the unit, ask students to complete three sketches and one painting in which they use at least two of the techniques discussed to convey personal meaning. Have students share their final products with each other.

Evaluation

1. Assess students' understanding of the concepts presented through discussion of the slides. With practice, students are better able to identify the important elements in the paintings.

2. Assess students' understanding of the concepts presented through their sketches and paintings.

AFTER

Techniques of Painting[*]

Subject Area: Art

Grade Level: 7–9

Time: Two weeks

Objectives

1. Students will express emotion through sketching and painting, using at least two of the techniques of color, contrast, perspective, form, line, subject matter, and texture to give meaning to an art form.

2. Students will learn that different ethnic groups use art to convey meaning across cultural barriers, regardless of the time period in which the art work is completed.

Suggested Procedures

1. Tell students that they will examine six U.S. American paintings from the 1930s. Also note that, as they study U.S. American cultural history of the 1930s during the next week in their U.S. American history class, they will learn how these paintings portray the styles of the period.

2. Have prints or posters of works by the following U.S. American artists displayed around the room (these artists are of diverse racial and ethnic backgrounds and sexual orientations and of both sexes): Consuelo Gonzalez Amezcua, Mary Cassatt, Helen Frankenthaler, H. N. Han, Keith Haring, Richard Hunt, Frida Kahlo, Jacob Lawrence, Piet Mondrian, Elie Nadelman, Louise Nevelson, Isamu Noguchi, Georgia O'Keefe, Lucas Samaras, Grandma Moses, Raphael Soyer, Joseph Stella, Yves Tanguy, Andy Warhol, and Charles White.

3. Review with students the following techniques of painting, using the works by the preceding artists as examples:

> Color
>
> Contrast
>
> Perspective or space
>
> Form or relationship of the shapes
>
> Line

---

[*]*Source:* David Castañeda, Waukesha Public Schools, Waukesha, WI.

      Meaning or subject matter

      Texture

4. Show the following pair of slides:

      Ben Shan, "Passion of Sacco and Vanzetti" (1931–1932)

      Raphael Soyer, "Under the Bridge" (1932)

Explain that both men were white immigrants from Russia, and tell why each came to the United States. Review each technique thoroughly as you compare and contrast the two paintings, making sure that students write down important information related to technique (sharp lines, dull colors, smooth textures, and so on). Ask students how each painting makes them feel (e.g., happy, sad, bored, angry, mixed up), and record their answers. Point out the elements in each painting that convey an emotional response and how these elements work together to convey the meaning of the work. If evident, emphasize how the artists reflect their cultural heritage.

5. Continue to the next pair of slides:

      Diego Rivera, "New Workers School" (mural, 1933)

      Antonio Garcia, "Woman Before a Mirror" (1935)

Explain that both artists were born in Mexico and that Garcia became a U.S. American citizen. Give the historical context of each painting. Repeat the procedure outlined in item 4.

6. Continue to the last pair of slides:

      Allan Crite, "Tyre Jumping" (1936)

      Charles White, "Fatigue" (1940)

Explain that both artists were African Americans, and briefly summarize the historical context of each painting. Repeat the procedure in item 4.

7. Hang all six prints on the wall. Have students discuss how the different artists used the techniques discussed earlier to convey emotion and meaning and how this transcends culture. Help students to recognize the particular ways an artist's cultural background influences his or her work, as well as the universals in art itself that transcend culture.

8. Over the remaining days of the unit, ask students to complete three sketches and one painting in which they use at least two of the techniques discussed to convey personal meaning. Have students share their final products with each other.

Evaluation

1. Assess students' understanding of the concepts presented through discussion of each pair of slides. With practice, students are better able to identify the important elements in the paintings.

2. Assess students' understanding of the concepts presented through their sketches and paintings.

3. Assess students' understanding of the cultural diversity and universality of art through class discussion.

WHY THE CHANGES?

Techniques of Painting

Curriculum Materials

The "Before" plan uses mainly paintings by white male artists, whereas the "After" plan presents the work of a variety of U.S. American artists, including white European Americans, Latinos, and African Americans, among others.

Curriculum Content

The "Before" plan focuses solely on the techniques of painting. In contrast, the "After" plan extends this focus into broader concepts involving art. One such concept is how art reflects its historical period; by linking the art class with the history class, the plan helps students learn an interdisciplinary concept. Another concept presented by the "After" plan is how culture is reflected in art, which is achieved by drawing on artists whose cultural backgrounds differ. And the concept of art as a universal, cross-cultural language is also taught through examples of artwork produced by members of diverse cultural groups.

Visuals

The "Before" plan does not specify the kinds of visuals to be displayed around the room. However, the "After" plan specifies that visuals should represent U.S. American artists of diverse racial and ethnic backgrounds and both sexes.

LESSON PLAN

BEFORE

Our National Anthem

Subject Area: Music

Grade Level: 6–10

Time: One class period

Objectives

1. Students will sing the national anthem.
2. Students will explain why the national anthem was written.

Suggested Procedures

1. Pass out the lyrics to "The Star-Spangled Banner" and ask students to read them. Review the song's history and discuss the types of events at which the anthem is commonly sung.
2. Play a recording of "The Star-Spangled Banner" and have students sing along. Then ask them to sing it without the aid of the recording.

Evaluation

Assess how well the class learns and sings the national anthem.

AFTER   ## Our National Anthems

Subject Area: Music
Grade Level: 5–10
Time: Two class periods

Objectives

1. Students will recognize the national anthems written by several U.S. American groups.
2. Students will describe the purpose of a national anthem.
3. Students will sing "The Star-Spangled Banner."

Suggested Procedures

1. Ask students to sing their school song. Have them discuss why they sing it and what their school song tells about the school. Use this discussion as a basis for examining anthems.
2. Pass out the lyrics to anthems such as the following (see Figure 5.5):
   "The Star-Spangled Banner"
   "Himno Nacional" (Mexican national anthem)
   "Lift Every Voice and Sing" (Black National Anthem)
   "Bread and Roses" (women's anthem)[*]

---

[*]To obtain "Bread and Roses," by Judy Collins, write to 1976 Electra 1076, 75 Rockefeller Plaza, New York, NY 10019.

The Star-Spangled Banner

Lyrics by Francis Scott Key
Music by J. Stafford Smith

O say can you see, by the dawn's early light,
What so proudly we hail'd at the twilight's last gleaming,
Whose broad stripes and bright stars, thro' the perilous fight,
O'er the ramparts we watch'd were so gallantly streaming?
And the rockets' red glare, the bombs bursting in air,
Gave proof thro' the night that our flag was still there.
O, say, does that Star-Spangled Banner yet wave
O'er the land of the free and the home of the brave.

On the shore, dimly seen thro' the mists of the deep,
Where the foe's haughty host in dread silence reposes,
What is that which the breeze, o'er the towering steep,
As it fitfully blows, half conceals, half discloses?
Now it catches the gleam of the morning's first beam,
In full glory reflected now shines on the stream;
'Tis the Star-Spangled Banner, O long may it wave
O'er the land of the free and home of the brave.

O thus be it ever when free man shall stand
Between their loved homes and the war's desolation!
Blest with vict'ry and peace, may the heav'n-rescued land
Praise the Pow'r that hath made and preserved us a nation.
Then conquer we must, for our cause it is just,
And this be our motto: "In God is our trust."
And the Star-Spangled Banner in triumph shall wave
O'er the land of the free and the home of the brave.

FIGURE 5.5   National Anthems

Arrange students into small groups and assign an anthem to each group. Have students write down what they think each anthem says about the group that wrote it and why they think the group wrote the anthem.

3. Have each group report to the class, writing down key points on the board. After they report on each anthem, tell of the history of the anthems.

4. Discuss the following question: If "The Star-Spangled Banner" is the anthem of all U.S. Americans, why have some groups written their own anthems?

5. Play recordings of the anthems, asking students to sing along. Choose some favorites to learn as a class.

The Black National Anthem
(Lift Every Voice and Sing)

Lyrics by James Weldon Johnson

Lift every voice and sing,
'Till earth and heaven ring,
Ring with the harmonies of Liberty.
Let our rejoicing rise,
High as the list'ning skies
Let it resound loud as the rolling sea
Sing a song full of the faith that the dark past has taught us
Sing a song full of the hope that the present has brought us;
Facing the rising sun of our new day begun,
Let us march on till victory is won.

Stony the road we trod,
Bitter the chast'ng rod,
Felt in the days when hope unborn had died;
Yet with a steady beat,
Have not our weary feet
Come to the place for which our fathers signed?
We have come over a way that with tears has been watered
We have come, treading our path thro' the blood of the slaughtered,
Out from the gloomy past, till now we stand at last
Where the white gleam of our bright star is cast.

God of our weary years,
God of our silent tears,
Thou who hast brought us thus far on our way;
Thou who has by Thy might,
Let us into the light,
Keep us forever in the path, we pray
Lest our feet stray from the places, our God, where we met Thee;
Lest our hearts drunk with the wine of the world we forget Thee;
Shadowed beneath Thy hand, may we forever stand
True to our God, True to our Native land.

Evaluation

1. Assess students' understanding of the purpose of a national anthem through class discussion.

2. Assess students' ability to sing the anthems.

WHY THE CHANGES?

Our National Anthems

Curriculum Content

The "Before" plan assumes that there is only one national anthem sung by U.S. Americans and uses it as the sole example of an anthem. The "After" plan

Himno Nacional

Lyrics by Francisco Gonzalez Bocanegra
Music by Jaime Nuno

Mexicans when the trumpet is calling,
Grasp your sword and your harness assemble.
Let the guns with their thunder appalling
Make the Earth's deep foundations to tremble.
Let the guns with their thunder appalling
Make the Earth's deep foundations to tremble.

Mexicanos al grito de guerra
El acero aprestad yel bridón.
Y retiemble en sus centros la tierra
Al sonoro rugir del cañón,
Y retiemble en sus centros la tierra
Al sonoro rugir del cañón,

May the angel divine, O Dear Homeland,
Crown thy brow with the olive branch of peace;
For thy destiny, traced by God's own hand
In the heavens, shall ever increase.
But shall ever the proud foe assail thee,
And with insolent foot profane thy ground,
Know, dear Country, thy sons shall not fail thee,
Ev'ry one thy soldier shall be found, Thy soldier ev'ry one shall be found.

¡Ciñe ¡Oh patria! tus sienes de oliva
De la paz el arcángel divino
Que en el cielo tueterno destino
Por el dedo de Dios se escribió
Mas si osare un extraño enemigo
Profanar con su planta tu suelo
Piensa ¡Oh patria querida! queel cielo
Un soldado en cada hijo te dió, Un soldado en cada hijo te dió.

Blessed Homeland, thy children have vowed them
If the bugle to battle should call,
They will fight with the last breath allowed them
Till on thy loved altars they fall.
Let the garland of olive thine be;
Unto them be deathless fame;
Let the laurel of victory be assigned thee,
Enough for them the tomb's honored name.

En sangrientos combates los viste
Por tu amor palpitando sus senos,
Arrostrar la metralla serenos,
Y la muerte o la gloria buscar.
Si el recuerdo de antiguas hazañas,
De tus hijos inflama la mente,
Los laureles del triunfo, tu frente
Volverán inmortales a ornar.

FIGURE 5.5, *continued*

makes several changes. First, it adds an analogue to an anthem from students' experience: the school song. Second, it draws on anthems sung by several different U.S. American groups to teach that there is more than one anthem sung by U.S. Americans, even though virtually all U.S. Americans also sing "The Star-Spangled Banner." Third, it teaches what an anthem is by offering several different examples and asking students to identify what they have in common.

Multiple Perspectives

The "After" plan includes multiple perspectives in two ways. First, students are provided with multiple anthems that were written from the perspectives of different groups for expressing group sentiment. Second, in small groups, students are encouraged to gain different perspectives from their peers on the purpose of an anthem.

Language Diversity

"Himno Nacional" is sung in Spanish; in our experience, it is useful in classes that contain Mexican American students. They appreciate hearing it. Other U.S. American cultural groups also have anthems that may not be in English; these can be translated for study or learned in their original language.

Instructional Strategies

Students are in a passive role in the "Before" plan, whereas small-group work places students in an active role in the "After" plan, allowing them to think together and to create part of what they are learning. The modalities used in the "Before" plan consist of reading, listening, and singing. The "After" plan adds small-group discussion and cooperative student–student interaction, which are not present in the "Before" plan.

Visuals

Although visuals are not described, the "After" plan can be modified to include such visuals as pictures of different artists singing "The Star-Spangled Banner," flags or emblems associated with different anthems to be studied, or pictures taken at events during which anthems are sung.

LESSON PLAN

BEFORE

U.S. History

Subject Area: Social Studies
Grade Level: 7–12
Time: Ongoing

Objectives

1. Students will identify the names associated with historic events.

2. Students will describe the causes of major historic events, such as the Mexican-American War.

3. Students will describe contributions that different sociocultural groups made to those historic events.

Suggested Procedures

1. Select a time period or event in history, such as the Mexican-American War of 1846. Ask students what they already know about that event, and brainstorm their responses on the board.

2. Have students read the textbook account of this war or other event being studied.

3. Supplement their reading with a lecture, film, or video that expands on significant parts of the material. For example, when studying the Mexican-American War, the story of "The Alamo" can be taught.

4. Identify four to six significant historical figures who played a part in the event being studied. For example, if the Mexican-American War is being studied, the historical figures could include Pres. James K. Polk, John C. Fremont, Kit Carson, Samuel Houston, Gen. Zachary Taylor, Gen. Mariano Vallejo, and Gen. Antonio Lopez de Santa Ana. Have each student select one figure and find out what kind of a person he or she was and what contribution he or she made to history. Students should write sketches of the person they select.

Evaluation

Evaluate students' ability to identify names and events and to explain causality through a written test as well as through oral class participation.

AFTER   ## HyperMedia History

Subject Area: Social Studies

Grade Level: 7–12

Time: Ongoing

Objectives

1. Students will identify the names associated with historic events.

2. Students will recognize that often different sociocultural groups perceive and experience the same historic event or time period differently.

3. Students will compare and contrast perspectives of dominant and subordinate groups historically.

4. Students will collect research information from diverse sources.

5. Students will represent different perspectives and experiences using hypertext and/or hypermedia.*

Suggested Procedures

1. Select a time period or event in history, such as the Mexican-American War of 1846. Have available a variety of history texts, such as a standard U.S. history textbook, *The Latino Experience in U.S. History* (Globe, 1994), *The African American Experience* (Globe, 1992), *Indian Country* (Harvey & Harjo, 1994), *A People's History of the United States* (Zinn, 1995), *A Different Mirror* (Takaki, 1993), *Caribbean Connections* (Sunshine & Menkart, 1991), *Japanese American Journey* (Japanese American Curriculum Project, 1985), and *Lies My Teacher Told Me* (Loewen, 1995).

2. Have students read the standard textbook account of this war (or any other event the class is studying). Then have them brainstorm as many different sociocultural groups as they can who may have viewed or experienced this event or time period differently from, as well as similarly to, the textbook account (including anyone in the textbook account). If they are studying the Mexican-American War, their list should include, for example, Pres. James K. Polk, the Mexican government, Mexican people in territory that is now part of the United States, different Native American nations in that same territory, Anglo Americans in that territory, African American leaders during that time period, and so forth.

3. Assign each item on the list to a small group of students whose task is to find out as much as they can about how the person or sociocultural group they are assigned experienced and/or perceived this war. In the process, students should note any significant differences within the group they are assigned (such as gender differences and tribal differences) that may emerge in their investigations.

4. The class will create a *Hyperstudio* program about this historic event. Each small group is responsible for creating one or more cards that include text information (such as excerpts from speeches and summaries of textbook accounts or other books) and can also include pictures, maps, diagrams, and so on. When scrollable text inserts are used, text information can be fairly extensive.

5. When students have completed their *Hyperstudio* cards, have each group present their cards. Then as a class determine how to link them electronically. To do this, students will need to consider what events relate most directly, how events relate, and so forth. Students can then enter appropriate buttons or

---

Note: This teaching process uses the computer program *Hyperstudio* and assumes that students know how to use it. Teachers who do not have access to *Hyperstudio* or *Hypercard* can adapt this teaching process to more common text formats, although doing so will lose some of the multidimensionality of the process.

hypertext links into their cards to create links. Do not rush through this process, since determining how best to link cards will cause students to examine relationships between events and between groups.

6. Have each student view the linked package about this event and look for any significant patterns. Students may record and present their observations in a variety of ways, such as in a journal each student keeps to record her or his analysis of each historic event that is studied.

7. Hold a class discussion in which students present and discuss their own analyses of patterns they discovered. The class can then use insights from this discussion to finish its *Hyperstudio* package of this historic time frame or event.

Evaluation

1. Evaluate each group's card(s) for accuracy, comprehensiveness, and general success in locating and presenting appropriate information.

2. Evaluate each individual student's analysis of historic patterns, such as the student's ability to identify patterns of aggression or to connect nationalism and military power.

3. Evaluate the class's success in identifying and representing different perspectives and experiences, linking these in a meaningful way and abstracting historic insights from the process of doing this.

WHY THE CHANGES?

HyperMedia History

Curriculum Materials and Multiple Perspectives

History textbooks today include a wider diversity of people than they did previously, and many educators assume that this is enough to make history multicultural. The "Before" plan makes the assumption that materials are already multicultural and that by including a few Mexican names in studying an event (such as the Mexican-American War) that event is being taught fairly.

What is missing from any single text, however, are diverse perspectives not only presented in depth but used to organize the entire account of U.S. history. There are several books available that provide teachers and students with diverse perspectives, although each book presents mainly the perspective of the authors of that book. Some of these are included with the "After" lesson plan. No single book represents a plurality of perspectives, but the collection taken together does.

In addition, the "After" plan provides a way for students to examine and acknowledge diverse interpretations and perspectives, without having to reduce them to one main "storyline" on history. Hypertext or hypermedia programs lend themselves well to representing different experiences, linking these where appropriate and leaving them unlinked where appropriate. Students can juxtapose three or four different experiences taking place at the same time in the same geographic area, without having to reduce these to one story.

Instructional Strategies

The "Before" plan depends on the textbook, lecture, additional reading, and possibly a film or video for instruction. This presents students with a rather limited array of ways to learn. The "After" plan expands ways of learning considerably. Students find *Hyperstudio* very engaging to use. As a multimedia program, it allows students to learn and create through text, pictures, maps, diagrams, and so forth. Students can work alone or cooperatively on their cards. The final product is a complex multimedia package that can be burned onto a CD-ROM disk. Completing this kind of project lends itself to different student talents and interests and is inherently motivating to many students today.

Resources

Harley, S., Middleton, S., & Stokes, C. (Consultants). (1992). *The African American experience*. Paramus, NJ: Globe Fearon.

Harvey, K. D., & Harjo, L. D. (1994). *Indian country*. Golden, CO: North American Press.

Japanese American Curriculum Project. (1985). *Japanese American journey*. Sacramento, CA: Spilman Printing.

Caban, Pedro A. (Ed.). (1994). *The Latino experience in U.S. history*. Paramus, NJ: Globe Fearon.

Loewen, J. W. (1995). *Lies my teacher told me*. New York: New Press.

Sunshine, C. A., & Menkart, D. (1991). *Caribbean connections*. Washington, DC: Network of Educators on Central America.

Takaki, R. (1993). *A different mirror*. Boston: Little, Brown.

Zinn, H. (1995). *A people's history of the United States* (rev. ed.). New York: Harper & Row.

LESSON PLAN

BEFORE

John Steinbeck[*]

Subject Area: English

Grade Level: 9–12

Time: Five to six days

[*]*Source:* Anne Fairbrother, Salinas Union High School District, Salinas, CA.

Objectives

1. Students will appreciate John Steinbeck as an author who wrote about his concern for migrant workers and exploitation.

2. Students will identify the main features of Steinbeck's writing style and subject matter.

Suggested Procedures

1. Introduce Steinbeck. Tell students of Steinbeck's work and his concern for migrant workers. He was concerned with social exploitation wherever he found it, and he chronicled the life of the poor and downtrodden. He was banned in Salinas for many years because he wrote an exposé of the owners of the land where the migrant workers were treated badly, and also because it was a small town—people did not like to read about themselves in his accurate stories!

2. Let students self-select into groups of no more than four students, and assign them a research project: to use the school library, the public library, computer resources, and textbook sources to prepare a multimedia presentation (with speeches, enactments, illustrations, video, audio, etc.) about Steinbeck's life and his major works. Set up a time line for group work in class, for the declaration of each member's research focus, and for presentations. Let students know that there will be two grades, one for the group presentation and one for the individual research handed in. Explain the criteria for a good presentation.

3. Read two stories by Steinbeck: "The Leader of the People," from *The Red Pony*, and a selection from *Travels with Charley*.

   Prepare quizzes, discussion questions, and free write topics as appropriate.

Evaluation

1. Assess students' comprehension of Steinbeck's writing style and subject matter through graded quizzes, individual free writes, and group discussions.

2. Assess students' understanding of Steinbeck's life and concerns through their presentation. Students will receive two grades for the presentation: one grade for the quality of presentation and one grade for the written research.

Resources

"The leader of the people," from *The red pony*. (1973). In J. E. Miller, R. Hayden, & R. O'Neal (Eds.), *The United States in literature*. Glenview, IL: Scott Foresman.

"*Travels with Charley.*" (1989). In David W. Foote (Ed.), *Literature: Blue level.* Evanston, IL: McDougal, Littell.

AFTER

Literature on Migrant Workers and Exploitation

Subject Area: English

Grade Level: 9–12

Time: Seven to eight days

Objectives

1. Students will examine conditions of working and living for migrant workers in rural California from different cultural perspectives.

2. Students will describe the main features of the writing styles of Carlos Bulosan, Raymund Barrio, and John Steinbeck.

3. Students will identify and understand rich metaphorical language.

Suggested Procedures

1. Find out what students know about the Philippines. its Independence Day? length of Spanish rule? length of U.S. American occupation? nature and extent of resistance? Tell of Filipino involvement with the United Farm Workers in Delano before César Chavez was involved.

2. Tell students that they will be reading three chapters from the book *America Is in the Heart*, an autobiography by Carlos Bulosan. In the book, Bulosan recounts his life in the Philippines, his journey to the United States, and his experiences working in the canneries in Alaska and in California fields and orchards. (Carlos Bulosan was born in 1913, came to the United States in 1930, and died in 1956).

3. Read the first chapter of *America Is in the Heart* aloud or silently. Afterward, students will take a quiz, part of which will involve a description of life in the Philippines as Bulosan was growing up there: "Describe—paint a picture with words—what you remember of the life of the peasant farmer and his family."

4. After the quiz, students will create a booklet for work to be done in response to this and two more chapters from *America Is in the Heart*, the booklet should have three to six lined pages, three blank pages, and a blank cover.

5. Students will write a double entry journal response to three self-selected quotes from the chapter. Then they will draw a picture illustrating one scene from the chapter, and they will create a title for the chapter.

6. Read Chapter 13 of *America Is in the Heart*, which tells of Bulosan's journey to the United States in 1930, when he was seventeen years old. Afterward, students will write a double entry journal response to three quotes from the chapter. Then they will draw a picture illustrating one scene from the chapter, and they will create a title for the chapter.

7. Read Chapter 19 of the book, which is set in the California fields and orchards in 1941, when there was great anti-Asian sentiment in the United States. Afterward, students will write a double entry journal response to three quotes from the chapter. Then they will draw a picture illustrating one scene from the chapter, and they will create a title for the chapter.

8. Students will then create a cover for their responses to the three chapters from the book.

9. Read Chapter 10 from *The Plum Plum Pickers*, by Raymund Barrio. After reading, have students work in groups to answer questions about what happens in the story and about some of the major images in the story.

10. As a last assignment in the group, ask students to identify and explain images and metaphors in the story: "As the story was read aloud, you should have noted that throughout the story there is vivid imagery. Find one vivid image each and explain what the image is and how or why it is effective."

11. When you give students back their work, go over many of the images as a class, on the board, showing denotations and connotations of images, and assess power and vividness of the metaphors.

12. Introduce Steinbeck. Discuss the realities of life for farm workers as seen in the stories we have just read. Tell students of Steinbeck's work and concern for migrant workers. He was concerned with social exploitation wherever he found it, and he chronicled the life of the poor and downtrodden. He was banned in Salinas for many years because he wrote an exposé of the owners of the land where the migrant workers were treated so badly, and also because it was a small town—people did not like to read about themselves in his accurate stories!

13. Read one of Steinbeck's novels: *Grapes of Wrath*, *In Dubious Battle*, or *Of Mice and Men* are suggested. Specific suggestions for teaching his work are not developed here, as they will be familiar to most English teachers.

Evaluation

1. Assess students' understanding of rural life in the Philippines in the early twentieth century through the quiz on Chapter 1 of *America Is in the Heart*.

2. Assess students' comprehension of living and working conditions for migrant workers in rural California through their booklets containing their journal

responses, drawings, and titles and their group work on *The Plum Plum Pickers*; these assignments should be graded.

3. Assess students' identification of the main features of the writing styles of Carlos Bulosan, Raymund Barrio, and John Steinbeck through their writing assignments and class discussion.

4. Assess students' understanding of rich metaphorical language through their group work on *The Plum Plum Pickers*.

Resources

Barrio, R. (1971). *The plum plum pickers* (2nd ed.). Binghamton, NY: Bilingual Press.

Bulosan, C. (1946). *America is in the heart: A personal history*. New York: Harcourt, Brace.

WHY THE CHANGES?

Literature on Migrant Workers and Exploitation

Curriculum Content and Materials

John Steinbeck is commonly taught in English classes. As in the "Before" lesson, students could prepare to read novels by Steinbeck by researching his life and reading some of his short stories. The "After" lesson retains Steinbeck's work but shifts the focus from the person of Steinbeck to the issues he and others wrote about. By widening the context to include the experiences of other California migrant workers, the students have a richer experience—often one that includes them more easily.

My Filipino students were enchanted by the chapters from Bulosan's book, since it was the first time they had ever seen themselves included in the curriculum! The students were a source of elucidation for some parts of the story and an inspiration to me to include more Filipino literature. I have learned in my studies that the Filipino American experience is a rich part of this country's history and hence should be addressed in any U.S. American Literature class. My Mexican American students also need to see themselves reflected in the curriculum, and others need to encounter Mexican American experiences in a way that leads to empathy and understanding—with a respect for differences and an appreciation of commonalities. Chicano literature allows for this if used by a teacher who is comfortable with the stories and sensitive to the culture. Students whose first language is Spanish are empowered when a story contains a few words in Spanish and they are then the expert of translation or pronunciation. It seems a little thing, but I cannot tell you how often the quiet boy comes alive when he sees his life mirrored in the story; a light comes into his eyes that ever is my inspiration to bring more Chicano literature into my classroom, where 50 percent of my students are Mexican American.

Yes, this route "into" to Steinbeck's work takes longer now, but when you decide as a teacher to bring multicultural perspective into your curriculum, you are revisioning the whole curriculum. As you bring in more good, diverse literature, some other pieces, favorites over the years, will have to go. That does not mean that an author like Steinbeck goes, but his work is recontextualized. Maybe it will now take longer to "teach" a particular book because you have transformed your approach to focus on a theme, enriched by multiple perspectives! Clustering your curriculum around themes, dipping into the rich veins of literature that reflect many cultural experiences, will be such a rewarding experience for you and your students that you will not miss the way you used to teach. I promise!

LESSON PLAN

BEFORE

Clothing in Spanish[*]

Subject Area: Elementary Spanish

Grade Level: 9–12

Time: One class period

Objectives

1. Students will use clothing vocabulary orally and the present indicative of the verb *to wear* in declarative, negative, and interrogative sentences.

2. Students will use this language in writing.

Suggested Procedures

1. Review colors by displaying crayons one at a time and asking students to identify them by color name in Spanish.

2. Describe what you are wearing in Spanish, using a story to make it interesting (e.g., "It's summer so I'm wearing shorts. But this is Seattle and, surprise—it's raining and I'm cold"). Continue describing your clothing, making sure everyone understands the vocabulary.

3. Choose a student to describe his or her clothing in Spanish. Continue with several students, letting them gradually take over the descriptions. Make sure everyone practices the declarative, negative, and interrogative forms. For example:

---

[*]Note: It is important that students learn colors in Spanish before this lesson.

FIRST STUDENT: Is Peter wearing blue jeans?

SECOND STUDENT: No, Peter's not wearing blue jeans. He's wearing black pants.

Also make sure all forms of the verb *to wear* are learned. For example:

Jack *is wearing* blue jeans. You *are wearing* blue jeans. They *are wearing* blue jeans.

If anyone has trouble understanding the idea of *to wear* in Spanish, remove your watch and say, "I'm not wearing a watch." Put the watch back on and say, "I'm wearing a watch." The students should catch on.

4. Tell the students to close their eyes. Choose one student to leave the room. The other students open their eyes and together try to remember what the missing student is wearing. As the items are named in Spanish, one student can draw them with crayons on butcher paper tacked on the wall. This reinforces the vocabulary visually and helps everyone remember what items have been named. When students have listed all the items they can, the missing student returns and the remaining items are named. Repeat this procedure with several students.

5. Give half the students pictures of people from magazines and the other half descriptions written in Spanish that each match one picture. The students move around the room, matching pictures with descriptions. Displaying their picture, one of each pair reads the description to the class.

6. Distribute magazines. Each student cuts out a picture of a person and writes a description in Spanish. This can be done as homework.

Evaluation

1. Evaluate students' comprehension and oral mastery of the language presented through oral participation.

2. Evaluate students' ability to use the language in writing through their written descriptions.

AFTER

Clothing in the Spanish-Speaking World*

Subject Area: Elementary Spanish

Grade Level: 9–12

Time: Two class periods

Source: Claire Alldred, Seattle, WA.

Objectives

1. Students will use clothing vocabulary orally and the present indicative of the verb *to wear* in declarative, negative, and interrogative sentences.

2. Students will use this language in writing.

3. Students will combine new language with previously learned language: colors, professions, and weather.

4. Students will appreciate the cultural diversity of the people who speak the target language.

5. Students will appreciate clothing different from their own.

Suggested Procedures

1. Pre-activity: Each student reads a different article in Spanish, written or adapted by the teacher, about the way of life of a certain Spanish-speaking community. The communities should be in Spain, Central America, South America, the United States, and the Caribbean. The articles may or may not refer directly to clothing but should include information that allows students to form ideas of the clothing worn by the people. For example, an article about Galicia (the north-western region of Spain) could inform students that farming is an important industry in Galicia and that the farmlands are divided into small plots so that many people own some land; that the climate is temperate, rainy, and unpredictable; and that in the larger towns, people are fashion conscious and several of Spain's most famous fashion designers are from Galicia. Students can deduce that work clothes, rain gear, and high-fashion clothes are all likely to be worn by people living in Galicia.

2. Review colors by displaying crayons one at a time and asking students to identify them in Spanish by color name. Review professions and weather by displaying relevant pictures and asking students to describe them.

3. Describe your own clothing in Spanish, relating it to your gender, age, nationality, region, and occupation, as appropriate. After enumerating all items of clothing, return to each item and ask, "Why?" Elicit ideas from students, supplying them when necessary. For example:

TEACHER:	I'm wearing a skirt. Why?
STUDENT:	You're a woman, you work, you're a teacher.
TEACHER:	Why am I wearing boots?
STUDENT:	You're wearing boots because it's cold out. It's raining. You live in Seattle.

If anyone has trouble understanding the idea of *to wear*, remove your watch and say, "I'm not wearing a watch." Put the watch back on and say, "I'm wearing a watch." The students should catch on.

4. Choose a student to elicit from class, in Spanish, what he or she is wearing and why. You may need to supply vocabulary. Note that while each item of clothing should be described, there will not always be a clear reason why the student is wearing it. Continue with several students, making sure everyone practices the declarative, negative, and interrogative forms. For example:

> FIRST STUDENT: Is Peter wearing blue jeans?
>
> SECOND STUDENT: No, Peter's not wearing blue jeans. He's wearing black pants.

Also make sure all forms of the verb *to wear* are learned. For example:

> Jack *is wearing* blue jeans. You *are wearing* blue jeans. They *are wearing* blue jeans.

5. Tell students to close their eyes. Choose one student to leave the room. The other students open their eyes and together try to remember what the missing student is wearing. As the items are named in Spanish, one student can draw them with crayons on butcher paper tacked to the wall. This reinforces the Spanish vocabulary visually and helps everyone remember what items have been named. When students have listed all the items they can, the missing student returns and the remaining items are named. Repeat this procedure with several students.

6. Give half the students pictures of people from magazines, representing Spanish speakers of different ages, sexes, and nationalities. Give the other half descriptions written in Spanish. Students move around the room, matching pictures with descriptions. Displaying their picture, one of each pair of students reads the description to the class.

7. Divide students into groups of five, making sure each group contains more able and less able students. Give each group a packet containing five photos of Spanish speakers, mounted on tagboard and labeled with name, age, country, region or town, and occupation. The packet should also contain cut-out photos of articles of clothing, some of which are suitable for each person. The students' task is to decide which clothes each person wears. Assembling the packets requires careful planning. Each person pictured must correspond to the culture described in one of the students' articles in the pre-activity (see procedure 1). One student in each group will be the expert on the clothing worn by one of the people pictured. However, while some connections may be direct and unquestionable (e.g., the traditional clothing of some American Indians), others will be more open to interpretation and discussion. Rain gear, for example, may be appropriate for several people in the same packet. The choice of pictures will determine how many different combinations are possible in each packet. Pictures can also be chosen to raise specific points about Spanish-speaking cultures. For example:

> Spanish-speaking communities within the United States have points in common with those in foreign countries.

American Indians live in varying degrees of separation and integration within Latino cultures.

While countries may differ widely, their large cities are often similar.

(These ideas can be expanded in future lessons, perhaps in social studies lessons conducted in English.)

8. After each group has matched people and clothing, the group presents its choices with its reasons to the rest of the class. For example, "Mari Carmen is a university student in Granada. She is 20 years old. Granada is very hot. Mari Carmen wears a white T-shirt, a blue skirt, espadrilles, white earrings, and a wristwatch." This example challenges the common assumption that everyone in the south of Spain is either a bullfighter or a flamenco dancer. A university student there may wear something traditional and particularly suited to the climate (espadrilles) but also clothing similar to that worn by students in the United States. Her occupation eliminates possible choices of clothing more than it demands a certain kind. This could be exploited to practice negative sentences. For example:

| TEACHER: | Does Mari Carmen wear a business suit? |
| STUDENT: | No, she doesn't wear a business suit. |

9. Each student can write a description of one of the people in their packet.

10. Distribute old magazines. Each student cuts out a picture of a person and writes a description. Steps 9 and 10 can be done as homework.

Evaluation

1. Evaluate students' comprehension and oral mastery of the language presented through their oral participation.

2. Evaluate students' ability to use the language through their written descriptions.

3. Evaluate students' acceptance of different kinds of people as Spanish speakers through the choices they make in step 10.

WHY THE CHANGES?

Clothing in the Spanish-Speaking World

Curriculum Content

Foreign language classes often do not teach enough about the culture of the people who speak the target language, especially people in countries other than where the language originated. For example, while many Spanish teachers teach some information about the culture of Spain, fewer teach about the cultures of Spanish-speaking people in the Americas or about Latino Americans. Neglecting to teach about culture, and especially the culture of speakers of the target language in the United States, encourages students to retain false stereotypes and may keep them from cultivating opportunities to practice the language close to home.

In the "Before" lesson, the teacher is concerned only with teaching vocabulary and grammar; no attempt is made to relate it to culture. In the "After" lesson, however, the teacher uses the vocabulary to teach about the cultural diversity of Spanish speakers. In the process, students are asked to think about why people wear what they wear and to do so in Spanish. Students not only learn more about cultural diversity among Spanish speakers, but their language practice is richer than in the "Before" plan. Clothing is not the only area in which cultural diversity can be taught. Many areas of vocabulary, such as foods, transportation, family, and so forth, lend themselves to this teaching.

Instructional Strategies

Both plans use a variety of modalities and grouping patterns. The "After" plan uses heterogeneous grouping to solve problems in addition to practicing language, which fosters higher-level thinking skills.

LESSON PLAN

BEFORE

Introduction to Native American Literature*

Subject Area: English

Grade Level: 9–12

Time: One to two periods

Objectives

1. Students will describe the historical dispossession of some specific American Indian nations.

2. Students will make connections between this history and Native American literature.

Suggested Procedures

1. Show the first 20 minutes of part 7 of *500 Nations*, looking at Californian American Indians, or show the section appropriate to your geographic region. Students should make notes on what happens for later group discussion. This video is part

---

*Source: Anne Fairbrother, Salinas Union High School District, Salinas, CA.

of an eight-video series, which is an excellent resource. This part focuses on the Chumash experience as Spanish missions were built with the labor of enslaved and brutalized American Indians, destroying their original way of life. With Mexican independence the various American Indian nations were freed from the missions, but their villages and homes were gone and they were reduced to a dispossessed servant class. Also, as a result of the addition of California to the Union, and of the ensuing Gold Rush, it was "open season" on American Indians, who were massacred en masse, the children being taken into legal slavery. The events are portrayed with historical accuracy and authentic testament, and the facts of the death of 90 percent of the people in what was the most densely populated region of Native America are clearly and movingly portrayed.

2. Give students group questions to answer from the video, followed by a quiz for them to answer individually.

3. In preparation for a unit on Native American literature, ask students to do a free write: "What do you know about American Indians in what is now the United States?"

4. After about 20 minutes of writing, have students share what they know, and elaborate and elucidate as you write students' information on the board. Free writes should be given back to students at the end of the unit, when students can write what they *now* know!

Evaluation

1. Assess students' understanding of the dispossession through their group work and their quiz.

2. Assess students' connection of history with literature through their free writes and participation in the discussions.

Resources

Video

500 nations. (1995). Burbank, CA: Warner Home Video. Hosted by Kevin Costner, narrated by Gregory Harrison.

AFTER

Introduction to Native American Literature

Subject Area: English

Grade Level: 9–12

Time: One to two periods

Objectives

1. Students will describe the historical dispossession of some specific American Indian nations.

2. Students will be able to look at an event from different perspectives, placing themselves in others' shoes.

3. Students will make connections between this history and Native American literature.

Suggested Procedures

1. Show the first 20 minutes of part 7 of *500 Nations*, looking at Californian American Indians, or show sections appropriate to your geographic region. Students should make notes on what happens for later group discussion. This video is part of an eight-video series, which is an excellent resource. This part focuses on the Chumash experience as Spanish missions were built with the labor of enslaved and brutalized American Indians, destroying their original way of life. With Mexican independence the various Indian nations were freed from the missions, but their villages and homes were gone and they were reduced to a dispossessed servant class. Also, as a result of the addition of California to the Union, and of the ensuing Gold Rush, it was "open season" on American Indians, who were massacred en masse, the children being taken into legal slavery. The events are portrayed with historical accuracy and authentic testament, and the facts of the death of 90 percent of the people in what was the most densely populated region of Native America are clearly and movingly portrayed.

2. After the video, students should work in groups and write their responses, after discussion, to *all* of these simulated situations, using their notes:

   a. You are a Californian American Indian—how might you feel after hearing this story? Give different possible scenarios; explain, but don't judge.

   b. You are an American Indian, but not from California—how might you feel after hearing this story? Give different possible scenarios; explain, but don't judge.

   c. You are a Mexican American—how might you feel after hearing this story? Give different possible scenarios; explain, but don't judge.

   d. You are an African American—how might you feel after hearing this story? Give different possible scenarios; explain, but don't judge.

   e. You are a white European American—how might you feel after hearing this story? Give different possible scenarios; explain, but don't judge.

   f. What do you think are the most helpful and sensitive responses that we can all have, as human beings? List them, giving your explanations.

3. Before the next day, use students' responses to all the situations to arrange a continuum of possible responses, ranging from negative/least sensitive to positive/most sensitive, with a range in between.

4. Put this on the board before class so that students see it. Tell students that all the responses are theirs, and all are valid responses, but some are more positive or sensitive than others. Discuss all the entries, validating *all* the responses. Somewhere on the continuum will be a sense of guilt, which can be addressed by letting students know that there have always been people, of all ethnic backgrounds, who have spoken out against injustice. No one is personally responsible for what happened in the past; everyone can decide where they stand, now, in the present.

5. In preparation for a unit on Native American literature and the issues raised in those stories and poems, ask students to do a free write: "What do you know about American Indians in what is now the United States? What questions do you have? Write up to five questions that you will answer at the end of the unit."

6. After about 20 minutes of writing, have students share what they know, and elaborate and elucidate as you write students' information on the board. Free writes should be given back to students at the end of the unit, when students can write what they *now* know!

Evaluation

1. Assess students' understanding of the dispossession, and their ability to look at an event from different perspectives, through their group work and individual notes. It is important, wherever possible, to individualize group grades by including individual work that they brought to their group work or individual work done afterward and based on the group work.

2. Assess students' connection of history with literature through their free write and participation in the discussions.

Resources

Video

500 nations. (1995). Burbank, CA: Warner Home Video. Hosted by Kevin Costner, narrated by Gregory Harrison.

WHY THE CHANGES?

Introduction to Native American Literature

Multiple Perspectives

In the "Before" lesson, students are learning about what happened to some of the indigenous people in this land. But although it is hard not to be moved by this video, hard not to hear the American Indians' voices, students are still basically just learning the facts without being given the chance to look at the events from different perspectives. The "After" lesson allows for a discussion, looking at the events from different perspectives. This is important because it enables students from a wide variety of backgrounds to connect one group's experiences with their own experiences and to see connections across groups.

For some students, especially white European American students, it is hard to hear the story of the way Native Americans were treated by the Europeans without feeling blamed, responsible, and sometimes guilty, which often results in hostility. If students are to be comfortable exploring a multicultural perspective, this problem really must be addressed. Rather than talking about this directly, this lesson plan allows all students to examine all the possible reactions to these events. Thus, issues of blame and guilt can be looked at as valid responses, and all students can learn how to move toward other responses on the continuum, provided by the students themselves! Some students will have written that they are not responsible, since it happened so long ago, and that they would not condone such treatment of others. The teacher can point out that there have always been those who stood up against injustice: that the Underground Railroad could not have been so successful without the participation of some European Americans, or that European Americans worked alongside African Americans in the south and the north during the Civil Rights Movement. Even Malcolm X realized that it was not whites as individual people who were the enemy but the system and its proponents. Students can realize that they can take a stand by their attitudes and actions *now*!

I found that this assignment was very liberating for my European American students, and after starting early in the school year with this, I experienced none of the hostility to multicultural works that I had been distressed and perplexed by in previous years. This exercise validated *all* perspectives, while showing that some responses were more sensitive and enlightened than others, and it allowed students to move their perspective to a more comfortable place.

LESSON PLAN

BEFORE

The Vietnam War

Subject Area: U.S. History

Grade Level: 10–12

Time: One week

Objectives

1. Students will describe U.S. foreign policy in Southeast Asia during the Johnson presidency.

2. Students will appreciate the pros and cons of U.S. involvement in Southeast Asia.

3. Students will learn of the major political and military events that took place during the Vietnam War.

Suggested Procedures

1. Discuss how the United States first became involved with Vietnam.

2. Have students read about reasons for Johnson's policy of escalation of the Vietnam War in their history textbook.

3. Have students debate the pros and cons of President Johnson's authorization of military forces in Vietnam without a declaration of war from Congress.

4. Have students prepare reports about one of the following topics: the Gulf of Tonkin Resolution, the Tet Offensive, the Ho Chi Minh Trail, Congressional Hawks versus Congressional Doves, the Green Berets, the Geneva Agreement of 1954, and Operation Plan 34A.

5. Discuss with students why the Vietnam War divided our nation.

6. Have students interview their parents about their role in and feelings about the Vietnam War. Have them share this with the rest of the class.

Evaluation

1. Assess students' understanding of U.S. foreign policy in Southeast Asia and the major events of the Vietnam War through a quiz.

2. Assess students' appreciation of the pros and cons of U.S. involvement in Southeast Asia through discussion.

3. Assess students' knowledge of a major event of the Vietnam War through their research reports.

AFTER

The Vietnam War and Desert Storm

Subject Area: U.S. History

Grade Level: 10–12

Time: Two weeks

Objectives

1. Students will describe U.S. foreign policy in Southeast Asia and in the Middle East.

2. Students will compare and contrast how those policies affected domestic policy during the Johnson and Bush presidencies.

3. Students will appreciate the pros and cons of U.S. involvement in Southeast Asia and the Middle East.

4. Students will describe the role of U.S. American soldiers during the Vietnam War and Desert Storm, including female soldiers and soldiers of color.

5. Students will describe the reactions of the U.S. American people to the Vietnam War and to Operation Desert Storm; they will examine how the reactions to these military engagements differ from each other.

6. Students will appreciate how soldiers who served in the Vietnam War were and still are affected—medically, economically, socially, and politically.

7. Students will examine the impact of the Vietnam War on Southeast Asian people (e.g., becoming refugees, living in camps for extended periods of time, immigrating to other countries) and develop an appreciation of their friendship and loyalty to the United States.

Suggested Procedures

1. Have students read in their history text about Johnson's policy of escalation of the Vietnam War. Have them also read the comments of Sen. J. William Fulbright concerning his opposition to the war. Ask students to examine the merits and weaknesses of both of these arguments. Have other students retrieve and examine the editorial page of several U.S. newspapers at the beginning of Desert Storm.

2. Have students research the number of soldiers and other military personnel involved in the Vietnam War and Desert Storm and organize these data along race, class, and gender lines. Have students compare the number of soldiers of color and the number of white soldiers involved in the war with their representation in the total U.S. population. Discuss reasons why so many people of color and poor rural whites participated in these military actions.

3. Have students investigate the role of women in the wars, both in the war area and at home. Discuss ways that women's involvement in these military actions made an impact on the status of women in U.S. society.

4. Invite members of a veterans' support group to class to discuss their feelings about the two military actions and why they joined the service (e.g., the Vietnam Veterans of America).

5. Have some students research the attitudes of civil rights advocates (e.g., Martin Luther King Jr.) and peace advocates such as Jane Fonda about the Vietnam War and the reasons they felt as they did. Have students interview or invite as guest speakers some conscientious objectors, to find out their views and reasons for their actions.

6. Have some students research Mohammed Ali's position toward the Vietnam War and how his attitude affected his boxing career. Also, compare that time in his life with how he was received at the 1996 Olympic Games.

7. Have students explore and analyze the differences in news coverage between the Vietnam War and Desert Storm.

8. Have some students prepare reports about the following topics: interviews with (if possible) recent arrivals from Southeast Asia about their feelings on the Vietnam War and the effect it had on the average citizen of Southeast Asia; the experiences of Amerasians, Vietnamese children whose fathers are U.S. American soldiers who served in Vietnam, particularly their current struggle to find their fathers in the United States.

Evaluation

1. Assess students' knowledge and understanding of the Vietnam War and Desert Storm by having them (as individuals, in pairs, or in small groups) present oral reports on a project they prepared about the military actions.

WHY THE CHANGES?

The Vietnam War and Desert Storm

Curriculum Content

The "After" plan helps students to understand how race, class, and gender factors relate to war. For example, people of color often disproportionately occupy the front lines during war and experience more death than whites. Also, the "After" plan has students examine two recent military actions that were for the most part perceived differently by U.S. citizens. Many people regard these as separate, unrelated wars that differ mainly in that one was long and drawn out, with media coverage contributing to domestic dissention, while the other was quick, efficient, and highly successful. The "After" lesson encourages students to probe beyond these simplistic judgments.

Multiple Perspectives

For many years, U.S. Americans have debated the outcome of the Vietnam War and the role of the United States during the war. The "After" plan provides students with a pro-and-con perspective on the war from two policymakers' (President Johnson and Senator Fulbright) points of view. The plan also presents the perspectives of U.S. American soldiers who served in the war, of objectors and peace activists, of ordinary citizens, and of Southeast Asian people on whose territory the war was fought. The plan encourages students to examine these multiple perspectives and to form their own opinions about the war.

In addition, the "After" plan, by comparing the two military actions, allows students to examine how groups who usually have diverse and varying opinions come together to support the country when the people believe they are fighting for the "right" thing.

Instructional Strategies

The "After" plan provides greater sensitivity than the "Before" plan to the ways students learn by offering more ways for students to collect information on the war. For example, interviewing recent arrivals from Southeast Asia can serve as strong motivating factors for getting students "turned on" to learning.

Evaluation

The "Before" and "After" plans have similar forms of evaluation. The advantage of the "After" plan, however, is that students present their reports in small groups, which fosters cooperative learning.

THE MANY FACES OF SELF-INTEREST: A MULTIDISCIPLINARY AND MULTIGRADE UNIT*

The concept of **self-interest** is associated with many behaviors carried out by a person or a group of people. Self-interest can be associated with personal or collective gain (e.g., greed or generosity and kindness). In this unit, students examine economic, political, national, group, and personal self-interest.

Subject Areas: Economics, Social Studies, Language Arts, Computer Literacy

Grade Level: 8–12

Time: Ongoing throughout the semester

Lesson Plan 1: Self-Interest

Objectives

1. Students will understand that self-interest is a motivating force in people's economic behavior.

Sources: Deborah Bicksler, Stoughton, WI, and Carl A. Grant, University of Wisconsin–Madison, Madison, WI.

Authors' note: Since the publication of the first edition of *Turning on Learning*, we have been encouraged to include some teaching units. However, to conserve space, we include here only the "After" plans.

2. Students will identify a number of different human behaviors that indicate that people make choices based on self-interest.

3. Students will define the following concepts: self-interest, pure market, competition, bargaining power, substitutes, and wealth.

4. Students will examine the economic behavior of individuals.

Suggested Procedures

1. Have students use the text *Economics Today and Tomorrow* to research and write about the meaning of these concepts: self-interest, pure market, competition, and bargaining power.

2. Divide the students into five groups. Have each group assume one of the five occupations listed in the chart in Figure 5.6. Each group should discuss the self-interest of the person in that occupation with regard to price/cost of the product being made, safety of the workplace/product, durability of the product, fashionability of the product, and competition of the market for the product. After the initial discussion, have each group do some research on the market behavior of the person they are representing. Resources for research information can include television talk shows and newspaper articles (e.g., talk shows about money; articles written during the debates over raising the minimum wage; articles on the manufacturing of celebrity-endorsed products in so-called Third World countries at extremely low wages; Kathy Lee Gifford's and others' testimonies before Congress on the low pay and use of child labor to make products).

3. After the groups have completed their research from item 2, have them fill in the self-interest chart.

4. After completing the chart, each group should describe in one or two paragraphs how self-interest helps or hinders society to function better.

Evaluation

1. Assess students' understanding of the concepts through their short essay assignment and discussions.

2. Evaluate each group's completion of the self-interest chart to which they were assigned.

Resource

Miller, Roger Le Roy. (1995). *Economics today and tomorrow* (4th ed., chap. 2). New York: Glencoe.

	Cloth Mill Operator	Garment Worker	Clothing Manufacturer	Consumer	Retail Merchant
Price/Cost	Low Cost, High Price	High Wages	Low Cost, High Price	Low Price	Low Cost, High Price
Safety					
Durability					
Fashion					
Competition					

FIGURE 5.6   Self-Interest Chart

Lesson Plan 2: Personal Self-Interest

Objectives

1. Students will relate their own self-interest with their social attitude and behavior.

2. Students will discuss how their own self-interest can affect their economic, national, and political behavior and behavior toward other groups.

3. Students will relate the self-interest behavior of literary characters to their own behavior or that of friends.

Suggested Procedures

1. Have students report on two literary characters whose self-interest affected their circumstances or the circumstances of their family or friends. They should tell whether the self-interest was to achieve economic, political, and/or personal gain.

2. Have students discuss in their working groups the times in life when it is important to consider one's self-interest.

3. Have students write a short essay on a time in their life when self-interest served as a motivating force. Have them answer the following questions: Was the outcome gratifying? Why or why not?

4. Discuss the implications from procedure 3 in terms of whether their decision making was self-serving with or without a concern for the common good.

Evaluation

1. Evaluate students' reports on two literary characters whose self-interest affected the circumstances of their family or friends.

2. Assess students' understanding of self-interest through their short essay assignment on a time in their life when self-interest was a motivating force.

Lesson Plan 3: National Interest

Objectives

1. Students will learn that national interest is a motivating force that affects a country's economic behavior.

2. Students will identify a number of different responses that a country will make to protect its national (self-)interest.

3. Students will examine the economic (self-)interest of countries.

4. Students will learn that sometimes actions taken on behalf of the entire country may have differential effects on groups of people living in that country (e.g., farmers).

Suggested Procedures

1. Discuss with students U.S. policies on protectionism and free trade in terms of national interest.

2. Organize students into six groups and have each group report the reason(s) given to a country by its leaders before the country dealt with a national or international crisis. For example:

> Pres. Franklin D. Roosevelt's first inaugural address, in 1933, to a depression-weary nation, when he said: "Let me assert my firm belief that the only thing we have to fear is fear itself—nameless, unreasoning, unjustified terror."

> Pres. Abraham Lincoln's second inaugural address, in 1865, when he said: "With malice toward none, with charity for all, with firmness in the right as God gives us to see the right, let us strive on to finish the work we are in, to bind up the nation's wounds."

Other examples could include:

> Pres. George Bush's comments on Desert Storm

> Shawnee leader Tecumseh's addresses in 1809–1811 to other American Indian tribal leaders to prevent further encroachment of tribal land

> Winston Churchill's address to the British people during World War II

Lincoln's Gettysburg Address

Corazon Aquino's address to the Philippine people after her election as president

Roosevelt's address to the United States at the beginning of World War II

Nelson Mandela's address to the South African people upon being elected president

Wilma P. Mankiller's initial inaugural address to the Cherokee Nation in 1987

3. Have students examine the reasons given by each of the leaders (e.g., military, economic, humanitarian; producer versus consumer welfare; the policy of free trade versus the policy of protectionism, or protection of national interest, which sets up a forced choice between the welfare of two groups). **Free trade** favors the welfare of consumers. **Protectionism** favors the welfare of producers. When one economic policy is employed by a government regarding a particular industry, the "costs" will vary. It matters greatly whether we favor policies that benefit almost everyone to some degree or policies that help or hurt a few people to a considerable degree. For example, there is a trade-off when we weigh the gains from trade that accrue as lower prices for textiles or cars against the impact of protectionism on the jobs of textile workers or auto workers. Another way to view the choice is the cost of inflation, which affects all, versus the cost of unemployment, borne by a few. The political voice of inflation drowns out the voice of unemployment. The injuries of those affected by foreign competition overshadow the "whisper" of consumers who would benefit from lower prices.

Have students work individually or in groups to complete the National Interest Chart in Figure 5.7. Remind them that newspapers and newsmagazines are excellent sources of information.

Evaluation

1. Assess students' understanding of national interest in a written essay and oral presentation.

2. Assess students' group reports on a country's demonstration of national self-interest versus a broader interest.

Resources

Blanche, Jerry D. (1990). *Native American reader: Stories, speeches and poems*. Juneau, AK: Denali Press. (for Mankiller's address)

Josephy, Alvin M., Jr. (1969). *The patriot chiefs*. New York: Viking Press. (for Tecumseh's speech)

Country: _____			
Problem/Issue	**Action 1**	**Action 2**	**Action 3**
1. Protectionism of domestic families	ban imports from Mexico	continue open import of vegetables	import tax placed on all vegetables
(vegetable vs. free trade)	Who does this policy help or hurt and why?	Who does this policy help or hurt and why?	Who does this policy policy help or hurt?
2.			
3.			
4.			

FIGURE 5.7   National Interest Chart

Lesson Plan 4: Political Interest

Objectives

1. Students will describe self-interest as a motivating force in a politician's behavior.
2. Students will examine the political behavior of politicians from different political parties.

Suggested Procedures

1. Organize students into pairs and have them report on how political party leaders respond to national concern (e.g., Clinton, Dole, and Perot on welfare reform; the Republican leadership and the Democratic leadership's position on the minimum wage).
2. Have the pairs use computer research methods (e.g., *NewsBank*) to retrieve from various newspapers across the country politicians' responses to different legislation (e.g., on Thursday, August 1, 1996, the headline in the *San Francisco Chronicle* read, "Clinton Backs Welfare Overhaul," and the lead article stated, "GOP joyful, liberal glum as House approves bill"; on Thursday, August 1, 1996, the headline in the *New York Times* read, "Clinton Signs Welfare Bill That Ends U.S. Aid: Guarantees and Gives States Broad Power," and the title of one lead article read, "Millions affected," and another read, "Master move in campaign").
3. Have students watch C-Span channels and take notes on the information given in speeches by members of Congress discussing their positions on issues.

Politician:_____

Political Position	Action 1	Action 2	Action 3
1.			
2.			
3.			

FIGURE 5.8   Political Interest Chart

4. Have student groups identify an interest group within their community and ascertain how and why it has taken a position on a certain problem or issue. Have the student group seek to discover the group motivation for its actions.

5. Have students complete the Political Interest Chart in Figure 5.8 with information collected from suggested procedures 2, 3, and 4. Also, students may wish to keep this chart active throughout the semester, including information as it becomes available.

Evaluation

1. Assess students' understanding of political interest in their written reports and oral discussion.

2. Assess students' research skills by the success they have locating information for their assignment.

3. In a short essay, assess whether students understand why and how politicians make decisions to satisfy their political interest.

Lesson Plan 5: Self-Interest/Self-Determination of Marginalized Groups

Objectives

1. Students will learn how the self-interest and self-determination of marginalized groups served as a sustaining factor in their determination to survive and become socially (i.e., economically and politically) successful.

2. Students will learn how some groups in this country have been marginalized.

Suggested Procedures

1. Discuss with students the sensitivity that needs to be exercised when students begin to examine issues that may be personal.

2. Organize students into five or six groups, and have each group select a historical or contemporary group that fought major obstacles to survive as a group (e.g., Amish; Pilgrims; Cherokee tribe's 1830s fight against relocation; Chinese who were recruited to the United States in the 1860s to work as contract laborers on the transcontinental railroad; German Jews who survived the Holocaust; African Americans who survived enslavement; women who fought to achieve voting rights; Cambodian and Laotian refugees who were displaced from their homes and country; Japanese Americans who survived internment).

3. Have students complete the chart in Figure 5.9 with information collected from procedures 1 and 2 (e.g., for women as the marginalized group, the problem could be listed as suffrage and the issue could be listed as mobilizing and heightening of awareness and activism [overt demonstrations and political pressure on state and federal government]). Also, have students keep this chart active throughout the semester.

Evaluation

1. Assess students' sensitivity toward one another by the way they ask questions and interact with each other.

2. Assess student groups' success completing the Marginalized Group Self-Interest/Self-Determination Chart.

Marginalized Group:_____

Problem/Issue	Action 1	Action 2	Action 3
1.			
2.			
3.			

FIGURE 5.9   Marginalized Group Self-Interest/Self-Determination Chart

3. Assess each student group's written and oral reports.

Features of This Unit

Curriculum Materials

During this unit, students will be asked to use a variety of curriculum resources, including newspapers, the World Wide Web, television, magazines, and textbooks.

Curriculum Content

The curriculum materials will provide students with varying points of view, utilizing national and international perspectives from men and women. The material is designed to appeal to students' interests by suggesting the use of current topics and topics that are relevant to their life circumstances.

Multiple Perspectives

The unit is designed to engage students in an examination of how the self-interests of individuals and groups of people influence the perspectives that they hold.

Instructional Strategies

The unit is designed to appeal to the many different ways that students like to learn. It makes use of the World Wide Web. (We know that all students may not have access to the Web, but we hope an increasing number will.) Students work in pairs and small groups to discuss and research topics to complete charts or prepare reports based on their findings. Oral and written reports are requested to strengthen both methods of presentation. Research other than the typical hunting-up something in the encyclopedia or textbooks is included to introduce and strengthen students' research skills and avenues of investigation.

Student Evaluation

The unit allows for a comprehensive and continuous evaluation over an extended period of time. Students are afforded greater opportunity to learn concepts and to demonstrate their knowledge of these concepts. Students' knowledge and procedures for conducting research should show improvement throughout the duration of the unit; their critical thinking skills should be increasingly sophisticated as they learn how "interest" influences many human actions.

Home and Community Relationships

Oftentimes, home and community relationships are discussed in terms of "partnerships" and "working together," without exploring why members in a community feel and act as they do. This unit has students examining why community groups take the positions they take on certain issues and how certain groups and/or workers within a community may be particularly affected by policy decisions made for national interest.

Education That Is Multicultural
and Social Reconstructionist

W hat can schools do to help bring about a fairer world, or can they do anything? Do issues of poverty, discrimination, and oppression require a more vigorous solution than just promoting cross-cultural understanding and mutual respect? As we head into the 21st century, what does it mean to be a citizen in a large democratic society, one that still has major unresolved issues involving fairness and social justice?

These are among the concerns addressed by this last educational approach. The name of the approach is challenging, while descriptive. The term *social reconstructionist* refers to the philosophical roots of the approach—the belief that schools in a democracy can and should prepare citizens to work actively and collectively on problems facing society. Individuals often feel powerless to institute significant social changes, believing that their only source of major government and social participation is through voting, and even then, they wonder whether their single votes will make a difference. But history—the histories of our country and other countries—teaches us that, when people organize interest groups, coalesce with other existing advocacy groups, and mobilize other individuals with similar concerns, they can make a significant difference. However, to do so successfully requires the ability to identify manageable aspects of social problems, which takes practice and commitment. Consider, for example, our country's increased awareness of drunk driving because of groups like MADD (Mothers Against Drunk Driving) that have gained national visibility, or parents' greater concern for the education of their children with disabilities, which brought about Public Law 94-142. Social changes such as these are the result of the efforts of individuals working together to achieve a goal.

Social reconstructionists believe that political participatory skills should be learned in school. We develop this argument more fully in our companion text, *Making Choices for Multicultural Education* (Sleeter & Grant, 1994). The school is the primary social institution, outside the immediate family and perhaps religious institutions, in which young people spend most of their time. As such, the school is an ideal place for young people to learn collectively how to make an impact on social institutions. To some extent, schools already do this when they develop a student government or teach conflict resolution skills. Social reconstructionism develops this line of participation skills further than schools usually take it. In addition, the school has always had the responsibility of preparing citizens for participation in society. Most of us would agree that social participation should include more than voting and obeying and that the passive obedience schools generally demand of students contradicts our belief in an active, democratic society. Thus, social reconstructionists believe the school should consciously and regularly teach and model democratic living to prepare our young people for active political participation as adults.

The phrase "education that is multicultural" refers to the kinds of social issues of greatest concern in a democracy and to the belief that the entire school experience should be reoriented to address these issues. They include social inequality based on race, social class, language, disability, sexual orientation, and gender, and the primary concern is whether we are practicing our democratic and egalitarian ideals if certain groups of people continue to oppress and control other groups. Some people argue that racism in our country is slowly withering away and will disappear altogether with time, but this argument ignores the poverty and powerlessness that people of color continue to experience. It also ignores the increasing degree to which people of color, immigrants, poor people, gay men, lesbians, and bisexuals have felt under assault during the last decade. Further, even though U.S. Americans recognize that racial and gender inequality are unjust, most accept our highly class-stratified society, in which both poverty and extreme wealth exist. Additionally, as a society, we remain perplexed about how to deal with homophobia, even though we know that the gay, lesbian, and bisexual population make up a significant portion of our society.

The **Education That is Multicultural and Social Reconstructionist approach** deals with all forms of group oppression as a whole. For example, the approach would not concentrate solely on the issue of sexism because sexism does not address fully the needs and concerns of women of color and women living at or below the poverty level. By not focusing on only an individual group, the approach deals with oppression as a whole and as such does not perpetuate other forms of oppression. Also, like the Multicultural Education approach described in Chapter 5, this approach involves coalition building.

GOALS AND OBJECTIVES

The approach discussed in this chapter attempts to prepare students to be citizens able to actualize the egalitarian ideology that is the cornerstone of our democracy. It teaches students about issues of social equality and power, fosters an appreciation of the diversity of the U.S. population, and teaches political action skills that students may use to deal actively with these issues. Although the approach is similar to the Multicultural Education approach, it is more action oriented.

Model and Celebrate Diversity and Equal Opportunity

The goals of the Multicultural Education approach apply to this approach as well. However, although the approach may address citizen participation and issues such as peace and ecology, these activities are not considered multicultural if they do not deal specifically with racism, sexism, classism, heterosexism, and ablism in school and society. Connecting issues such as ecology to other social issues is actually not difficult. For example, environmental racism connects ecology with racism by critiquing the use of communities of color and American Indian reservations as waste dump sites for affluent European American communities. A prerequisite of dealing with these issues is to restructure the school experience so that it models and celebrates the rich diversity and ideals of equality in this country. Examples of lessons that involve such restructuring include "Story Time" (p. 264) and "Conflict over Western Land" (p. 287).

Practice Democracy

Democracy in the United States means different things to different people. For some it means having access to societal institutions and participation in the decision-making process (e.g., the right to vote or sit at a lunch counter). For others, such as ourselves, it means, in addition to access, being able to actually benefit from what one has access to without the barriers of formal and informal racism, sexism, classism, and other forms of marginalization. For example, not only does one have the right to vote and make choices and the opportunity to participate in the democratic process at varying levels (e.g., as a voter, campaign assistant, or any type of public representative), one is also welcomed because of the excellence and diverse perspective he or she brings. In addition to having the right to sit at a lunch counter, one is accepted and treated as an equal human being and a valuable customer at any type of commercial establishment, from a fast-food restaurant to private golf courses in country clubs.

To practice democracy, the approach suggests that in the classroom and school, students collectively learn to make substantive decisions that will prepare them to not only have access to democracy but also to benefit from what one has access to. This does not mean giving free rein to students; rather, it means opening up considerably more avenues for student decision making than are generally found in schools. Of course, structure and learning to respect authority are important, but real growth and maturity come from an understanding of why structure is needed and from participation in forming and establishing that structure.

Analyze Social Inequality

Most school curricula do not relate directly to students' own lives, which many account for much of their boredom with and alienation from school. Students often ask why they must learn about things that are unrelated to their own experiences. In this approach, the teacher deals with issues in students' own lives and helps them to connect broader social issues with their own experiences. For example, most adolescents consciously attempt to develop gender identity and a way of preparing for the future and understanding gender construction within this society. As students become curious about sex, they also become concerned about diseases such as AIDS. This curiosity (and fear) provides an excellent opportunity for examining people's feelings about AIDS and the way those feelings have translated into inadequate funding of research on cures.

Another social issue is the rapidly changing role of women and the slower, more reluctantly changing role of men. In a study that we conducted (Grant & Sleeter, 1996), we noticed that many of the junior high girls who were from the lower middle class were not strongly interested in patterning their gender identity after their mothers and were more thoughtful about their futures than the boys. The girls argued that, although they admired and loved their mothers, they wanted a different kind of life. They were not mainly interested in raising kids, taking care of their husbands, and providing part of the family income. Instead, they wanted professional careers and more control of their lives. Many of the boys, on the other hand, held unrealistic dreams of playing professional sports and gave little consideration to other professional alternatives. Complicating the girls' pursuit of their goals, however, was their lack of consistent and careful analysis about their choice of boyfriends and how they at times downplayed their intellectual side to appeal to the boys. For many girls, the selection of boyfriends was more based on the boy's popularity, coolness, or romantic pursuit than the boy's dedication to a realistic career-oriented future.

The school involved in this study missed a chance to connect with these issues, which were of real concern to the students. It did little to help the girls develop their new identity (e.g., by inspiring them to pursue their professional dreams). It gave them little counseling on the courses they needed, the hard work and perseverance necessary for success, and strategies needed to succeed. Also, the school did little to help the boys deal with the reality of their slim opportunity to play professional sports. The curriculum included few life stories of contemporary women, and it did not explain how some of these women struggled against societal odds to become successful. Similarly, the curriculum and courses offered little to teach the boys about the changing world economy or to explain how they would need to adjust and respond to the changing role of women.

To teach about these aspects of society, the teacher may also use students' own experiences with issues of race and class or with unequal opportunities and resources available to dominant (versus dominated) groups. We know of a teacher in a farm working community who encouraged students to find out about pesticides that were being used in the fields and causing health problems to farm workers (including students' family members). On the basis of their investigation, students began to speak out on issues of pesticides and farm worker health.

Social issues become more real and meaningful to students when they are encouraged to examine them from a personal viewpoint, and students are more likely to act on issues that have meaning than on distant, abstract ones. For example, that European Americans in general have greater access to jobs than African Americans or Latinos is a significant social issue but one that is difficult to resolve in the abstract. However, European American teenagers being more actively recruited by employers than African American or Latino teenagers may be an issue that students are actually experiencing. Also, male teenagers being more actively recruited for employment and/or for positions that provide some managerial training than female teenagers may be another issue. When teachers involve experiences that have personal meaning in students' lives, students' interest is likely to be great. Lessons in which students analyze issues in their own life experiences include "Language Experience" (p. 260), "The Court System" (p. 299), and "Music Appreciation" (p. 290). Action Research Activity 6.2 is designed to help teachers identify the social issues of most concern within the local community.

Encourage Social Action

The approach we discuss here encourages social action by having students actually work on social issues. Student involvement can take many forms, including writing letters, engaging in community service, and producing and distributing information about a community problem. The teacher must investigate the suitability of various forms of action in the local community (see Action Research Activity 6.2). In addition, the teacher must be careful not to pressure students into doing or saying anything that is contrary to their beliefs. Rather, the teacher should show students how they can act constructively on issues and needs that exist within the community. A lesson illustrating social action is "African American Literature" (p. 307).

Many schools are teaching students the skills of conflict resolution. By itself, conflict resolution is not necessarily the same as social action, but when conflict resolution is combined with political awareness it leads to social action skills. Let us give an example. A school experiences student fighting and implements a conflict resolution program. In that program, students are taught to express their feelings using "I" statements, to actively listen to feelings that other students express, and to cooperatively develop solutions for conflicts in which no student loses. Peer mediators may be trained to assist in this process.

When we examine them politically, we can see that many of the conflicts erupting within the school stem from community conflicts or issues related to powerlessness in the community. For example, students who lack access to jobs and meaningful recreational opportunities often "hang out" on the streets and become involved in gang activities. Conflict resolution may mean examining issues in the community that affect students' lives and figuring out how to do something constructive to meet students' needs. If recreational activities are lacking, students can organize to get the city to provide more recreational opportunities. One of our colleagues spent years organizing urban gang youth to produce murals articulating their concerns publicly. In so doing, she helped students work through conflicts they had with each other, learn to identify larger social origins of their frustrations and conflicts, and learn to collaborate to voice their needs and concerns to larger audiences. In so doing, she was able to channel the energy of conflict into social advocacy and action.

Another colleague told us about teaching her first-grade class the use of conflict resolution to settle their disputes. She described how these first graders taught older students (third and fourth grade) to use conflict resolution to resolve disagreements on the playground and arguments with older brothers and sisters.

ACTION RESEARCH ACTIVITY 6.1

Student Decision Making

Use Table 6.1 to help you analyze your classroom or school in terms of the extent to which students are involved in decision making, as well as to identify the areas in which decision making can be broadened and for which students. Pay attention to which students are hindered from decision making and why. Also determine the extent to which students are invited to make decisions on an individual versus a group basis.

ACTION RESEARCH ACTIVITY 6.2

Discovering Issues of Concern to the Community

This approach to multicultural education suggests that teachers become familiar with issues of concern to the communities their school serves. Student demographic changes, school boundary changes, and the growth of specialized schools (such as magnet schools) make it increasingly difficult to determine a school's community and to familiarize oneself or keep up with the concerns of the different groups of people the school serves.

To learn more about the community, first find out who local residents of the community see as their leaders and/or spokespeople. Find out what religious institutions and local organizations people in the neighborhood affiliate with. Also find out what media (newsletters, local and/or ethnic newspapers, religious institution bulletins) serve the neighborhood.

To find out the main issues currently facing the community, interview two or three community leaders or parents and pay attention to media that represent the community, or organize teams of teachers to visit different neighborhood centers

TABLE 6.1   Analyzing Students' Opportunities to Make Decisions

Situations Requiring Decision Making	Decisions Are Made by		Which Students Are Involved?			How Often?		
	Individual	**Group**	**All**	**Some**	**A Few**	**Often**	**Sometimes**	**Never**
1. Where to sit								
2. Whom to work with; whether to work alone or with someone								
3. What order to accomplish or to work on tasks								
4. Due dates								
5. What materials or procedures to use in accomplishing assignments								
6. Classroom rules								
7. What assignments must be completed								
8. Grading policies and procedures								
9. Supplementary or "extra" content to learn or study								
10. Main content to study								
11. Schoolwide behavior rules								
12. School policies								

and community organizations and report back to the entire staff what they learned. Some questions that can help your investigation include:

1. What problems or issues are currently facing the community?

2. What main improvements would community members like to see?

3. What kinds of additional resources could the community best use, and for what?

4. What resources does the community currently have for addressing these issues, and what is the community currently trying to do about them?

5. What are the community's greatest strengths?

6. What should future citizens be learning to contribute best to the local community's growth, development, and improvement?

LESSON PLAN

Language Experience

Subject Area: Reading

Grade Level: 1–6

Time: Ongoing

Objectives

1. Students will express themselves orally.

2. Students will read orally with accuracy and expression.

3. Students will distinguish between fact and fiction.

Suggested Procedures

1. Discuss with students the difference between fiction and nonfiction, emphasizing that fictional characters are made up even though they are often portrayed to act like real people.

2. Tell students to create a fictional story about children their own age in a fictional school. They should begin the story with an opener such as, "Once upon a time, a fourth-grade class was working on spelling, when suddenly something happened." Ask students to dictate the story while you write it on the board or type it into a computer with a display screen large enough for all students to view. Students can contribute lines to the story in round-robin fashion so that everyone is included.

3. Distribute a copy of the story to each student. Discuss elements of the story that make it fiction rather than fact.

4. Have students practice reading their completed story. Ask each student to add new words from the story to his or her own collection of flash cards of new words to practice.

5. When students have mastered the story to the best of their ability, repeat the procedure. (This activity may be integrated with other approaches to teaching reading.)

Evaluation

1. Assess students' reading skills by listening to them read the class's story.

2. Assess students' oral skills through their contributions to the stories.

3. Assess students' ability to distinguish between fact and fiction through the content of their stories and through class discussion.

AFTER

Language Experience

Subject Area: Reading

Grade Level: 3–6

Time: Three or four days

Objectives

1. Students will express themselves orally.

2. Students will read orally with accuracy and expression.

3. Students will distinguish between fact and fiction.

4. Students will analyze how student groups oppress each other.

Suggested Procedures

1. Discuss with students the difference between fiction and nonfiction, emphasizing that fictional characters are made up even though they are often portrayed to act like real people.

2. Tell students to create a fictional story about children their own age in a fictional school; the story should be about a real event that occurs in the classroom or on the playground. Ask them to discuss and to choose collectively from the following list of events (the teacher can offer other choices, but all choices should relate to students' experiences):

    a. At recess, some students try to join an activity or use equipment that other students usually dominate; however, they are unwelcome.

    b. When teachers are not present, some students tease others, putting them down and trying to hurt or anger them.

    c. During a classroom activity, some students manage to "hog" the most and best resources.

    d. When choosing teams for an activity, some students are always chosen first and others are always chosen last.

    e. At recess, some large students pick on some of the smaller students.

    f. At recess, boys do not allow girls to play; they tell them that girls are not strong enough or skilled enough to play.

Tell students that the story should portray fictional characters who act like real children.

3. Ask students to dictate the story while you write it on the board or type it into a computer with a display screen large enough for all students to view. Students can contribute lines to the story in round-robin fashion so that everyone is included.

4. Have students practice reading their completed story. Ask each student to add new words from the story to his or her own collection of flash cards of new words to practice.

5. Through class discussion, analyze the students' story using the following questions (reword them as needed so that students comprehend):

    a. Which children lose in the story? Is there anything about them that may lead to their losing? (Probe for descriptors, not evaluative judgments.)

    b. Which students gain something? (Probe in the same way.)

    c. Is there anything about the students that may lead to their winning?

    d. Of the children that gain, who are the leaders and who just go along for what they can gain from the situation?

    e. How do the students who gain something work things so they can keep controlling situations like this?

6. Ask students whether it might be possible to resolve this situation so that everyone is treated fairly and equally. After discussing some possibilities, using the language experience approach again, have students make up a story about the same fictional characters in which the losers resolve the problem fairly and successfully.

7. Have students practice reading the new story.

8. Ask students if similar problems happen at their school. If so, discuss ways of resolving them and of establishing rules or procedures for students that promote fairness.

9. Pay attention to race, class, gender, and disability dynamics in what students talk about, and use this as a basis for helping them understand more about these areas. For example, if the "losers" tend to include special education students, regular education students probably know and appreciate little about their peers' needs and characteristics; the school may also unintentionally reinforce the low status of special students and the relatively higher status and "normalcy" of regular education students.

Evaluation

1. Assess students' reading skills by listening to them read the class's stories.

2. Assess students' oral skills through their contributions to the stories and to class discussion.

3. Assess students' understanding of oppression among peer groups through class discussion.

4. Assess students' skills at resolving group conflicts through class discussion and through the action they take on real conflicts in the school.

WHY THE CHANGES?

Language Experience

Practicing Democracy

Democracy plays no role in the "Before" plan. In the "After" plan, students democratically select the topic for the story, and the teacher encourages students to consider and use democratic means to resolve group conflicts.

Analyzing Social Inequality

In the "Before" plan, the content of the story is practically irrelevant; rather, students are encouraged to talk for the purpose of developing oral skill and to produce something to practice reading. In the "After" plan, however, content is important. The teacher uses a story based on students' own experiences to examine how groups of students oppress one another. The story itself is fictional, so students may analyze a problem from an objective perspective. Thus, the teacher specifies that the characters and the school be fictional but that the story revolve around how one group controls or puts down another group and that the characters behave like real people.

Class discussion of the story is also important in that the teacher helps students to identify the oppressors and the oppressed as groups (as opposed to a few individual bullies or victims with no shared characteristics), as well as to determine how the oppressors use a situation to their own benefit. The teacher must decide the extent to which race, class, gender, and disability dynamics are reflected in the story and discussion; although care should be taken not to force the students' experience into these categories, careful thought should be given to what the students' story tells about how these are operating in the school. As students become aware of race, class, gender, and disability dynamics in their own relationships with each other, this can be extended to lessons about diversity and oppression in the neighborhood, the community, and the wider society.

Encouraging Social Action

The "After" plan encourages social action in two related ways. First, the second story that students dictate is one in which the oppressed group acts successfully in its own interest. The teacher should encourage students to make this story reflect some of the real problems, obstacles, and strategies that people use to defend themselves. Second, the discussion moves to real problems in the school and what can be done about them. Democratic processes should be encouraged here, and students should be actively supported in their attempts to resolve group conflicts fairly.

LESSON PLAN

BEFORE

Story Time

Subject Area: Reading

Grade Level: 1–8

Time: Ongoing

Objectives

1. Students will become interested in reading highly acclaimed books.

2. Students will gain an appreciation for and an enjoyment of reading through being read to.

3. Students will enjoy books that are at or above their instructional levels.

Suggested Procedures

1. Select trade books that are considered "classics" to read to students throughout the year (e.g., *Charlotte's Web*, by E. B. White; *Tales of a Fourth Grade Nothing*, by Judy Blume; and *Curious George*, by H. A. Rey).

2. As time permits, read a portion of the chosen book to the class each day.

Evaluation

Assess students' enthusiasm for the books through their attentiveness to the teacher as books are read and through their own selection of books at a later date.

Resources

Blume, J. (1986). *Tales of a fourth grade nothing*. New York: Dell.

Rey, H. A. (1973). *Curious George*. Boston: Houghton Mifflin.
White, E. B. (1952). *Charlotte's web*. New York: Harper & Row.

| **AFTER** | # Story Time* |

Subject Area: Reading

Grade Level: 3–8

Time: Ongoing

Objectives

1. Students will become interested in reading highly acclaimed books that represent diverse peoples in both text and illustrations.

2. Students will enjoy a variety of books both above and below their instructional levels.

3. Students will learn that some groups of people are oppressed and that oppression can manifest itself in many forms.

4. Students will analyze and synthesize ideas in stories.

5. Students will understand that reading is a prerequisite to the acquisition of certain types of knowledge, as well as a necessity for taking advantage of certain types of opportunities.

6. Students will generate alternatives to social conditions that restrict opportunities for oppressed groups of people and develop strategies for their accomplishment.

Suggested Procedures

1. Select trade books, especially those dealing with issues pertaining to race, class, gender, or disability, to read to students throughout the school year. For example: *Baseball Saved Us*, by K. Mochizuki; *The Hot and Cold Summer*, by J. Hurwitz; *My Friend Jacob*, by L. Clifton; *Smoky Night*, by E. Bunting; *Tar Beach*, by A. Getz; *Tar Beach*, by F. Ringgold; and *The Well*, by M. D. Taylor.

Source: Maureen Gillette, College of St. Rose, Albany, NY.

   Note: It may be helpful for the teacher to keep a journal of students' reactions to the books and to the discussions generated in class, as well as of ongoing evidence of improvement in their reading ability. The journal will help the teacher to see visible evidence of change in the students as individuals, in the class as a whole, and in the teacher's own practice.

2. Develop a set of discussion questions related to the issues presented in the book. If the book is lengthy and will span two or three weeks, develop a series of questions to follow sections of the book.

3. As time permits, read a book (or a portion of a book) to students each day. Following the reading, have the class discuss issues raised in the reading, guided by the teacher's preplanned questions. This can be done in small groups or with the whole class. Focus specifically on issues related to race, class, gender, or disability in the story, probing for their relationship to story events. For example, probe the causes that led the boys in *The Hot and Cold Summer* to have preconceived stereotypic ideas about what the girl who was coming to visit would be like. It is often necessary to role-play parts of the story to give students a feeling for events from the viewpoint of the characters, especially when using stories outside children's experiential background, such as having a disability or living in the inner city when they do not.

4. Encourage students to generate alternative courses of action for the story characters based on earlier discussions of story events and to consider all applicable consequences to these alternatives. The teacher may want to ask for volunteers to state the alternative they prefer and to explain their rationale. Discussion follows as other volunteers agree and disagree and offer alternative rationales. The teacher will be able to assess the extent to which students are critically analyzing and synthesizing issues related to race, class, gender, and disability. The teacher needs to provide a nonthreatening environment for doing this. Since much of what one believes comes from one's experiential background, the teacher must be aware of students' ability to understand the issues and should guide the discussion so that students experience a wide variety of ideas and rationales. The teacher also should help students to analyze their own backgrounds for experiences with oppression, either as oppressors or oppressed, which is best done in a nonthreatening way using examples from the story.

5. On completion of a book, give students a choice of projects related to the story. The class, either as a whole or in small groups, should decide in a democratic fashion on a follow-up activity that they believe is suitable for that particular book. The teacher should provide a short list of alternative projects and explore with the class the pros and cons of each one. The list of activities may vary but should end with allowing students to design their own project. The following are some examples:

   a. After reading *The Hot and Cold Summer*, students will have discussed the origins of sex-role stereotypes and how those stereotypes are broken down, and they will have speculated about the ability of the boys in the story to apply what they have learned about one female to all females. A small group of students then interviews younger students about their nontraditional roles (e.g., boys who enjoy playing with dolls or girls who enjoy playing with cars and trucks). The older students work with their younger partners to create a language experience book about that child. The finished product may be bound or laminated and shared with the younger student's peers. The younger child reads the book to a small group of his or her class-mates, and the older child leads a discussion of nontraditional roles in an effort to break down stereotypes held by those children and to reinforce issues of equity. This activity not only gives older students an opportunity to become actively involved in promoting change but can open the door for ongoing cooperative partnerships between older and younger students as well.

b. A small group of students reads another book dealing with the same issue as the book discussed in class and then prepares a comparison between the two books. They may choose to read the book to the class and lead a discussion, or they may meet with the teacher to discuss their analysis.

c. In small groups, students rewrite the story (or part of the story) in play form, incorporating one or more of the alternatives and its consequences as discussed in class. As students rewrite the story, they should role-play the scenes to get a feel for the dialogue and the feasibility of the chosen alternative. The finished play can be produced with costumes and scenery and performed for the rest of the class.

d. The class can compile a list of issue-related questions that they would like to ask the author of the book they have read. The list can be sent to the author or publisher with a cover letter written by the group that explains their discussion of the issue and their interest in the book. If feasible, they could invite the author to the school.

e. Two or three students prepare the story and a plan for discussion. The story is then read and discussed in another class with the students as readers and discussion leaders.

f. Students rewrite the story (or part of it) from another person's perspective (e.g., having a disability versus not having a disability), with a different ending (perhaps more realistic), with a different protagonist (e.g., Latino instead of European American), or in a different setting (e.g., suburban rather than inner city).

g. Older students rewrite difficult or longer stories for younger students. Pages may be illustrated, laminated, and bound. The books are read to and discussed with younger children by older children.

6. If the projects are done in small groups rather than as a class, students should meet as a whole class and share their projects. They should tell their classmates what they did, explain how and why they chose their project, and detail their analysis of the results.

Evaluation

1. Assess students' enthusiasm for the books being read to them through their attentiveness and their own selection of books at later dates.

2. Assess students' levels of discussion following the readings.

3. Assess the quality of students' project activities and the sharing of projects.

4. Determine the extent of students' carryover discussion of issues related to oppressed groups and social inequality into other content areas.

5. Assess students' improvement in reading ability as evidenced in all subject areas.

Resources

Bunting, E. (1994). *Smoky night*. San Diego: Harcourt Brace.

Clifton, L. (1980). *My friend Jacob*. New York: E. P. Dutton.

Getz, A. (1979). *Tar beach*. New York: Dial Press.

Hurwitz, J. (1985). *The hot and cold summer*. New York: Scholastic.

Mochizuki, K. (1993). *Baseball saved us*. New York: Lee & Low Books.

Ringgold, F. (1991). *Tar beach*. New York: Crown.

Taylor, M. D. (1995). *The well*. New York: Dial Books for Young Readers.

WHY THE CHANGES?

Story Time

Modeling and Celebrating Diversity and Equal Opportunity

Students who enter school with what has been termed **school knowledge** often do well from the start, especially in reading. Students who enter school without this knowledge are often members of an oppressed group, and many times they are of the "low-reading group" or characterized as "corrective readers." Once behind, they tend to fall further below their grade levels. We all know how strongly a teacher's words and actions can influence students. Further, reading to students of all ages has a positive impact on how they view reading. It is imperative that all students reach their full reading potential because reading is such an essential life skill, a prerequisite for taking advantage of existing opportunities and for engaging in work to change societal inequalities.

In both plans, the teacher models reading. The "After" plan, however, avoids what Smith, Greenlaw, and Scott (1987) found in their study of books most often read in elementary classrooms—that they maintain stereotypic sex roles and are void of people of color and those with mental or physical disabilities. The "After" plan uses books that offer a more equitable view of society while tapping the experiential background of a wide range of students.

Practicing Democracy

The "After" plan allows for both collective decision making and student choice in the design of follow-up projects. Through a collective process of choosing a follow-up project, either as a class or in small groups with the teacher as guide, students learn to choose from among alternatives in a manner that is fair to all participants. By sharing projects, students become aware of alternative methods for goal accomplishment and gain an appreciation of the learning styles of their peers.

Analyzing Social Inequality

The use of books is a nonthreatening way for students to probe oppression. By using the story plot and the characters, the teacher can develop issues of social inequity outside students' own lives. As students feel comfortable with the issues, the teacher can gradually lead the discussion to the lives of the students. As children begin to recognize incidents involving oppression in their own lives, they can see them in context rather than as a personal statement about themselves.

Encouraging Social Action

Each follow-up activity, whether suggested by the teacher or students, should require students to apply what they have discussed to another situation. For many students, the ideas will be new and may need to be further thought out and assimilated; these students may benefit from a project that opens avenues for discussion with others. The "After" plan places students in the active roles of critical thinkers and problem solvers as they consider conditions that structure inequality. Thus, the reading becomes not only exciting and enjoyable to students but a communicative process as well. Only when reading reaches this level can students use it to take advantage of opportunities and to generate workable alternatives for action based on choice.

LESSON PLAN

BEFORE

Foreign Languages

Subject Area: Language Arts

Grade Level: 4–8

Time: Ongoing

Objectives

1. Students will carry on a simple conversation in languages other than English.

2. Students will appreciate the importance of learning another language.

Suggested Procedures

1. Teach students the basic words and phrases of another language (e.g., greetings, numbers, colors).

2. Teach students the elements of a simple conversation in this language, such as how to ask and answer about the location of objects in the classroom. Create games that allow students to practice; do not let the activity become a dull drill session.

3. When students are proficient, teach the same things in yet another language. Sign language is often enjoyed by students.

4. During the school year, teach one or two songs in each language and gradually add vocabulary words.

5. Discuss the uses for learning these languages (e.g., where one would use them, jobs making use of language skills, and so on).

Evaluation

1. Assess each student's skill through oral conversation.

2. Assess students' appreciation of other languages through their willingness to learn them.

AFTER

U.S. American Languages

Subject Area: Language Arts

Grade Level: 4–8

Time: Ongoing

Objectives

1. Students will name the various languages and dialects spoken by U.S. Americans.

2. Students will appreciate that controversy over language policy involves power and in–out group relationships.

3. Students will empathize with language-minority people in the national language issue.

4. Students will value languages—their own as well as others.

5. Students will carry on a simple conversation in another U.S. American language.

Suggested Procedures

1. Ask students if they can name U.S. American languages and dialects other than Standard English. List some on the board and briefly describe them. Languages and dialects used most commonly include Spanish, French, German, Cantonese, Italian, Amslan (American Sign Language), Black English, Tex-Mex, Appalachian, Mandarin, and Hawaiian pidgin.

2. Ask students whether the United States should have an English-only policy; let students express their views—do not take a stand.

3. Tell students that they will role-play this issue. Divide the class into two groups. Teach each group a code (e.g., fingerspelling, Morse Code) and give the group several days to practice it. Once students become reasonably proficient in using the codes, have them use the codes to develop a group activity, such as singing a song or acting out a skit. Use the activity to develop cohesiveness within each group.

4. Bring both groups together. Explain that one group is dominant in this "society"; you decide which. The dominant group sits in front and has access to paper, pencils, and other materials for a portion of the school day. The dominant group also must teach its code to the other group, but only until they are able to understand most of what is being said in it; fluency or proficiency is not to be stressed.

5. Hold a group discussion in the dominant group's code on whether the class should encourage the use of one or both codes during recess (English is not used, since it would make the debate pointless). It is likely that each group will defend its own code and rally around the issue and that the dominant group will try to impose their own code.

6. Discuss students' reactions to the simulation activity using the following questions:

    a. How did the subordinate group feel about the idea of giving up their own code?

    b. What kinds of arguments did the dominant group use to impose their code?

    c. What kinds of advantages did the dominant group have to help them?

    d. If the subordinate group lost its code, what else would it lose?

    e. How did language serve to unify each group? Was this good, bad, or some of both?

    f. What might be a reasonable policy that respects the interests of both groups?

7. Share with students information on the current English-only policy debate. Ask students to determine who would benefit most from an English-only policy, what the policy would sacrifice, and whether the costs would be worth the gains.

8. Select one or two languages or dialects spoken by U.S. Americans and teach students the basic words, phrases, and elements of a simple conversation. Create games that allow students to practice; do not let this activity become a dull drill session. Teach one or two songs in the language. If possible, arrange for students to interact with people who use the language (such as organizing a social event with a bilingual or deaf class).

9. Help students identify key actors in the current language policy debate and to write letters or essays expressing their views.

Evaluation

1. Evaluate students' understanding of language policy issues through their discussions of the role-play activity.

2. Assess students' skills in carrying on a simple conversation in another language spoken by U.S. Americans through their class participation.

3. Assess students' appreciation of other languages through their interest in learning and practicing them.

WHY THE CHANGES?

U.S. American Languages

Modeling Diversity

The "Before" plan implicitly assumes that all U.S. Americans speak Standard English and that the other languages and dialects spoken by U.S. Americans are foreign. The existence of dialects is not mentioned, nor is the fact that many U.S. Americans use languages other than English as their primary language. In contrast, the "After" plan recognizes the multilingual, multidialectal character of U.S. society by teaching about the various languages of U.S. Americans.

Practicing Democracy

Democracy plays no role in the "Before" plan, whereas the "After" plan invites students to discuss and attempt to resolve the issue of language policy in a democratic society. In the simulation activity, a democratic procedure is used, although it is biased in favor of the dominant group. In the discussion that follows, this problem is addressed openly and students are encouraged to think about how to handle group living in a culturally pluralistic democratic society more fairly.

Analyzing Social Inequality

The "After" plan assumes that the student body is linguistically homogeneous and uses simulation to make language diversity a real part of their lives for a period of time. (If the student body is linguistically pluralistic, the simulation may not be needed.) The simulation is given enough time and attention so that students take it seriously. Each group in the simulation is encouraged to complete a group-building activity using their language to develop a sense of ownership and solidarity among students; as a result, they experience the tensions and conflict that result when one group attempts to control another. The cross-cultural simulation *BaFa BaFa* developed by Shirts (1977) operates on the same principles and can be used to achieve similar purposes, although it does not deal directly with language policy or issues of oppression.

Encouraging Social Action

Once the issue is examined in relationship to both the simulation and real debates about a language policy, students are invited to take action by writing letters or essays.

LESSON PLAN

BEFORE

Environmental Studies

Subject Area: Science

Grade Level: 5–10

Time: One to two weeks and throughout the semester

Objectives

1. Students will research the environmental/ecological problems in their area.

2. Students will list things they can do to become more involved in eliminating environmental/ecological problems

Suggested procedures

1. Upon prior investigation the teacher will initiate this lesson by taking the students on a walk to two teacher-selected contrasting areas in the community that illustrate a polluted area and a carefully monitored environment that shows good ecological management. Upon returning to the classroom, the students will discuss, compare, and contrast what they have seen and brainstorm the causes of the polluted area and why pollution is a detriment to the community and society.

2. The teacher and students will set up an ecological interest center complete with research material (e.g., newspaper and magazine articles, books, films, videotapes). The center can also house the computer. Students working alone or in study pairs should examine the material in the center. At this time the teacher will introduce the environmental/ecological unit.

3. Organize students into cooperative groups, and have each group choose an environmental/ecological problem they wish to research in the Learning Material Center (LMC).

4. Lead a group discussion pertaining to the three Rs of environmental care: reduce, reuse, and recycle. Ask students to think of ways that they can work toward solving environmental problems in their community via the three Rs.

5. Have students prepare a written report in which they outline their suggestions for environmental improvement in their community.

Evaluation

1. Evaluate the students' knowledge of the environmental/ecological problems in their community through a written test or short essay.

2. Evaluate the reports that students present to the class.

AFTER

Environmental/Ecological Studies: A Local, National, and Global Concern[*]

Subject Area: Science

Grade Level: 5–10

Time: Three weeks and throughout the semester

Objectives

1. Students will define the terms *environment* and *ecology* and discuss the importance of each to the welfare of an area.

2. Students will describe interrelationships between organisms and their environments.

3. Students will research their immediate environment and another environmental area outside the United States.

4. Students will value conservation and describe what they can do to promote good conservation.

_____

Sources: Carl A. Grant, Lola Ferguson, Jo Richards, University of Wisconsin–Madison, Madison, WI.

5. Using computers, students will research what students throughout the world are doing to solve the environmental/ecological problems in their communities.

6. Students will show respect for how people deal with environmental issues in other countries that have different ethnic, socioeconomic, religious, and political views from theirs.

Suggested Procedures

1. Brainstorm and record what students know about the terms *environment* and *ecology*.

2. Look up the words in a dictionary, then review what the students have brainstormed and make whatever changes they determine are necessary. Discuss why the terms have been confused in the past and suggest that the students devise a method that will help them use the terms correctly.

3. Take a walk to two contrasting areas in the community that illustrate an area that is polluted and an area that exhibits good ecological management. (*Note*: Observe the areas throughout the school year periodically and discuss/record the changes.) Back in the classroom, students brainstorm the causes of the polluted area and why pollution is a detriment to the community and society. Develop a K–W–L chart (What We Know, What We Want to Know, and What We Have Learned) on which the students record their responses as they progress in the unit.

4. Set up an ecological interest center complete with research material (e.g., newspaper and magazine articles, science and reference books, trade books, bulletin boards, posters, films, and videotapes). The center can also house the computer. Students working alone or in study pairs will examine/study the material in the center through individual and/or group projects and during their free time.

5. Organize students into cooperative groups, each of which will choose an environmental/ecological problem (determined from their field trips or from class assignments/study) that they wish to research in the Learning Material Center (LMC).

6. Write and illustrate a guidebook to local plants and animals and their dependency on one another.

7. Study local pollution problems; have speakers from a nature reserve, a greenhouse, a local park, and/or the local or state EPA agency address the class.

8. Color key a state or local map according to the major water resources and indicate waterfalls, lakes, rivers, streams, and reservoirs. Determine which resources are for commercial use and which are for human consumption. Note the effects on the water source(s) by commercial use.

9. Study the depletion of resources in the community; brainstorm why it is happening, what the economical impact is, how to contain it, what the students can do

about it, and how they can encourage/lead the community to participate; plant a tree, tend to it, advise other classes how the tree will improve the school's aesthetic/physical environment, keep a log of its care and growth and write/produce an Arbor Day celebration to present to all the classes (poems, stories, songs, etc.).

10. Write a letter to the community newspaper presenting an environmental/ecological problem and offer solutions to the problem; write a federal representative (in Congress, in the Senate) about environmental/ecological concerns and possible solutions.

11. Bring in supermarket products and discuss their environmental impact (many claim to be from recycled materials but are not biodegradable); research 100%-recycled materials, make a list to send to students' families, and encourage their use as often as possible.

12. Discuss, research, and prepare informative addresses to school assemblies or other classrooms about the depletion of the ozone layer, its causes, and things that can be done to prevent more damage.

13. Tour a local factory to learn what steps the owners had to take to reduce emissions for pollution control, how it affects the local community, and what the financial price tag for such action will be for the owners and social/financial price tag will be for the community.

14. Study garbage and discuss what happens when garbage is burned in incinerators or is dumped into landfills. Conduct experiments to determine what conditions are necessary to "break down" garbage into reusable nutrients. Work in groups to predict, then observe and compare what happens to apple slices that are sealed in plastic bags and that are buried in loose, damp soil that is periodically turned (compost). Survey the class about how their families dispose of garbage and discuss pros and cons of alternative methods (paper bags, no bags, recycling pails, and composting). Test how quickly a variety of materials decompose (paper, aluminum foil, cotton cloth, and a piece of banana and wiener) after the students have predicted the outcomes and observe/record changes over a two-week period. Write conclusions that members of the class have made from the experiments.

15. Write environmentally conscious mottos for displays around the school (e.g., Don't Feed the Trash—Feed the Hungry; students concentrate on diminishing school lunch waste and ways the wasted food can be put to better use).

16. Demonstrate the balance of life with an aquarium in the room. Note the effects of water temperature, balance of plants, the lack of/overabundance of food, balance of fish and other animals and plants, and the availability of food, plants, and oxygen. Note the role of snails, plants, and supply of oxygen pumped into the aquarium. Graph the number of fish–gill movements at different temperature readings and problem-solve when/why there are more or less.

17. Use a variety of resources that report on current, prevalent worldwide environmental/ecological problems (e.g., global warming, pollution of lakes and streams, depletion of the rain forest and other resources, and soil erosion).

18. Divide the class into seven teams and assign each a continent. Each team will choose a country on their continent to research the environmental/ecological problems. Each group will present their research to the total class on the nature of the environmental/ecological problem(s) and the strategies that the country is employing to prevent or eliminate the problem. Probe for connections between environmental problems in Third World nations, and actions of western nations that may have caused or aggravated these problems.

19. With the assistance of the World Wide Web, have students learn about environmental problems in different parts of the world (especially the country they are studying) and ways they are being resolved.

20. Have students make a curriculum web on environmental concerns, including ways to address these concerns.

Evaluation

1. Based on students' suggestions, develop and implement a class or all-school plan to improve the local environment.

2. Assess students' understanding of worldwide environmental problems through group presentations and/or written essays.

3. Evaluate students' curriculum web on environmental concerns, causes, and possible solutions.

4. During small- and large-group discussions, assess students' understanding of and appreciation for cultural values and the steps a country might take to deal with the concerns (e.g., excess use of fuel consumption that may cause smog and other environmental problems).

5. Assess the value of the unit by the students' changed attitudes and behaviors that demonstrate concern and respect for their environment and the students' efforts to monitor themselves and others in protecting and conserving it.

WHY THE CHANGES?

Environmental/Ecological Studies

Multiple Perspectives

The "After" plan has students examining environmental/ecological problems in their community, as well as in another country. The challenge of discovering environmental problems in their country and relating and comparing these problems to environmental problems in other countries will foster an esprit among the students. Also, the way the "After" plan is structured (i.e., student groups presenting reports on environmental/ecological problems in different countries) will lead students to understand how the issue is important to *all* people. Additionally, the "After" plan teaches respect for how environmental/ecological problems are dealt with in other countries, and asks students to identify

U. S. policies and practices that may be creating or aggravating problems else-where.

Practicing Democracy

An important tenet of democracy is listening to multiple points of view. The "After" plan teaches students to show respect for the way different countries deal with their environmental and ecological problems. Also, as students retrieve information on environmental problems from a Web page that has been prepared by someone in another country, they may have the opportunity to learn how decisions are made in different countries to deal with environmental/ecological problems.

Analyze Social Inequity and Take Action

The "After" plan has students investigating and attempting to eliminate environmental problems and issues in their own community.

Instructional Strategies and Grouping Students

Although the "Before" plan uses student groups and several instructional strategies, the "After" plan uses student groups with a wealth of different student activities. Students are provided numerous opportunities and multiple ways to acquire interest in this topic.

LESSON PLAN

BEFORE

Rate and Line Graph

Subject Area: Mathematics

Grade Level: 6–8

Time: One class period

Objectives

1. Students will complete a rate table that expresses rate as a percentage.
2. Students will construct a segmented line graph showing relationships among rates.

Suggested Procedures

1. Review the concept of rate and the rate table from your previous lessons.
2. Explain that rate can be expressed as a percentage. On the board, complete the rate table shown in Table 6.2, with student input.

TABLE 6.2　Rate: 35% Discount ($0.35 \times M = D$)

Marked price (M), in dollars	$100.00	$150.00	?	$75.80	?
Discount (D)	?	?	$425.00	?	$113.65

TABLE 6.3　$R_m = M - D$

	Store A	Store B	Store C	Store D	Store E
Marked price (M), in dollars	$450.00	$450.00	$450.00	$450.00	$450.00
Discount price (D), in dollars	$431.00	$382.50	$414.00	$261.00	$279.00
Discount rate (R)	?	?	?	?	?

3. Ask students to name some discount stores in the area. Ask them whether all the stores charge the same price for the same item; point out that prices usually vary somewhat among stores.

4. Explain that the discount rates on television sets in different stores will be compared. In the rate table shown in Table 6.3, each column refers to a different store, and the marked and discount prices of each store's television set are given. With student input, compute the discount rate for each store on the board.

5. Distribute graph paper. Explain that rates can be graphed and compared visually. Have each student construct a segmented line graph of the discount rates in Table 6.3.

Evaluation

1. From class discussion, assess students' understanding of the concept of rate.

2. Check students' line graphs for accuracy.

AFTER

Rate and Line Graph

Subject Area: Mathematics

Grade Level: 6–8

Time: Two class periods

Objectives

1. Students will complete a rate table that expresses rate as a percentage.

2. Students will construct a segmented line graph showing relationships among rates.

3. Students will compare poverty rates among different racial groups.

Suggested Procedures

1. Ask students whether they know if poverty in the United States has increased, decreased, or remained the same in the last two decades. Ask whether people are more likely to be poor if they are white or of color. Ask also how well students believe U.S. society has reduced economic racism over the past two decades. The concepts of rate and line graph can help students examine these issues.

2. Review the concept of rate and the rate table from your previous lessons. Explain that rate can be expressed as a percentage. On the board and with student input, complete the rate table shown in Table 6.4. Population data are expressed in thousands in the table; have students convert the statistics to thousands.

3. Give each student a copy of a table such as the one shown in Table 6.5. Explain that each column refers to a different racial group within the United States and that the numbers refer to 1983 census population data. Ask students to describe population concepts that might be expressed as rate (e.g., unemployment rate, high school dropout rate, poverty rate).

TABLE 6.4   Rate: 22% of a Population ($0.22 \times P = s$)

Population (P), in thousands	100	?	820	5,550	?	?	30,800
Subgroup (s), in thousands	?	44	?	?	128	1,262	?

TABLE 6.5   Rate: 15%

	Asian American	African American	Latino	Native American	European American
Population (P), in thousands	3,726	27,263	14,609	1,534	196,036
Subgroup (s), in thousands	?	?	?	?	?

4. Explain that the rate of any population concept can vary among different racial groups. Using Table 6.5, have students compute the subgroup when the following rates apply to each racial group: Asian American, 13 percent; African American, 36 percent; Latino, 30 percent; Native American, 28 percent; European American, 12 percent.

5. Explain that these rates refer to the poverty rate of each racial group during 1983 and discuss this in terms of how many people lived in poverty during that year. Explain that census data on poverty rates among African Americans and European Americans have been recorded since 1960 and among Latinos since 1972.

6. Distribute a table such as Table 6.6. Explain that the figures in the table refer to poverty rates; make sure students understand that the figures do not refer to numbers of people. You can access 1990 census data on the World Wide Web at the following Web site, to keep this kind of table current:

    http://venus.census.gov/cdrom/lookup

   Distribute graph paper. Review how a segmented line graph is constructed. Have students work in pairs to construct segmented line graphs of poverty rates over time, using different colors to represent different racial groups.

TABLE 6.6   Poverty Rates in the United States, 1960–1993 (in percentages)

Year	All Races	White	Black	Hispanic
1960	22.4	17.8	—	—
1966	14.7	11.3	41.8	—
1969	12.1	9.5	32.2	—
1970	12.6	9.9	33.5	—
1975	12.3	9.7	31.3	23.0
1976	11.8	9.1	31.1	26.9
1977	11.6	8.9	31.3	24.7
1978	11.4	8.7	30.6	22.4
1979	11.7	9.0	31.0	21.6
1980	13.0	10.2	32.5	21.8
1981	14.0	11.1	34.2	25.7
1982	15.0	12.0	35.6	26.5
1983	15.2	12.1	35.7	29.9
1984	14.4	11.5	33.8	28.0
1985	14.0	11.4	31.3	28.4
1986	14.6	11.0	31.1	29.0
1987	13.4	10.4	32.4	27.3
1988	13.0	10.1	31.3	28.0
1989	12.8	10.0	30.7	26.7
1990	13.5	10.7	31.9	26.2
1991	14.2	11.3	32.7	28.1
1992	14.8	11.9	33.4	29.6
1993	15.1	12.2	33.1	30.6

Statistical Abstract of the United States. (1995). Lanham, MD: Bernan Press.

7. Discuss the persistence of poverty over time and the reasons poverty rates seem to be higher among African Americans and Latinos than among European Americans and Asian Americans.

8. Collect state and/or city data on the same type of poverty rates. Have students compute local poverty rates over time and construct segmented line graphs. As part of another class, students should investigate the specific policies and practices that have contributed to poverty and racism locally. Students can then prepare a report for a local newspaper that includes rate tables, line graphs, and results of their investigation, along with suggestions for how poverty and racism might be dealt with more constructively.

Evaluation

1. Check students' rate tables and line graphs for accuracy.

2. From class discussion, assess students' understanding of the concept of rate and of rate changes over time.

3. From class discussion, assess students' awareness of poverty and inequality in the United States.

WHY THE CHANGES?

Rate and Line Graph

Modeling Diversity and Equal Opportunity

Rate tables and line graphs can be constructed using any set of quantities that express rates. The "Before" plan is concerned only with teaching these mathematical concepts and uses discount rate as a meaningful set of quantities that students would understand. However, it is not truly concerned with teaching about discounts. The "After" plan, however, teaches a social issue and mathematical concepts simultaneously. Poverty rate lends itself well to the concepts of rate and line graphs. The lesson encourages students to consider whether society actually values racial diversity and equal opportunity when it continues to allow a sizable percentage of citizens to live in poverty and to sustain particularly high rates of poverty among U.S. Americans of color.

Before teaching this lesson, the teacher should be ready to deal with the "blame the victim" reasoning that students may use to explain poverty. The teacher is encouraged to coordinate with other teachers on efforts to help students understand institutional racism and classism. This lesson alone will not do that, but it can be a valuable one when taught in conjunction with other lessons on these issues.

Analyzing Social Inequality

Data on national poverty rates give a global picture of racism and classism in our society over time but may appear abstract and removed from students' own lives. Therefore, the teacher is encouraged to locate similar data from the state and local levels. Often such data are available through state and city governments or local social service agencies. The teacher may find that these local data have not been prepared into rate tables and line graphs, which may depict local trends over time.

Encouraging Social Action

Although the math teacher may not feel comfortable with having students investigate reasons for institutionalized poverty in their city, working with teachers in other disciplines is important for helping students link math with other areas of living. In this case, math and social studies could be linked well, and these could be linked with English in the preparation of a written research report. Such interdisciplinary teaching helps subjects gain relevance and meaning to students and makes social action projects such as the one illustrated in this lesson possible.

LESSON PLAN

BEFORE

City Government

Subject Area: Social Studies

Grade Level: 7–9

Time: One week

Objectives

1. Students will identify important city services and explain their functions.

2. Students will identify the typical problems of a given city.

3. Students will recognize that various decisions are necessary to run a city.

4. Students will recognize that the quality of urban life can vary.

Suggested Procedures

1. Discuss with students how government plays an important role in a city and determines the types of city services that are available.

2. Determine as a group the types of services available in most major cities. Read about city services in a textbook.

3. Have guest speakers from two or three different city services visit and speak to the class.

4. In groups of four, ask students to develop a paragraph that outlines the problems of a city. They should also identify what city services they consider important and how those services could offer a solution to the problems. A final summary statement should express how city services affect the quality of urban life.

Evaluation

Assess students' mastery of the objectives through a quiz.

AFTER

City Government*

Subject Area: Social Studies

Grade Level: 7–9

Time: One or two weeks

Objectives

1. Students will learn that an urban area consists of a variety of ethnic, racial, age, and religious groups, each with its own needs.

2. Students will demonstrate sensitivity to these diverse needs.

3. Students will identify necessary city services.

4. Students will recognize that cities should make city services equally available to a diverse city population.

5. Students will view decisions as a necessary part of running a city.

6. Students will learn that mutual cooperation is one method of solving common urban problems.

7. Students will recognize that city services have an impact on the quality of urban life.

8. Students will appreciate that cultural diversity makes a city a "better place."

Suggested Procedures

1. In groups of three or four, have students discuss who lives in any given city (e.g., those with physical disabilities; the aged; racial, ethnic, and religious groups). Have the groups present their findings to the class and record their responses for the class to see.

2. As a class, discuss how the needs of a diverse population vary from group to group (e.g., neighborhoods with large numbers of children need more schools;

Source: Virginia Kester, Madison Public Schools, Madison, WI.

limited-English-speaking communities need services in their own languages; a neighborhood center could serve the young after school and the elderly during the day).

3. As a group, have students determine what city services could meet these diverse needs.

4. Present the following scenario to the class: "You are all members of a city council. It is your job to determine what city services will be funded in the neighborhood described in the accompanying packet. You may not go over budget and you will have to make decisions. There is not enough money for everything this area needs. As a group, you should give attention to how you solve this problem (through bullying, cooperation, and so on) as well as to solving the problem itself. Be prepared to describe to the class how you resolved this issue and what you actually decided."

5. Give each group a packet that includes the following items:
   a. Map of the area
   b. List of needs for the area
   c. Population (who lives there?)
   d. Possible city services that could meet needs. Each city service should be given a fixed dollar amount that it would cost to implement.
   e. Amount of money the council has to spend (must be less than what is needed for all services, so decisions have to be made)

6. In small groups, have students discuss and decide which city services they feel should be implemented in "their neighborhood." Remind them that they should decide how they want to make these decisions and present their findings. Their presentations should include the city services that should be implemented in the area, an explanation of how each service will meet the needs of the area, reasons the service was chosen over other services, and the way the group arrived at its decision (i.e., the group decision-making process).

7. Once all group projects have been presented, the teacher should guide the class in drawing some conclusions. Discuss the following questions and ideas:
   a. How does availability of city services affect the quality of your lives (e.g., how good would your education be if it was in a language you did not understand? is a new bus good for you if it stops six or seven blocks from your house or is impossible for you to get on?) and the quality of city life as a whole (e.g., health clinics that reduce the spread of communicable diseases)?
   b. How do the city services available to you make your lives better in the long term versus the short term (e.g., if the school is two blocks from your house, how does its close proximity affect your feelings about it)?
   c. City governments always have to make some kind of decision about which service to supply and how it will be implemented in a city. This has the

potential to be a heated, emotional decision in real life, and students need to discuss the kinds of behaviors that help ensure a fair decision-making process. They should refer back to their own discussions and identify behaviors that allowed for an open discussion (discuss also why an open discussion is in the best interest of all people).

8. Have students collect newspaper articles about current city service issues. They should present in written or oral form what they consider the issue to be and how it relates to quality of life within their city.

Evaluation

1. Assess students' appreciation of the diversity of an urban population through initial class discussion and their participation in the mock city council.

2. Assess students' understanding of city services through their solutions to the groups' problems.

3. Assess students' decision-making skills through their small-group work.

WHY THE CHANGES?

City Government

Modeling Diversity

The "Before" plan does not mention the diversity that characterizes a city's population, whereas the "After" plan makes this its focus topic. In the "After" plan, students examine what diverse groups compose a city and then analyze competing claims that different groups have on city service resources.

Practicing Democracy

In the "After" plan, students role-play a city council and must collectively decide how to allocate resources. The "Before" plan does not provide this type of active democratic simulation.

Analyzing Social Inequality

By examining the allocation of resources of a city and by role-playing a city council, students in the "After" plan learn that resources are often distributed unequally and that the decision-making process can produce that result. Then, by collecting and discussing newspaper articles on city services in their own city, students can begin to apply this analysis to where they live.

The lesson is usually successful with middle school students, who enjoy issue-oriented activities in which they can express values that are important to them. It is extremely important to follow through on the final discussion, in that students internalize more readily concepts that are applied to their daily lives.

LESSON PLAN

BEFORE

Settling the West

Subject Area: Social Studies

Grade Level: 8–9

Time: One week

Objectives

1. Students will identify and describe the goals of the western settlers during the 1800s.

2. Students will analyze the effect of the increase of settlers on Native American culture.

3. Students will describe what settlers found on arriving in the west.

Suggested Procedures

1. Outline for students the reasons why people went west (e.g., economic reasons).

2. Read the selected U.S. American history textbook for a description of the trip west and the things people found on arriving there.

3. Use study sheets to reinforce key concepts.

4. Through class discussion and appropriate films or texts, discuss the effect of the increase of settlers on Native American life-style.

Evaluation

Assess students' mastery of the concepts through a quiz.

AFTER

Conflict over Western Land*

Subject Area: Social Studies

Grade Level: 8–9

Time: Two weeks

———————

*Source: Virginia Kester, Madison Public Schools, Madison, WI.

Objectives

1. Students will recognize that the settlers who went west were from a variety of ethnic, religious, and racial backgrounds.

2. Students will identify that the reasons for going west varied with the settlers.

3. Students will describe the hardships of those who moved west.

4. Students will recognize that the land and its use was a major source of conflict among different cultural groups.

5. Students will identify and describe the various Native American nations indigenous to the U.S. American west.

6. Students will appreciate that the western lands were already "home" to many Mexican and native peoples.

7. Students will identify a variety of approaches to solving a conflict and recognize that individuals always have a choice.

Suggested Procedures

1. Read available material on Native American nations west of the Mississippi River. Films or guest speakers can also be engaged to give students necessary historical background. Have students take notes on the mainstream native economy and culture as well as various Native American viewpoints toward their land.

2. Discuss as a group how Native American groups would have felt about their land and life-style. Have students infer responses of these groups to others with varied purposes moving into their area. Have students role-play what might be said at a meeting of Native Americans discussing "rumors" of settlers (or invaders) and possible responses to them.

3. View filmstrips on the Mexican life-style of the southwest as well as Mexican viewpoints of new settlers. (The filmstrips available through La Raza or other Latino organizations will give the Mexican point of view, which is essential.) Have students note, as they did with Native American people, what the mainstay of the southwestern economy would be as well as the Mexican attitude toward the land.

4. Have students role-play what might be discussed at a meeting of Mexicans concerning the incoming settlers. They should note possible responses.

5. Students should read or view available material on the settlers who went west. (The material should cover the various ethnic groups who traveled west.)

6. Discuss with the class how these different groups would view the land of the west and what needs they would hope to meet by moving there.

7. Divide the class into small groups. Have each group choose two viewpoints and develop each viewpoint toward the land as well as the methods they plan to use if others challenge this viewpoint.

8. Have each group present its viewpoint and methods.

9. Summarize with the class that conflict occurred in the west because different people wanted a limited amount of land for different uses and they had different cultural views about land ownership. The class should also read and discuss selections on the conflicts that occurred between the various groups in the 1800s (e.g., Mexican-American War, Indian War) and identify the causes of these conflicts.

10. Locate and share with students current examples of conflict over land. These can be arguments over land use, urban renewal versus renovation, "gentrification" of a city, landlord or tenant rights, or other examples from their own neighborhoods. Discuss how land and its distribution have remained a focus of conflict in our society. Students can also discuss other current conflicts caused by varied interest groups desiring a limited resource such as employment or housing (e.g., the recent immigration law and its impact on the economy of the southwest). Students should try to draw parallels between these current examples and the conflicts of the past.

11. Refer back to students' discussion of the methods of coping with conflict. Rank order the methods that worked toward ending the conflict. Discuss how the methods of resolving conflict can be applied to today's issues.

Evaluation

1. Assess students' mastery of the main ideas through a quiz or essay.

2. Have students choose one of the current conflicts and develop a plan for resolving it.

WHY THE CHANGES?

Conflict over Western Land

Modeling Diversity

The "Before" plan represents the perspective usually taken in studying the west, in that it focuses on white European American settlers and mentions only in context other groups—mainly Native Americans. In contrast, the "After" plan gives equal attention to Native Americans, Mexicans, and European Americans. That is, the lesson's focus is not on only one group's story but on the ways various groups interacted in conflict over control of the land and on their diverse viewpoints about land use. The "After" plan also uses a wider variety of teaching strategies than the "Before" plan. In the "Before" plan, students mainly read, listen, and watch, whereas they also role-play and discuss in the "After" plan.

Practicing Democracy

The "After" plan provides more opportunity for students to practice democracy than the "Before" plan. Students role-play meetings of Native Americans and

Mexicans, discussing the advancing settlers. These meetings can and should be run democratically.

Analyzing Social Inequality

After studying conflict over western land, in the "After" plan students examine conflict over other limited resources, including land, in their own community. They are encouraged to discover who has how much of the best land and to examine how this came to be and how current struggles for land and other resources take place.

LESSON PLAN

BEFORE

Music Appreciation

Subject Area: Vocal Music

Grade Level: 8–12

Time: One week

Objectives

1. Students will describe and identify musical characteristics particular to a genre of contemporary music (e.g., pop).

2. Students will sing songs representative of a genre.

Suggested Procedures

1. Select three to five songs that represent a particular genre of contemporary music. Explain to students that they will study the genre for the next few days.

2. Provide students with background information on the genre and on key composers and performers. Students will already have some knowledge here that they may wish to share with the class. Provide an overview of the salient characteristics of the genre of music and of the songs with which students should become familiar.

3. Play recordings of each song. After each one, help students identify how the song exemplifies the characteristics of the genre. Help them identify specific examples of these characteristics (e.g., repetition, rhythm, and so on).

4. Using your usual procedure for teaching the class to sing a piece of music, teach them some of the songs.

Evaluation

1. Assess students' ability to identify musical selections through a quiz.

2. Assess students' mastery of a song through their performances.

AFTER

Music Appreciation

Subject Area: Vocal Music

Grade Level: 8–12

Time: One week

Objectives

1. Students will describe and identify genres of contemporary music.

2. Students will analyze popular music for portrayal of sex roles and gender relationships.

3. Students will analyze peer-group norms for sex roles and gender relationships.

4. Students will identify who profits by reinforcing sexism among the young through popular music and music videos.

5. Students will sing contemporary nonsexist music selections.

Suggested Procedures

1. Explain what is meant by the term *genre*. Provide background information on genres of contemporary music and the salient characteristics of each. Find out which genres are preferred by the students in the class.

2. Ask students to name some of their favorite popular songs and rock videos. Ask what appeals to them about these songs and videos.

3. Ask students what these songs and videos say about relationships between men and women. Explain that the class will analyze messages about this.

4. On the board, develop with the class a list of questions for analyzing media portrayal of male–female relationships. For example:

   What image is given of the ideal woman? The ideal man?

   What image is given of what a man gains from a relationship with a woman? of what a woman gains from a relationship with a man?

   To what extent are sharing and friendship portrayed as a central part of a love relationship?

> To what extent are love relationships portrayed as heterosexual? As homosexual?
>
> What image is given of power relationships between men and women?
>
> Who wields what kind of power and over what aspects of the relationship?
>
> How do race and social class factors interact with gender relationships?

5. Have students select five to ten popular songs and/or videos* that portray male–female relationships. Provide or have students bring to class the lyrics to the songs and copies of the videos. In small groups, have students analyze the songs and videos according to the questions developed earlier. Then ask them to share their findings with the class.

6. Ask students to consider how their peer group deals with male–female relationships. Have them discuss questions such as these:

> What does it mean to be "feminine"? "masculine"?
>
> In male–female relationships, who wields power over what aspects of the relationship?
>
> To what extent are friendship and sharing a central part of love relationships?
>
> How are female–male relationships exploitative?
>
> Do male–female relationships vary in their dynamics with different social classes? with different racial groups?
>
> Are particular role or power dynamics involved in interracial or cross-social class girl–boy relationships?

Be careful that students avoid finger-pointing and name-calling; they should stick to the issues. You might precede this with a discussion of ground rules for keeping it constructive.

7. Ask students to consider the extent to which popular songs and videos reinforce unequal and exploitative gender, racial, and class relationships. Or, to what extent do they suggest equality? How does this vary among artists? Do any artists or businesses (record companies, record stores, television stations) profit by selling youth images that reinforce unequal relationships? Have students brainstorm ways they might deal with such businesses, including refusing to buy (boycotting), writing letters, and publishing critical reviews in newspapers.

8. With input from the class, identify some contemporary music selections that are not exploitative. Using your usual procedure for teaching the class to sing a piece of music, teach them these songs. Students may also prepare a concert that focuses on positive intergroup relationships and that tells the audience what they have learned about exploitative images in music.

---

*Note: Adherence to copyright laws is important.

Evaluation

1. Assess students' ability to analyze sexism critically in their peer group and in music through class discussion.

2. Assess students' mastery of the songs through their performances.

WHY THE CHANGES?

Music Appreciation

Practicing Democracy

The "Before" plan does not involve students in decision making; rather, the teacher determines the music to study, the way it will be studied, and the selections students will learn to sing. In contrast, the "After" plan involves student decision making—students select the music to analyze, help develop the questions to guide their analysis, and help select songs to learn. This gives students more ownership in the learning process and helps them develop decision-making skills. The "After" lesson suggests that students learn on their own and examine critically their own real-life experiences. Thus, it is essential that students have input into the lesson and become active participants in helping to construct the lesson itself.

Analyzing Social Inequality

The "Before" plan may or may not relate to students' own lives. Often music is taught in schools as if it is not a part of students' lives, and a sharp distinction is made between school music and students' popular music. Even a unit on contemporary music can focus on music that adults enjoy more than adolescents. However, much of what students internalize about music is learned through their experience with popular music. Teachers may not enjoy much of the music that students enjoy, but such music can be used as a vehicle for teaching students a greater understanding and appreciation of music.

The "After" plan helps students critically analyze messages in music. Adolescents expend considerable energy and attention working out gender identities and relationships with the opposite sex, and this is informed to some extent by students' ethnic and class identities. However, this area is rarely addressed at all in the school curriculum, even by educators who teach about sexism and women's contributions. The "After" lesson takes gender identity and boy–girl relationships—topics of interest to students—and popular music and uses these topics to help students openly examine sexism and exploitation. Students are helped to understand how male–female relationships can be exploitative and how youth can be exploited by the music industry catering to sexism in the lives of the young. In addition, the lesson helps students examine how race and class connect with inequality and can be enmeshed in gender relationships (e.g., why

African American male–European American female relationships are more common than European American male–African American female relationships).

Encouraging Social Action

The "After" lesson asks students to consider how they can resist being exploited by those in the music industry who profit by selling them music that reinforces inequality. It also suggests incorporating the idea of critical analysis of messages in music into a concert.

LESSON PLAN

BEFORE

Creating a Newspaper

Subject Areas: English, Journalism

Grade Level: 8–12

Time: Four weeks

Objectives

1. Students will describe the purposes and forms of various parts of the newspaper.
2. Students will describe roles and responsibilities of news professionals.
3. Students will communicate effectively, using correct writing conventions.
4. Students will examine implications of audience for newspaper content.
5. Students will create a school newspaper.

Suggested Procedures

1. Find out the extent to which students use the newspaper and, if they do, which section(s). Then distribute several community newspapers and, if possible, school newspapers from several schools. Have students skim these, then discuss why people use newspapers and what the common sections are in a newspaper. Tell them that they will be creating a newspaper for their own school.

2. Invite a panel of guest speakers who work for local newspapers, magazines, and TV stations. Have them talk about the purpose of the newspaper, magazine, or TV station they work for, what they do in their own jobs, what a typical day for them is like, how knowledge of the audience influences stories and coverage to the audience, and what trends they foresee in their work.

3. Gather information about interests of students in the school. Have students each interview one or two people in the school to find out (a) what they would like to see in a newspaper, (b) what they don't like in a newspaper (or on TV), and (c) what would make them want to pick up a student-created newspaper and read it. Discuss how these interests should be reflected in a school newspaper.

4. Determine what the main sections of the newspaper will be, and divide students into groups accordingly. The sections may include, for example, a main section, entertainment, editorials, and sports. Each group should decide what stories or features they could create or gather for that section. Have each group then report to the class as a whole for feedback.

5. Give students a few days to complete writing their articles or other entries. Students should put their articles into a computer for editing and later for merging into one document. Each section should have a "section editor," who ensures that the articles get written. Section editors should collect the articles and redistribute them within the section to read carefully and provide feedback. Encourage students to rework their submissions. Then collect all the articles.

6. There are various methods for compiling the articles into one document; teachers will need to determine what is feasible in their own situations. Some teachers have access to computer programs for doing a real newspaper layout; others will assemble the articles in the form of an informal newsletter.

7. Students should design an audience feedback questionnaire to include with the newspaper to gather information about how well their newspaper responds to a diverse audience.

8. Duplicate and distribute the newspaper; collect as many feedback questionnaires as possible. Analyze feedback questionnaires. Have students examine the results and write recommendations for how to improve the newspaper.

Evaluation

1. Evaluate each section of the students' newspaper for its reflection of purposes of that section of the newspaper.

2. Evaluate each student's written contribution for effective communication and use of correct writing conventions.

3. Evaluate the newspaper for how well it interests readers in the school.

AFTER | ## Creating a Newspaper

Subject Areas: English, Journalism

Grade Level: 8–12

Time: Four weeks

Objectives

1. Students will describe the purposes and forms of various parts of the newspaper.

2. Students will communicate effectively, using correct writing conventions.

3. Students will analyze diverse interests and viewpoints of a multicultural community and issues of concern to them.

4. Students will recognize biases in the media.

5. Students will critique relationships between institutional power, economic power, and media.

6. Students will create a newspaper that effectively serves a multicultural community and advances its interests.

Suggested Procedures

1. Find out the extent to which students use the newspaper and, if they do, which section(s). Then distribute several community newspapers and, if possible, school newspapers from several schools. Have students skim these, then discuss why people use newspapers and what the common sections are in a newspaper. Tell them that they will be creating a newspaper for their own community, both as a way of learning about newspapers and a way of creating something that serves a diverse community well.

2. Invite a panel of guest speakers who work for local newspapers, magazines, and TV stations. Try to get speakers who represent a diversity of sociocultural groups. Have them talk about the purpose of the newspaper or TV station they work for, who the audience is, how knowledge of the audience influences stories and coverage, how closely they pay attention to the audience, and how much advertisers influence stories and coverage. Also ask about how much they investigate controversial issues beyond what the major news services provide.

3. Decide who will be the audience of the newspaper the class will create; it might be the school, it might be the local neighborhood and the school. Gather information about the racial and ethnic composition of the audience, the socioeconomic composition, languages spoken, the age composition, and any other demographic variables that might be significant in terms of audience analysis.

4. Assign students to analyze a TV show or a newspaper section. Divide the class so that a small group looks particularly at the representation of a particular segment of their audience (from the previous procedure). For example, you may assign three students to look for representation of Asian American adults, three to look for representation of Asian American children and youth, and so forth.

5. Have students share their findings, and determine which sociocultural groups are best represented and best served by the media they analyzed. Who is invisi-

ble? Who is represented negatively? Whose perspectives predominate? Whose issues are discussed and advanced?

6. Gather several alternative media (media produced by groups other than the dominant society, such as African American newspapers or magazines, Latino news media, feminist media, gay/lesbian media). Distribute these; after students have browsed them, discuss how the viewpoints represented are similar to or different from those in media they examined earlier, and the degree to which issues discussed in them are different and investigated differently. Discuss why alternative media arise.

7. Older students can examine relationships between power and media by exploring how advertisers affect content and substance of media. View the first half of the video *Manufacturing Consent*, which presents Noam Chomsky's theory of propaganda. Then have students in small groups create a poster, skit, or short essay expressing what they learned. Use their work to discuss how one can find out in one's own community the degree to which advertising affects the substance of news.

8. Have students each interview one or two people in the target audience to find out (a) what they would like to see in a newspaper, (b) what they don't like in a newspaper (or on TV), (c) what would make them want to pick up a student-created newspaper and read it, and (d) their suggestions for making the newspaper respond well to a diverse audience. Make sure people from all subgroups in the target audience are interviewed. Have students share their findings.

9. Based on these various investigations (of the audience, of biases in media, and of alternative media), have students develop a purpose for the newspaper they will create. Their purpose may be partially to entertain and respond to consumer demand; it might also be to educate, examine issues, and address concerns of a multicultural community.

10. Determine what the main sections of the newspaper will be, and divide students into groups accordingly. The sections may include, for example, a main section, entertainment, editorials, and sports. Each group should decide what stories or features they could create or gather for that section. Have each group then report to the class as a whole for feedback, paying particular attention to how well their ideas fit the expressed desires of the audience. Desires of groups that are numerically small often get lost at this point; draw students' attention to any such groups in their audience and have them consider how to make the newspaper relevant to these groups. If students are not sure at this point, they may need to do a few more interviews.

11. Give students a few days to complete writing their articles or other entries. Students should put their articles into a computer for editing and later for merging into one document. Each section should have a "section editor," who ensures that the articles get written. Section editors should collect the articles and redistribute them within the section to read carefully and provide feedback. Encour-

age students to rework their submissions. It is up to the section editor to deter-mine when each article is finished.

12. There are various methods for compiling the articles into one document; teach-ers will need to determine what is feasible in their own situations. Some teach-ers have access to computer programs for doing a real newspaper layout; others will assemble the articles in the form of an informal newsletter.

13. Students should design an audience feedback questionnaire to include with the newspaper to gather information about how well their newspaper responds to a diverse audience. The questionnaire should include the most important demo-graphic variables, so that responses can be grouped according to who the respondents are (such as by sex).

14. Duplicate and distribute the newspaper; collect as many feedback question-naires as possible.

15. Analyze feedback questionnaires, dividing them for analysis by key demographic variables. Have students examine the results to find out how well their newspa-per served the various subgroups in the audience. Have the class write recom-mendations for how to build a newspaper that serves a diverse community audi-ence. If they wish, their recommendations can be sent to local news media.

Evaluation

1. Evaluate each section of the students' newspaper for its reflection of its pur-poses.

2. Evaluate each student's written contribution for effective communication and use of correct writing conventions.

3. Evaluate the newspaper for how well it addresses and reflects the diversity of its audience and the viewpoints and interests of people in the audience.

WHY THE CHANGES?

Creating a Newspaper

Modeling Diversity

In the "Before" lesson, while audience is acknowledged, the diverse perspec-tives and interests of the audience are not necessarily attended to. The "After" lesson focuses on diversity within the audience. Students may at first feel uncomfortable with that focus, until they realize that there are some real differ-ences in perspectives among people in the audience, which they cannot neces-sarily anticipate without finding out specifically about their audience.

   The "After" lesson also attempts to make sure guest speakers are diverse. Not only does this present a diversity of role models, but issues related to diver-sity are much more likely to be discussed when the speakers are diverse.

Analyzing Social Inequality

Newspapers are a great way to examine what bias there is in media, whose viewpoints predominate in media, and how media connect with power and control issues. The "Before" plan does not address these issues at all. The "After" plan has students examine media they consume, then use the results of their examination to attempt to build a newspaper that is more inclusive. Using alternative media (such as ethnic or feminist media) helps students to see limitations in the perspectives of mainstream media and to see what it means to advocate for interests other than those students may be used to seeing advocated in media. It is particularly effective to find different treatments of the same event or issue, such as immigration.

The "After" plan also suggests examining relationships among economic power, advertising, and media content. This is a complex issue that can become an entire unit in and of itself. However, even a short lesson such as using the suggested Chomsky videotape to help analyze local newspapers can raise students' level of awareness about the power of advertising and cause students to examine their advertisers critically.

Encouraging Social Action

Part of social action entails learning to build new institutions that work for everyone. The entire focus of the "After" lesson is on building a newspaper that actually works for everyone in the community, based on some analysis of why newspapers often exclude or distort parts of their audience. In addition, in the "After" plan, students are encouraged to communicate their recommendations for building a newspaper, based on an analysis of their own newspaper, to a wider audience.

LESSON PLAN

BEFORE

The Court System

Subject Area: Social Studies

Grade Level: 8–12

Time: One week

Objectives

1. Students will describe how the court system works and how a trial takes place.

2. Students will describe the roles of the main persons involved in a trial.

3. Students will distinguish between the different kinds of courts and identify the kinds of legal issues that each type deals with.

Suggested Procedures

1. Ask students to describe how the court system works and how a trial takes place, based on what they have learned through the media or during any visits to court.

2. Have students read pages in a textbook on the court system, the kinds of courts, and the kinds of legal issues with which each deals. Discuss this material with the class, providing additional examples and explanations.

3. Have students read pages in a textbook on how a trial takes place. Discuss this with the class, making a list on the board of each of the main persons involved in a trial and describing his or her role: judge, bailiff, prosecutor, plaintiff, defendant, defense counsel, witness, jury, and court reporter.

4. Arrange a visit to the local courthouse to watch a trial in action. Have students develop questions, based on their observation, that they would like to ask a member of the legal profession.

5. Invite a member of the legal profession to talk with the class as a guest speaker. The talk should center on the questions that students generate.

Evaluation

Assess students' knowledge of how the court system works, of the different kinds of courts and their functions, of how a trial takes place, and of the roles of the main persons involved in a trial through a test.

AFTER

The Court System[*]

Subject Area: Social Studies

Grade Level: 8–12

Time: Ongoing

Objectives

1. Students will use democratic procedures to establish classroom rules.

2. Students will use courtroom procedures to enforce classroom rules.

3. Students will describe how the court system works and how a trial takes place.

4. Students will describe local agencies that help low-income families and families of color with legal problems.

---

[*]*Source:* Mary F. Braun, Kenosha, WI.

5. Students will analyze local legal conflicts involving race, class, gender, sexual orientation, or disability issues.

6. Students will examine how many people of color, women, and people with disabilities hold positions of judge or bailiff in their local court system.

Suggested Procedures

1. Ask students to brainstorm a list of the classroom conditions that they need for optimum studying and learning (e.g., lighting, heat, room, noise level, and so on); write the list on the board. Beside the list, record students' suggestions for rules or classroom laws that help provide the conditions for good learning. Ask them to discuss the lists and to suggest any additions or corrections.

2. Explain that students will select the rules that they will follow daily in the classroom. Take a secret ballot vote to give each student the chance to express his or her opinion. If the rules receive a majority vote, they are passed. If they do not pass, return to the list and discuss changes. This may be time consuming, but students' time is not wasted if the teacher explains that this is the way laws are passed and that discussion is important. The students are also more apt to follow rules that they establish themselves.

3. Ask students if they have ever seen a courtroom—either a real one or one on television. Explain that in a democratic society, courts are considered a fair way to decide an individual's guilt. Ask why it is better for a court and judge/jury rather than an individual citizen to decide guilt (e.g., "Why shouldn't citizens take the law into their own hands?").

4. Explain that since the students set up the rules for the classroom, they will set up enforcement procedures as well. Each student will be selected as a judge for a week. On Monday of that week, the names of seven students will be chosen randomly to serve as jurors. Any student who violates a classroom rule will receive a summons to appear before the student court. The teacher will act as arresting officer. Trial will be held every Friday for the students who misbehave. If the weekly judge is sick on that day, the next judge (alphabetical order) will preside. If one of the jury is sick, another will be randomly selected at that time. The defendant may speak in his or her own defense or select another student to act as a lawyer. In selecting punishments, the punishment must be fair and should fit the crime. It can be a creative punishment but cannot be humiliating or painful to the student. The punishments must follow school rules, of course. But any reasonable punishment meted out to the student will be followed as if the teacher had given out the punishment.

5. Arrange a visit to the local courthouse to watch a real trial in action. Ask students to answer questions comparing this courtroom with media portrayals of courtrooms and with their own student court. If at all possible, try to select a trial presided by a female judge and/or a judge of color (e.g., Asian American, Latina) and/or in which the attorneys are of color and/or female.

6. For homework, ask students to write an essay showing how they think the legal system works and its possible problems. These will be opinion essays and will not be graded.

7. Have students read pages in a textbook on the court system. Then invite a member or members of the legal profession to talk with the class. These speakers should include, if possible, women and people of color. Use students' essays on the legal system and the elements that students see as its problems for the focus of the talk.

8. Ask students what they would do if they were in legal trouble and had no money to pay a lawyer. Probe to find out what agencies they are familiar with. Discuss the various agencies, describing the functions of each one. Pass out brochures from these agencies and ask each student to choose one he or she finds interesting. Each student will contact that agency and find out more about it, inquire about services in legal matters and in translations for non-English-speaking persons, and inquire about ways to volunteer and help such an agency. Each student will have a week to find out this information and report back to the class.

9. Have the class role-play a local trial involving an issue of race, social class, disability, sexual orientation, or gender. Help students gather information on the case. Assign the following roles: judge, bailiff, prosecutor, plaintiff, defendant, defense counsel, witnesses, jury, and court reporter. The role-playing can include the following steps: opening of the court, selection of the jury, opening instructions by the judge, opening statements by the attorneys, direct examination and cross-examination of the defendant and witnesses, closing statements, jury deliberation, and verdict. Then have the class discuss ways the legal system supports fairness and equality and ways it can be biased.

Evaluation

1. Assess students' skills in using democratic and legal procedures through their development and enforcement of classroom rules.

2. Assess students' understanding of how the court system operates and how trials take place through a quiz.

3. Assess students' analyses of race, class, gender, and disability issues in legal conflicts and their knowledge of local agencies that deal specifically with these issues through class discussion and a quiz.

WHY THE CHANGES?

The Court System

Modeling Diversity

The "After" plan includes issues related to race, social class, gender, and disability that are not attended to in the "Before" plan. First, the teacher tries to select a courtroom to visit in which the judge and/or attorneys are of color and/or female. Second, the guest speakers are to be women and/or people of color as much as possible. Third, agencies are studied that specifically help people living at or below the poverty level, gay and lesbian people, and people of color. Fourth, the trial that students role-play is selected so that it deals with a race, class, gender, sexual orientation, or disability issue.

The "After" plan also uses a greater variety of teaching strategies than the "Before" plan, especially those that actively involve students. In the "Before" plan, students read, listen to the teacher, observe, and listen to a guest speaker. The "After" plan adds to this role-playing, performing volunteer work, and discussing. The role-playing, in particular, appeals to students who learn best through active involvement and working with their peers.

Practicing Democracy

In the "Before" plan, students learn about the legal system but do not practice it. In the "After" plan, students use democratic and court procedures for governing themselves in their classroom. In this way, they learn to make democracy a real part of their lives.

Analyzing Social Inequality

In the "After" plan, students examine how race, class, sexual orientation, gender, and disability interact with the local court system, primarily by learning about local agencies that deal with these issues and by role-playing a trial. The lesson then asks students to discuss the extent to which the existing local system promotes fairness as well as ways it is biased or used unfairly.

LESSON PLAN

BEFORE

Heredity

Subject Area: Biology

Grade Level: 10–12

Time: Two or three days

Objectives

1. Students will describe Mendel's experiments and their significance.

2. Students will define the terms *dominant trait, recessive trait, genes, genotype, phenotype,* and *hybrid*.

3. Students will differentiate among theory, hypothesis, and fact.

Suggested Procedures

1. Discuss with students the types of traits that seem to run in families. Ask them to name the traits that seem to run in their families.

2. Have students read the pages in a textbook on Mendel's work.

3. Discuss the concepts from the textbook, illustrating them in terms of human eye color (brown/blue). Use a chart depicting several generations to illustrate dominant and recessive traits.

4. Have students construct a chart depicting the crossing of yellow and green peas. The chart should illustrate dominant and recessive traits, hybrids, genes, genotypes, and phenotypes.

5. Through discussion of students' charts, make sure students understand the distinction among theory, hypothesis, and fact. Point out that Mendel never saw chromosomes or genes; his theory of dominant and recessive traits started as a hypothesis based on casual observation and was later tested through scientific experimentation. Make sure students understand that theories are accepted only as long as they explain observations; when new evidence contradicts a theory, the theory is reconstructed.

Evaluation

Assess students' understanding of Mendel's work and of the terms through the charts they construct and through a quiz.

AFTER   ## Biological Determinism

Subject Area: Biology

Grade Level: 10–12

Time: Three days

Objectives

1. Students will explain the term *biological determinism*.

2. Students will describe political biases that can be embedded in scientific findings.

3. Students will learn alternative interpretations of scientific findings that support biological determinism.

4. Students will appreciate how biological determinism is used to support political interests and social relations.

Suggested Procedures

1. Distribute the worksheet shown in Figure 6.1. Ask students to mark the statements on the worksheet that they believe to be scientific fact. After students have completed the worksheet, point out that none of the statements has been conclusively proven by science, although research exists that both supports and refutes most of the statements.

2. Discuss with students that science is often thought to proceed in the following manner:

   a. The scientist develops a hypothesis.

   b. The scientist designs a perfect, definitive experiment to test the hypothesis.

   c. The scientist carries out the experiment, which works the first time and thereafter.

   d. The hypothesis is proven and is now fact.

   e. The fact is now presented in textbooks. (Whatley, 1986, p. 187)

3. Tell students that they will role-play scientists and attempt to verify the following hypothesis: "A sense of musical rhythm is inherited genetically and is more prevalent in some races than in others." Stress that they should pretend this is really true and expect to confirm it. Have the class suggest a procedure that could be used to test the hypothesis and that will probably confirm it. The class may wish actually to conduct the experiment.

Check the statements you believe are true and supported by scientific research.

_____   1. Men are innately stronger than women.

_____   2. Low intelligence is caused by some sort of brain deficiency.

_____   3. Brain deficiency is more prevalent among the lower class than the middle class.

_____   4. Women are more emotional than men because of hormones.

_____   5. As a group, African Americans are innately stronger than European Americans.

_____   6. A sense of musical rhythm is inherited genetically and is more prevalent among some races than among others.

_____   7. Homosexuality is caused mainly by hormone imbalance.

_____   8. Aborigines are lower on the evolutionary scale than Caucasians.

_____   9. Learning disabilities are caused by minor impairments to the brain or nervous system.

_____   10. Males, especially Asian males, are genetically better disposed to think quantitatively and spatially than are females.

FIGURE 6.1   Biological Determinism Worksheet

4. Have the class brainstorm biases built into their experiment that help them reach the desired conclusion. Have them suggest alternative interpretations for the findings of such an experiment. Explain that the same sorts of biases are built into most research on biological determinism. Biases such as the following are common:

> Scientists conducting research are almost always members of the group that is "proved" superior.
>
> A fairly limited repertoire of behavior (such as answering verbal questions) is often generalized to represent a global ability (such as intelligence).
>
> What is usually published or reported are experiments finding differences between groups, differences that readers of scientific research tend to support; research that does not find differences often is not reported.
>
> Scientists sometimes repeat an experiment, modifying the procedure until the desired results are found.
>
> Data can be analyzed statistically to support a variety of conclusions; which data are analyzed using which statistical tests can depend partly on the results one is seeking.
>
> Findings often can be interpreted several different ways, not just the way the experimenter interprets them.

5. Provide students with an account of research on at least one aspect of biological determinism, such as the inheritability of intelligence. Recommended source material includes Maccoby and Jacklin (1974) and Gould (1996).

6. Discuss with students how biological determinism is used to support some groups' interests. For each item on the worksheet, discuss the roles and social relationships that are reinforced if the statement is considered to be true.

7. Discuss the implications of this lesson for students, including (a) the need to think critically about what one reads; (b) the need to be aware of how science is used for political purposes; and (c) that students could aspire to become scientists who provide alternative viewpoints. If issues involving biological determinism are in the media, these can be studied and discussed as well.

Evaluation

In a description of a real or hypothetical research study, students are asked to suggest potential biases in the research, potential political uses of the findings, and alternative interpretations of the findings.

Resources

Gould, S. J. (1996). *The mismeasure of man* (3rd ed.). New York: Norton.

Maccoby, E. E., & Jacklin, C. N. (1974). *The psychology of sex differences*. Stanford, CA: Stanford University Press.

Whatley, M. H. (1986). Taking feminist science to the classroom: Where do we go from here? In Ruth Bleier (Ed.), *Feminist approaches to science* (pp. 181–190). New York: Pergamon Press.

WHY THE CHANGES?

Biological Determinism

Analyzing Social Inequality

The ideology of biological determinism continues to be used to rationalize social inequality. Often people simply accept it in the form of unexamined, assumed stereotypes. The traditional curriculum usually does not directly examine this ideology and the stereotypes and inequalities it supports. However, this lesson replaces or supplements the closet curriculum concept—heredity—with a critical examination of biological determinism. The study of heredity as it usually appears in biology tends to support the ideology of biological determinism. Some teachers present only the biological inheritance of obvious physical features such as eye color and do not address more complex things such as intelligence; whereas others explain that the connections between biology and intelligence, ability, and personality are not clearly understood. In either case, students' beliefs relating to biological determinism are left unexamined.

The "After" plan also teaches students about the social aspects of scientific inquiry. Social, human, and political biases are built into any field of scientific investigation, a fact that students should be aware of. The lessons taught about science in the "After" plan can be extended to an examination of scientific research in any current social area. The plan can be taught as a sequel to, rather than a replacement of, the "Before" plan. The two are not mutually exclusive, although the teacher may not have time to teach both.

LESSON PLAN

BEFORE

African American Literature[*]

Subject Area: English

Grade Level: 9–12

Time: Over the course of one month

---

[*]*Source:* Anne Fairbrother, Salinas Union High School District, Salinas, CA.

Objective

While reading the case work *Black Boy,* by Richard Wright, students will become familiar with three additional literary works dealing with the African American experience.

Suggested Procedures

1. Have students read the novel *Black Boy,* by Richard Wright. There are many issues raised in this novel that students probably have limited understanding of; while reading the novel, have them also read and discuss works such as those listed in Resources.

2. Have students read aloud "After You My Dear Alphonse," by Shirley Jackson, as a Readers' Theater. Afterward, have students identify Johnny's mother's problem. She makes assumptions based on the fact that her son's friend Boyd is black; these cause Mrs. Wilson to stereotype Boyd. Students will easily identify the stereotyping. Johnny's mother is apparently kind but is disappointed when Boyd doesn't fit her stereotype. Discuss this, and examine why these stereotypes are harmful even though the mother only wants to help Boyd.

3. Have students read "Everyday Use," by Alice Walker. After reading, pose the question: Why doesn't the mother want Dee/Wangero to have the two old quilts? Have students brainstorm this in groups, and then share their answers with the class for discussion.

4. Have students read "Thank You M'am," by Richard Wright, and come up with questions for the class to answer, as an individual quiz or in groups.

Evaluation

1. Informally, students' understanding of the main ideas in the stories will be assessed through their participation in class discussions.

2. A follow-up quiz on all four stories will be given and graded.

Resources

Jackson, Shirley. (1991). "After you my dear Alphonse." In S. Jackson, *The lottery and other stories*. New York: Noonday Press.

Walker, Alice. (1991). "Everyday use." In *Braided lives: An anthology of multicultural American writing*. St. Paul, MN: Minnesota Humanities Commission, Minnesota Council of Teachers of English.

Wright, Richard. (1993). "Thank you m'am." In A. Mazer (Ed.), *America street: A multicultural anthology of stories*. New York: Persea Books.

AFTER	## Taking Action Against Discrimination

Subject Area: English

Grade Level: 9–12

Time: Over the course of one month

Objectives

1. Students will become familiar with three or four literary works dealing with diverse U.S. American cultural experiences.

2. Students will recognize and identify similarities and differences between the different cultural experiences.

3. Students will see that discrimination and racism affect relations between other groups besides European Americans and African Americans.

4. Students will see that stereotyping and discrimination may or may not be related to issues of color or culture.

5. Students will examine their own experiences and look at issues of prejudice and discrimination in their school or community, devising and implementing strategies for combating the problem.

Suggested Procedures

1. Have students read the novel *Black Boy,* by Richard Wright, over the course of one month. There are many issues raised in this novel that students probably have limited understanding of. To help, students could watch *Patch of Blue*, identifying themes of physical and mental abuse, of prejudice and discrimination, and of goodness and love. An essay identifying the major theme could be assigned. In addition, have them also read and discuss works such as those listed in Resources.

2. After reading a portion of Part 1, Chapter 7, from the novel *Chicano* (excerpted in *From the Barrio*) aloud in class, students will answer discussion questions in groups that lead students to show an understanding of, and an evaluation of, the issues raised in the story.

3. Students then will do a free write: "Do you think Sammy was treated fairly? What wider social/racial issues are shown here? Can you relate to any of his

experiences?" These questions can then be discussed as a class. There is stereotyping and racial/cultural discrimination in this story.

(If *Chicano* cannot be found, two other stories dealing with Chicano experiences could also be used: "The Scholarship Jacket," by Marta Salinas; or Chapter 13 from *George Washington Gomez*, by Americo Paredes. Both deal with discrimination and issues of culture and class. Another suggested work to parallel *Black Boy* is *Living Up the Street*, by Gary Soto.)

4. Students will read the story "The Stolen Party," by Liliana Heker (set in Argentina), aloud in class; then, in groups they will answer comprehension and interpretive questions. The students will discuss if there is prejudice here. (It is a matter of class and color—not race, culture, or country.) As a class, students will discuss this story and what is happening and why, identifying parallels between the experiences of Hosaura and Richard: stereotyping and class/cultural/racial discrimination.

5. Students will read aloud "An Awakening . . . Summer 1956," by Nicholasa Mohr (Puerto Rican author), and, in groups, come up with one interpretive and one evaluative question about the story.

6. Students will send one person from one group to write the questions on the board. The teacher will go over the questions, only to establish whether they are truly interpretive and evaluative. Students will then answer the class's questions in groups. If the following questions are not generated, they can be added to the questions on the board:

   Why had the young woman come to Texas? (interpretive)

   How does she feel when she sees the sign in Nathan's Food and Groceries, and why? (interpretive)

   Why does Nathan give her a Pepsi after refusing to serve her? (interpretive)

   Do you think she did the right thing in breaking the bottle as she did? What would you have done in her position? (evaluative)

   How did she feel afterward? Why? (interpretive)

   What does she mean by: "A reminder . . . should I ever forget"? (interpretive)

   What does she mean by: " . . . now she was more than ready for the challenges"? (interpretive)

7. Have students write about their own experiences that relate to the literature and about parallels and contrasts among the different novels and stories.

8. Have students work in groups to identify problems involving prejudice and discrimination in their school or community. Have groups share their ideas with the class. As a class, discuss each problem and brainstorm solutions.

9. Have students decide on one or more problems in the school or the community that they are prepared to try to solve; then decide on strategies, time lines, and measures of success. Depending on the situations being tackled, set up time for feedback, written reports, and assessment of the results.

10. After finishing *Black Boy*, students could watch *Mask*, where the issue of discrimination and stereotyping pertains to disabilities. A quiz, to be taken in pairs, could be assigned to assess students' grasp of the plot and issues raised in the movie and similarities to the issues raised in *Black Boy*.

11. Have students discuss how various forms of discrimination affected characters in *Black Boy*. If action had been taken similar to the strategies students have proposed for addressing discrimination in their own school or community, how much better would the lives of the characters have been? Have students pretend they are Richard Wright, and write an evaluation of the strategies they are undertaking in their own communities.

Evaluation

1. Students' familiarity with the main themes of the literature and videos will be assessed through their essays and free writes.

2. Students' identification of similarities and differences between the different cultural experiences, and their analysis of discrimination and racism, will be assessed informally during class and group discussions.

3. Students' ability to identify and change perceived social injustices in their school or community will be assessed through the effectiveness of the action strategies they develop and implement.

Resources

Print

Heker, L. (1986). "The stolen party." In A. Manguel (Ed.), *Other fires: Short fiction by Latin American women*. New York: C. N. Potter.

Mohr, N. (1994). "An awakening . . . summer 1956." In Virginia Seeley (Ed.), *Latino Caribbean literature*. Paramus, NJ: Globe Fearon.

Paredes, A. (1990). *George Washington Gomez*. Houston: Arte Publico Press.

Salinas, M. (1984). "The scholarship jacket." In R. A. Anaya & A. Marquez (Eds.), *Cuentos Chicanos: A short story anthology* (rev. ed.). Albuquerque, NM: Published for New America by the University of New Mexico Press.

Soto, G. (1992). *Living up the street: Narrative recollections*. New York: Dell.

Vasquez, R. (1973). "Chicano." In L. O. Salinas & L. Faderman (Eds.), *From the barrio.* San Francisco: Canfield Press.

Wright, R. (1978). *Black boy: A record of childhood and youth.* London: Longman.

Audiovisual

Mask. (1996). Image Entertainment.

A patch of blue. (1965). Metro-Goldwyn-Mayer.

WHY THE CHANGES?

Taking Action Against Discrimination

Curriculum

In both the "Before" and "After" lessons, students read multiple works by African American authors to deepen their understanding of African American experiences. Obviously, one could teach a whole course focusing on African American literature! One novel does not fully represent any group, and in both plans, the teacher recognizes that issues in a novel such as *Black Boy* are complex and will not necessarily be understood simply through reading this one novel by itself. Further, instead of just hearing of the brutality of slavery, often written by white European American historians, students need to read of the events in books such as *Before the Mayflower,* by Lerone Bennett Jr. Then, to further focus on the struggle and courage of African American history, rather than the stereotypes of submission, students should read *Narrative of the Life of Frederick Douglass, an American Slave* or other slave narratives. At some point, especially if this course is integrated with U.S. American history, students should read poems from the wealth of black poetry from the 1950s and 1960s so they can see how the issues of heritage and assimilation were addressed. Books such as *The Autobiography of Malcolm X* would be important supplemental reading for students, along with at least one book written by one of the many prominent modern African American women writers.

Modeling Diversity

African American literature, as well as the literature of any other group, can be taught with a multicultural perspective. The problem in the classroom with a traditional curriculum on African American works is that students often only hear of racism and discrimination when reading African American literature, such as *Black Boy*, and this perpetuates a stereotype that racism is only a black/white issue, as well as the stereotype that African American experiences do not have additional dimensions. Only when students examine prejudice involving other groups in society can they clearly examine the underpinnings and extent of discrimination and racism. Only then can they can see it in their communities and work at trying to change it. Of course, a view of social injustice should include issues involving other peoples and groups not mentioned here: Native American and Asian American experiences; gender inequities; people with disabilities; ageism; heterosexism and homophobia; restrictions on youth, and so on.

Encouraging Social Action

All students know that problems involving prejudice and discrimination exist. To help them understand them more fully and to work to effect changes is an empowering process, which will probably cause the students to grow to be active and involved citizens.

Resources

Bennett, L. Jr. (1987). *Before the Mayflower: A history of black America* (6th ed.). Chicago: Johnson Publishing.

Douglass, F. (1845). *Narrative of the life of Frederick Douglass, an American slave.* Boston: Published in the Anti-Slavery Office.

X, Malcolm. (1992). *The autobiography of Malcolm X* (with the assistance of Alex Haley). New York: Ballantine Books.

References

Grant, C. A., & Sleeter, C. E. (1996). *After the school bell rings* (2nd ed.). New York: Falmer Press.

Shirts, G. R. (1977). *BaFa BaFa*. Del Mar, CA: Simile II.

Sleeter, C. E., & Grant, C. A. (1994). *Making choices for multicultural education: Five approaches to race, class, and gender* (2nd ed.). Upper Saddle River, NJ: Merrill/Prentice Hall.

Smith, N., Greenlaw, M., & Scott, C. (1987). Making the literature environment equitable. *The Reading Teacher, 40*(4), 400–407.

A FINAL WORD

Have you made your choice? Which approach to multicultural education fits you both in theory and practice? Do you prefer one or a combination of the approaches? Remember our warning about random selection—select one or two approaches and work with each one for a while. An important key to successful use is making the approach your own. Follow the framework for the approach as it is outlined, but do not hesitate to express yourself in using it.

Try to involve your colleagues by having them work with you. Meet with them to discuss how you can "turn on" your students to learning.

Have fun this school year, and "turn on" learning!

Carl A. Grant
Christine E. Sleeter

Index

315

Lesson Plan Index

BY SUBJECT AREA

BY GRADE LEVEL